Attorney General's Advisory Committee on
American Indian and Alaska Native Children Exposed to Violence:

Ending Violence So Children Can Thrive

NOVEMBER 2014

US Senator Byron L. Dorgan (ret.)

Joanne Shenandoah, PhD, *Iroquois*

Dolores Subia BigFoot, PhD, *Caddo Nation of Oklahoma*

Eric Broderick, DDS, MPH

Eddie F. Brown, DSW, *Pasqua Yaqui & Tohono O'odham*

Valerie Davidson, JD, *Yup'ik*

Anita Fineday, JD, MPA, *White Earth Band of Ojibwe*

Matthew L. M. Fletcher, JD, *Grand Traverse Band of Ottawa and Chippewa Indians*

Jefferson Keel, *Chickasaw Nation*

Ron Whitener, JD, *Squaxin Island Tribe*

Marilyn J. Bruguier Zimmerman, MSW, *Assiniboine-Sioux/Fort Peck Reservation*

This project was supported by Grant No. 2013-TY-FX-K002 awarded by the Office of Juvenile Justice and Delinquency Prevention, Office of Justice Programs, U.S. Department of Justice. Points of view in this document are those of the authors and do not necessarily reflect the official positions or policies of the U.S. Department of Justice.

U.S. Department of Justice

Eric Holder, Jr.
Attorney General

Karol Mason
Assistant Attorney General

Robert L. Listenbee Jr.
Administrator
Office of Juvenile Justice and Delinquency Prevention

This report was created as part of the Defending Childhood Initiative created by Attorney General Eric H. Holder, Jr. This initiative strives to harness resources from across the Department of Justice to:

- Prevent children's exposure to violence;

- Mitigate the negative impact of children's exposure to violence when it does occur; and

- Develop knowledge and spread awareness about children's exposure to violence.

Members of the Advisory Committee

Co-Chairs

US Senator Byron L. Dorgan (ret.), Chairman of the Board of Advisors, Center for Native American Youth; Former U.S. Senator; Former Chairman of the US Senate Indian Affairs Committee

Joanne Shenandoah, PhD (*Iroquois*), Composer and Singer

Members

Dolores Subia BigFoot, PhD (*Caddo Nation of Oklahoma*), Associate Professor, Department of Pediatrics, University of Oklahoma Health Sciences Center; Director, Native American Programs, University of Oklahoma

Eric Broderick, DDS, MPH, Former Deputy Administrator of the Substance Abuse and Mental Health Services Administration; Rear Admiral

Eddie F. Brown, DSW (*Pasqua Yaqui & Tohono O'odham*), Executive Director, American Indian Policy Institute; Professor of American Indian Studies and School of Social Work, Arizona State University

Valerie Davidson, JD (*Yup'ik*), Indian Health Advocate

Anita Fineday, JD, MPA (*White Earth Band of Ojibwe*), Managing Director, Indian Child Welfare Program, Casey Family Programs; Formerly Chief Judge for the White Earth Tribal Nation

Matthew L. M. Fletcher, JD (*Grand Traverse Band of Ottawa and Chippewa Indians*), Director, Indigenous Law and Policy Center, Michigan State University College of Law

Jefferson Keel (*Chickasaw Nation*), Lieutenant Governor of the Chickasaw Nation

Ron Whitener, JD (*Squaxin Island Tribe*), Affiliated Assistant Professor, University of Washington School of Law, Associate Judge, Tulalip Tribal Court

Marilyn J. Bruguier Zimmerman, MSW (*Assiniboine-Sioux/Fort Peck Reservation*), Director, National Native Children's Trauma Center, University of Montana

Acknowledgements

During the course of our work, the Attorney General's Advisory Committee on American Indian and Alaska Native Children Exposed to Violence received support and assistance from numerous individuals and organizations to whom we would like to express our deepest gratitude.

The U.S. Department of Justice's Office of Juvenile Justice and Delinquency Prevention, led by Administrator Robert Listenbee, provided the funding for this critical work as part of the Defending Childhood Initiative. We thank the department for the support it provided and its commitment to helping American Indian and Alaska Native children heal and thrive.

Our technical assistance provider, the Tribal Law and Policy Institute (TLPI), organized four public hearings and five Listening Sessions spanning the country and they assisted with the organization of this report. The hearings and Listening Sessions formed the backbone of our inquiry. We also would like to thank the following individuals and organizations who made it possible, through their generosity and time, for us to convene experts and community members to discuss children's exposure to violence: Salt River Pima-Maricopa Indian Community; Gila River Indian Community; Akimel O'odham/Pee-Posh Youth Council; All Nations Indian Church; National Congress of American Indians; National Indian Child Welfare Association; Seminole Tribe of Florida; Native Village of Napaskiak; Native Village of Emmonak; community of Bethel; National Indian Education Association; Little Earth of United Tribes; Center for Native American Youth; Casey Family Programs and the Ain Dah Yung Center. In addition, the following individuals provided assistance at hearings and Listening Sessions: Elders Jim and Bonnie Clairmont; Yago and Ina Evan; Mike Hoffman; John McDonald; and Vivian Korthuis.

We also gratefully acknowledge the many individuals who helped shape our thinking about this work and provided us with the support to complete this challenging task, including Professor Alicia Lieberman, who was appointed to the Advisory Committee but not able to participate in the hearings, Professor Sarah Deer and Erin Bailey.

Most importantly, this report and the work of this task force would not be what they are without the voices of those who shared their expertise, personal experience, passion, and commitment to ending American Indian and Alaska Native children's exposure to violence during the course of our hearings and Listening Sessions, as well as those who submitted written testimony. They are acknowledged individually in a separate section of this report, but their contributions bear mentioning again and we are greatly indebted to them. Ending American Indian and Alaska Native children's exposure to violence requires every one of us. The hundreds of people we heard from across this nation have demonstrated what profound change can occur when one person accepts the responsibility each of us has for ending this epidemic. On behalf of our sacred children, we thank you for your dedication.

Letter from the Co-Chairs

NOVEMBER 18, 2014

Today, a vast majority of American Indian and Alaska Native children live in communities with alarmingly high rates of poverty, homelessness, drug abuse, alcoholism, suicide, and victimization. Domestic violence, sexual assault, and child abuse are widespread. Continual exposure to violence has a devastating impact on child development and can have a lasting impact on basic cognitive, emotional, and neurological functions. We **cannot** stand by and watch these children—who are the future of American Indian and Alaska Native communities—destroyed by relentless violence and trauma. This Advisory Committee was charged by U.S. Attorney General Eric H. Holder Jr. with examining these issues and making recommendations for change that will heal and protect American Indian and Alaska Native children and foster environments in which they can thrive and develop to their full potential.

Over the course of several months this Advisory Committee listened to hours of testimony about the trauma and suffering endured by our Native people—past and present. We heard story after story of abuse, loss, and tragedy. We heard about the legacy of historical trauma caused by loss of home, land, culture, and language and the subsequent abuse of generations of Native children in American boarding schools. We heard that, through a tragic history of broken promises and chronic underfunding, our country has failed to meet its trust obligations to Native Americans and their children.

Yet at every hearing we also heard about the desire for healing and the importance of restoring traditional ceremonies and ancestral wisdom as ways of returning safety, dignity, respect, and well-being to our Indigenous people and their children. We discovered a remarkable core of resilience and love of children among Native people and a sense of urgency about changing their communities.

Throughout the testimony, we also heard stories of critical tribal funding that has been cut across sectors—housing, law enforcement, child welfare, juvenile justice, health care, and education—and how the lack of funding negatively impacts the children in those communities. And while there are state and federal programs intended to address the needs of Native American children and youth, the findings of this report illustrate that grant-making systems are cumbersome and resources for tribes are extremely limited. Too often tribes are forced to compete with one another for limited resources and the grant application process is subject to unrealistic time frames, overwhelming paperwork, and requirements that place unrealistic burdens on small or remote tribal communities.

A number of the recommendations in this report require substantial investment and new appropriations for programs that provide critical services and care to American Indian and Alaska Native children. Progress will not be made until Congress passes legislation requiring mandatory spending for tribal children and youth. Furthermore, treaties and existing law and trust responsibilities *demand* that Congress and the Executive Branch direct sufficient funds to American Indian and Alaska Native Nations to bring funding into parity with the rest of the United States so that tribal Nations can effectively address violence in their communities, prevent children from being exposed to violence, and respond to those children who need to heal.

This report is submitted to Attorney General Holder with a deep sense of responsibility, humility, commitment, and hope for change. We are extremely grateful to all the witnesses and others who generously shared their stories, wisdom, time, and recommendations with us. And we thank our fellow Advisory Committee members—an extraordinary group of people who have a deep commitment to American Indian and Alaska Native children.

Joanne Shenandoah, PhD, Co-Chair

US Senator Byron L. Dorgan (ret.), Co-Chair

Contents

Appendices

Preface

Public Hearings

*The Advisory Committee held four public hearings over the course of 2013–14 in North Dakota, Arizona, Florida, and Alaska. These hearings included testimony from more than **150 witnesses**. Thousands of pages of written testimony were reviewed for this report.*

The Attorney's General's Task Force on American Indian and Alaska Native Children Exposed to Violence was established in 2013, based upon a recommendation from the Attorney General's National Task Force on Children Exposed to Violence. This American Indian/Alaska Native (AI/AN) Task Force has been anchored by an Advisory Committee consisting of nonfederal experts in the area of AI/AN children exposed to violence and a federal working group that includes federal officials from key agencies involved in issues related to AI/AN children exposed to violence. The charge to the Advisory Committee on AI/AN Children Exposed to Violence (Advisory Committee) was to make high-level policy recommendations to Attorney General Eric Holder on ways to address issues around AI/AN children exposed to violence.

The charter mandated that members of the AI/AN Advisory Committee conduct four hearings and up to six Listening Sessions nationwide to learn from key practitioners, advocates, academicians, policy makers, and the public about the issue of AI/AN children exposed to violence in the United States in and outside of Indian country.[1]

The Advisory Committee was also directed to gather information on promising and evidence-based practices that could benefit these children and their communities. Finally, the Advisory Committee was directed to write a final report to the Attorney General presenting its policy recommendations. This Advisory Committee was charged with making recommendations to the Attorney General of the United States.

Many of the recommendations in this report are addressed to Congress and executive branch agencies outside the Department of Justice because solutions to the dire situation faced by AI/AN children must be comprehensive and will require efforts beyond the Department of Justice. Therefore, the Committee recommends that the Attorney General work with the Legislative and executive branches of government to implement the recommendations.

The recommendations are intended to serve as a blueprint for preventing Al/AN children's exposure to violence and for mitigating the negative effects experienced by Al/AN children exposed to violence across the United States and throughout Indian country. During 2013–14, the Advisory Committee convened four public hearings and multiple Listening Sessions across the nation to examine the scope and impact of violence facing AI/AN children exposed to violence in their homes, schools, and communities. The Advisory Committee heard from more than 150 witnesses. The hearings, attended by more than 580 people, were open to the public.[2]

The primary focus of this report is the findings and recommendations that emerged from those hearings. In addition, this report incorporates and builds on two highly relevant reports that preceded it. The 2012 Report of the Attorney General's National Task Force on Children Exposed to Violence[3] and the 2013 Indian Law and Order Commission (ILOC) report, *A Roadmap for Making Native America Safer.*[4]

The Attorney General's National Task Force on Children Exposed to Violence held hearings throughout the country and released its comprehensive final report on December 12, 2012. This final report includes fifty-six wide-ranging recommendations. One foundational recommendation was to establish a separate task force or commission to examine the unique needs of AI/AN children exposed to violence.[5]

Following the 2012 release of the Final Report of the Attorney General's National Task Force on Children Exposed to Violence, a second highly relevant report was released by the Indian Law and Order Commission (ILOC). The ILOC was a bipartisan commission created through the 2010 Tribal Law and Order Act (Public Law 111-211) (TLOA). The TLOA directed the commission to conduct a comprehensive study of the criminal justice system relating to Indian country and to develop recommendations on necessary modifications and improvements to the justice systems on the federal, tribal, and state levels. The final report, released in 2013, *A*

Roadmap for Making Native America Safer,[6] was unanimously approved by all nine bipartisan commissioners. The goals of the ILOC report are directly connected to this Advisory Committee's mission to address the needs of AI/AN children exposed to violence.

The Advisory Committee believes that the recommendations in the 2012 Final Report of the Attorney General's National Task Force on Children Exposed to Violence and the 2013 Indian Law and Order Commission reports complement the findings and recommendations in this report and encourage policy makers to consult all three reports as they implement policies that will improve the lives of AI/AN children.

Each of the five chapters in this report addresses a critical issue in protecting AI/AN children exposed to violence. Each chapter discusses the Advisory Committee's findings based on testimony offered at hearings, information gleaned at Listening Sessions, and additional research conducted by the committee members; and each chapter will conclude with the Advisory Committee's recommendations related to those findings. This report provides the Advisory Committee's vision of the development of effective, culturally appropriate programs and services to protect AI/AN children exposed to violence. The Advisory Committee believes that the implementation of these recommendations can make lasting change across the nation, fulfilling its vision of *Empowering Communities to Make Lasting and Positive Change for AI/AN Children Exposed to Violence.*

Notes

1. Holder, Eric H., Jr., *Charter for the Advisory Committee of the Attorney General's Task Force on American Indian/Alaska Native (AI/AN) Children Exposed to Violence,* available at: http://www.justice.gov/defendingchildhood/charter-adv-comm-aian.pdf.

2. Hearing #1: Bismarck, ND, December 9, 2013. Hearing #2: Phoenix, AZ, February 11, 2014. Hearing #3: Fort Lauderdale, FL, April 16–17, 2014. Hearing #4: Anchorage, AK, June 11–12, 2014. Listening Session #1: Phoenix, AZ, February 10, 2014. Listening Session #2: Minneapolis, MN, May 20–21, 2014. Listening Session #3: Bethel, AK, June 9, 2014.

3. Listenbee, Robert L., Jr., et al., *Report of the Attorney General's National Task Force on Children Exposed to Violence,* Washington, D.C.: U.S. Department of Justice, Office of Juvenile Justice and Delinquency Prevention, December 2012.

4. Indian Law and Order Commission, *A Roadmap for Making Native America Safer: Report to the President and Congress of the United States* (November 2013), available at: http://www.aisc.ucla.edu/iloc/report/index.html.

5. 5Listenbee, Robert L., Jr., et al., *Report of the Attorney General's National Task Force on Children Exposed to Violence,* Washington, D.C.: U.S. Department of Justice, Office of Juvenile Justice and Delinquency Prevention, December 2012: 38.

6. 6 The Indian Law and Order Commission was created in response to a mandate of the Tribal Law and Order Act, PL-111-211. The TLOA directed the commission to develop a comprehensive study of the criminal justice system relating to Indian country and to develop recommendations on necessary modifications and improvements to the justice systems and the federal, tribal, and state levels. *See* Indian Law and Order Commission, *A Roadmap for Making Native America Safer: Report to the President and Congress of the United States* (November 2013): vi, available at: http://www.aisc.ucla.edu/iloc/report/index.html.

Executive Summary

Day in and day out, despite the tremendous efforts of tribal[1] governments and community members, many of them hindered by insufficient funding, American Indian and Alaska Native (AI/AN) children suffer exposure to violence at rates higher than any other race in the United States. The immediate and long term effects of this exposure to violence includes increased rates of altered neurological development, poor physical and mental health, poor school performance, substance abuse, and overrepresentation in the juvenile justice system. This chronic exposure to violence often leads to toxic stress reactions and severe trauma; which is compounded by historical trauma. Sadly, AI/AN children experience posttraumatic stress disorder at the same rate as veterans returning from Iraq and Afghanistan and triple the rate of the general population.[2] With the convergence of exceptionally high crime rates, jurisdictional limitations, vastly under-resourced programs, and poverty, service providers and policy makers should assume that *all* AI/AN children have been exposed to violence.

Through hearings and Listening Sessions over the course of 2013–14, the Attorney General's Advisory Committee on American Indian and Alaska Native Children Exposed to Violence[3] examined the current epidemic of violence and evaluated suggestions for preventing violence and alleviating its impact on AI/AN children. This report presents the Advisory Committee's policy recommendations that are intended to serve as a blueprint for preventing AI/AN children's exposure to violence and for mitigating the negative effects experienced by AI/AN children exposed to violence across the United States and throughout Indian country. The primary focus of the report is the thirty-one wide-ranging findings and recommendations that emerged from hearings and Listening Sessions. The Advisory Committee also examines the reports of the Attorney General's National Task Force on Children Exposed to Violence in 2012[4] and the Indian Law and Order Commission (ILOC) in 2013,[5] and incorporates some of the recommendations from these important reports that most strongly impact AI/AN children exposed to violence.

This report contains five chapters: (1) "Building a Strong Foundation"; (2) "Promoting Well-Being for American Indian and Alaska Native Children in the Home"; (3) "Promoting Well-Being for American Indian and Alaska Native Children in the Community"; (4) "Creating a Juvenile Justice System that Focuses on Prevention, Treatment and Healing"; and (5) "Empowering Alaska Tribes,[6]

Removing Barriers, and Providing Resources." Each chapter contains a discussion of the topics, providing background information, data, examples of problems as well as promising practices, and the Advisory Committee's recommendations.

This Advisory Committee was charged with making recommendations to the Attorney General of the United States. Many of the recommendations in this report are addressed to Congress and executive branch agencies outside the Department of Justice because solutions to the dire situation faced by AI/AN children must be comprehensive and will require efforts beyond the Department of Justice. Therefore, the Committee recommends that the Attorney General work with the legislative and executive branches of government to implement the recommendations. A summary of each chapter is presented below.

Chapter 1—Building a Strong Foundation

We must transform the broken systems that re-traumatize children into systems where American Indian and Alaska Native (AI/AN) tribes are empowered with authority and resources to prevent exposure to violence and to respond to and promote healing of their children who have been exposed. Current barriers that prevent tribes from leading in protecting and healing their children must be eliminated before real change can begin.

1.1 Leaders at the highest levels of the executive and legislative branches of the federal government should coordinate and implement the recommendations in this report consistent with three core principles–Empowering Tribes, Removing Barriers, and Providing Resources–identified by the Advisory Committee.

There is a vital connection between tribal sovereignty and protecting AI/AN children. The Advisory Committee is convinced that state and federal governments must recognize and respect the primacy of tribal governments in responding to AI/AN children. Jurisdictional restrictions on tribes must be eliminated to allow Tribes to exercise their inherent sovereign authority to prevent AI/AN children's exposure to violence. Resource limitations must be adequately addressed. The barriers that currently limit tribes' response to exposure to violence must be removed. Tribes should be supported in this effort with the assistance, collaboration, and resources needed to build their capacity to fully implement and sustain tribal-controlled, trauma-informed prevention and treatment models and systems. These barriers must be removed in order to empower individual tribal communities to prevent their children from being exposed to violence along with sufficient tools to respond and promote healing in their children who have been exposed.

1.2 The White House should establish—no later than May 2015—a permanent fully-staffed Native American Affairs Office within the White House Domestic Policy Council. This new Native American Affairs Office should include a senior position specializing in AI/AN children exposed to violence. This office should be responsible for coordination across the executive branch of all services provided for the benefit and protection of AI/AN children and the office lead should report directly to the Director of the Domestic Policy Council as a Special Assistant to the President. The Native American Affairs Office should have overall executive branch responsibility for coordinating and implementing the recommendations in this report including conducting annual tribal consultations.

The Advisory Committee believes that a permanent fully-staffed Native American Affairs Office, including a senior position specializing in AI/AN children exposed to violence, is required in order to comply with the federal government's trust responsibility and to effectively address the current inability of the federal government to serve the needs of AI/AN children exposed to violence. The new White House Native American Affairs Office should provide the essential executive branch coordination and collaboration required to effectively implement the recommendations in this report. The current "stovepipe organizational structure" of the executive branch restricts the flow of information and cross-organizational communication, making essential collaboration extremely difficult.

The White House Native American Affairs Office should conduct annual consultations with tribal governments, including discussion of:

1. Administering tribal funds and programs;

2. Enhancing the safety of AI/AN children exposed to violence in the home and in the community;

3. Enhancing child protection services through trauma-informed practice;

4. Enhancing research and evaluation to address behavioral health needs and explore tribal cultural interventions and best practices;

5. Enhancing substance abuse services for caregivers and youth that addresses exposure to violence; and

6. Evaluating the implementation status of the recommendations in this report.

1.3 Congress should restore the inherent authority of American Indian and Alaska Native (AI/AN) tribes to assert full criminal jurisdiction over all persons who commit crimes against AI/AN children in Indian country

In May 2013, Congress passed the Violence against Women Reauthorization Act (VAWA).[7] Among its provisions, Congress amended the Indian Civil Rights Act (ICRA) to authorize "special domestic violence criminal jurisdiction" to tribal courts over non-Indian offenders who (1) commit domestic violence, (2) commit dating violence, or (3) violate a protection order. It is troubling that tribes have no criminal jurisdiction over non-Indians who commit heinous crimes of sexual and physical abuse of AI/AN children in Indian country. Congress has restored criminal jurisdiction over non-Indians who commit domestic violence, commit dating violence, and violate protection orders. Congress should now similarly restore the inherent authority of AI/AN tribes to assert full criminal jurisdiction over all persons who commit crimes against AI/AN children in Indian country including both child sexual abuse and child physical abuse.

1.4 Congress and the executive branch shall direct sufficient funds to AI/AN tribes to bring funding for tribal criminal and civil justice systems and tribal child protection systems into parity with the rest of the United States and shall remove the barriers that currently impede the ability of AI/AN Nations to effectively address violence in their communities. *The Advisory Committee believes that treaties, existing law and trust responsibilities are not discretionary and demand this action.*

The Advisory Committee believes that this investment is necessary to create an environment in which AI/AN children, today and for generations to come, may thrive. This investment is not only the right thing to do, but is part of the legal obligations of this nation to those communities. In order to more effectively address the needs of AI/AN children exposed to violence, substantial changes must be made in the methods by which AI/AN tribes are able to access federal funding. Substantially increased levels of federal funding will be required.

Funding for child maltreatment prevention and child protection efforts is especially limited in Indian country. Meanwhile, states receive proportionately more funding for prevention and child protection while tribes receive little to no federal support for these activities. Tribes are not even eligible for the two major programs that fund these state programs—Title XX of the Social Services Block Grant and the Child Abuse Prevention and Treatment Act.

The U.S. Department of the Interior (DOI) through the Bureau of Indian Affairs (BIA) provides limited funding for tribal court systems but the funding level is far too low. The BIA has historically denied any tribal law enforcement and tribal court funding to tribes in jurisdictions—such as Public Law 280 (PL-280) jurisdictions[8]— where congressionally authorized concurrent state jurisdiction has been established. Furthermore, efforts to fund tribal justice systems such as the Indian Tribal Justice Act of 1993 (which authorized an additional $50 million per year in tribal court base funding) have repeatedly *authorized* increased tribal court funding, but the long-promised funding has never materialized in the form of actual *appropriations.*

Since the late 1990s, the U.S. Department of Justice (DOJ) has also become a significant federal source of tribal justice funding. Tribes have utilized DOJ grant funding to enhance various and diverse aspects of their tribal justice systems, from tribal codes to Juvenile Healing to Wellness Courts (tribal drug courts) to unique tribal youth programs. While these grants have offered immense support, they are far from the consistent, tribally driven approach that is needed in Indian country. The Advisory Committee heard repeated frustration from hearing witnesses concerning the competitive funding approach that DOJ utilizes.

It is important to note that DOJ funding for tribal justice systems has been consistently decreasing in recent years. It is particularly troubling that the Consolidated Tribal Assistance Solicitation (CTAS) grant program with the closest direct connection to AI/AN children exposed to violence—the Office of Juvenile Justice and Delinquency Prevention (OJJDP) Tribal Youth Program (TYP)—has suffered the greatest decrease in funding levels. In a four-year period, OJJDP TYP funding has plummeted from $25 million in FY 2010 down to only $5 million in FY 2014. Tribes, like their state and local counterparts, deserve the benefit of reliability in their quest to build robust tribal justice systems that can adequately serve their youth. Base funding from resources pooled across various federal agencies would offer tribes the reliability and flexibility that is needed.

AI/AN children are generally served best when tribes have the opportunity to take ownership of the programs and resources that they provide. PL-93-638 contracts, self-governance compacts, and PL-102-477 funding agreements, are examples of successful federal programs that afford tribes the option to take over the management of federal funds for an array of programs. However, currently none of these programs applies to the DOJ.

> **1.4.A** **Congress and the executive branch shall provide recurring mandatory, not discretionary, base funding for all tribal programs that impact AI/AN children exposed to violence, including tribal criminal and civil justice systems and tribal child protection systems, and make it available on equal terms to all federally recognized tribes, whether their lands are under federal jurisdiction or congressionally authorized state jurisdiction.**

The United States' trust responsibility to AI/AN tribes requires the provision of basic governmental services in Indian country. Funding to fulfill this obligation, however, is currently provided in the *discretionary* portion of the federal budget despite the fact that the treaties that made promises to Indian tribes did not promise "*discretionary*" support and the trust responsibility is not *discretionary*. Because the spending is discretionary and not mandatory as it should be, public policies like sequestration reduce or eliminate programs that clearly should not be cut.

> **1.4.B** **Congress shall appropriate, not simply authorize, sufficient substantially increased funding to provide reliable tribal base funding for all tribal programs that impact**

AI/AN children exposed to violence. This includes tribal criminal and civil justice systems and tribal child protection systems. At a minimum, and as a helpful starting point, Congress shall enact the relevant funding level requests in the National Congress of American Indians (NCAI) Indian Country Budget Request for FY 2015.

Substantially increased levels of federal funding will be required to more effectively address the needs of AI/AN children exposed to violence. For the past ten years, NCAI has published an annual Indian Country Budget Request Report that reflects collaboration with tribal leaders, Native organizations, and tribal budget consultation bodies. That budget request should serve as a helpful starting point for the initial minimum levels of increased funding that will be needed. The annual NCAI budget reports also provide further insightful detail concerning a wide range of federal programs that will be required to implement these recommendations.

1.4.C   Congress shall authorize all federal agencies, beginning with the Department of Justice (DOJ), to enter into 638 self-determination and self-governance compacts with tribes to ensure that all tribal system funding, including both justice and child welfare, is subject to tribal management. Further, the Department of Health and Human Services (HHS) should fully utilize its current 638 self-determination and self-governance authority to the greatest extent feasible for flexible funding programs in the Department of Health and Human Services (HHS) beyond the Indian Health Service (IHS) and seek additional legislative authority where needed.

Expanding the option for self-governance would translate to greater flexibility for tribes to provide critical social services within agencies such as the Administration on Aging, Administration on Children and Families, Substance Abuse and Mental Health Services Administration, and the Health Resources and Services Administration. HHS must work closely with tribes to strengthen current self-governance programs and advance initiatives that will streamline and improve HHS program delivery in Indian country.

1.4.D **Congress shall end all grant-based and competitive Indian country criminal justice funding in the Department of Justice (DOJ) and instead establish a permanent, recurring base funding system for tribal law enforcement and justice services.**

As soon as possible, Congress should end all grant-based and competitive Indian country criminal justice funding in the DOJ and instead pool these monies to establish a permanent, recurring base funding system for tribal law enforcement and justice services. Federal base funding for tribal justice systems should be made available on equal terms to all federally recognized tribes, whether their lands are under federal jurisdiction or congressionally authorized state jurisdiction.

1.4.E **Congress shall establish a much larger commitment than currently exists to fund tribal programs through the Department of Justice's Office of Justice Programs (OJP) and the Victims of Crime Act (VOCA) funding. As an initial step towards the much larger commitment needed, Congress shall establish a minimum 10 percent tribal set-aside, as per the Violence Against Women Act (VAWA) tribal set-aside, from funding for all discretionary Office of Justice Programs (OJP) and Victims of Crime Act (VOCA) funding making clear that the tribal set-aside is the minimum tribal funding and not in any way a cap on tribal funding. President Obama's annual budget request to Congress has included a 7 percent tribal set-aside for the last few years. This is a very positive step and Congress should authorize this request immediately. However, the tribal set-aside should be increased to 10 percent in subsequent appropriations bills. Until Congress acts, the Department of Justice shall establish this minimum 10 percent tribal set-aside administratively.**

After determining that AI/AN women face the highest level of violence in the nation—along with the highest rate of unmet needs—Congress set aside a percentage of VAWA funding for tribal governments. Since the 2005 VAWA Reauthorization, the tribal set-aside has been 10 percent. The Advisory Committee finds that the 10 percent VAWA tribal set-aside is a highly relevant precedent that should be applied to all discretionary OJP programs that impact AI/AN children exposed to violence. The same rationale applies to the VOCA funding, which has served as a major funding source for states to provide services to victims of crime since its establishment in 1984. However, it should be noted that this is a minimum initial amount with the expectation that substantially increased levels of funding will be forthcoming.

> **1.4.F   The Department of Justice (DOJ) and Department of Interior (DOI) should, within one year, conduct tribal consultations to determine the feasibility of implementing Indian Law and Order Commission (ILOC) Recommendation 3.8 to consolidate all DOI tribal criminal justice programs and all DOJ Indian country programs and services into a single "Indian country component" in the DOJ and report back to the President and AI/AN Nations on how tribes want to move forward on it.**

While the Advisory Committee is in general agreement with the ILOC's Recommendation 3.8 to consolidate all DOI tribal criminal justice programs and all DOJ Indian country programs and services into a single DOJ "Indian country component," the Advisory Committee recommends that tribal consultation be conducted prior to making such a significant and far-reaching move.

1.5   The legislative branch of the federal government along with the executive branch, under the direction and oversight of the White House Native American Affairs Office, should provide adequate funding for and assistance with Indian country research and data collection.

Research and data collection is a critical component of developing effective responses to AI/AN children exposed to violence. Tribal governments, like every government, need the ability to track and access data involving their citizens across service areas and to accept the responsibility of gathering data. Tribal governments currently do not have adequate access to accurate, comprehensive data regarding key areas affecting AI/AN children exposed to violence. Even when data is gathered, it is often not shared with tribes. In order to remedy this situation, federal leadership is required and data should be co-owned with tribes.

Tribal Nations also need access to research initiatives that will help create and develop effective prevention and intervention strategies for children exposed to violence. Currently, many tribal communities are developing and implementing culturally based prevention and intervention programs. However, most do not have the resources necessary to evaluate the effectiveness of these programs.

1.6 The legislative and executive branches of the federal government should encourage tribal-state collaborations to meet the needs of AI/AN children exposed to violence.

The criminal justice, juvenile justice, and child welfare systems are too often ineffective because tribes and states do not always act collaboratively. The federal government should use its power and funds to encourage tribal-state collaborations.

1.7 The federal government should provide training for AI/AN Nations and for the federal agencies serving AI/AN communities on the needs of AI/AN children exposed to violence. Federal employees assigned to work on issues pertaining to AI/AN communities should be required to obtain training on tribal sovereignty, working with tribal governments, and the impact of historical trauma and colonization on tribal Nations within the first sixty days of their job assignment.

The federal trust responsibility should include ensuring that all service providers attending to the needs of AI/AN children receive appropriate training and technical assistance. Properly credentialed professionals who lack the cultural knowledge to identify and understand tribal familial needs face challenges in providing effective services. Further, AI/AN communities struggle to ensure access to a qualified AI/AN workforce in the trauma treatment area.

Chapter 2—Promoting Well-Being for American Indian and Alaska Native Children in the Home

Every single day, a majority of American Indian and Alaska Native (AI/AN) children are exposed to violence within the walls of their own homes. This exposure not only contradicts traditional understandings that children are to be protected and viewed as sacred, but it leaves hundreds of children traumatized and struggling to cope over the course of their lifetime. Despite leadership from tribal governments, parents and families, domestic violence in the homes of AI/AN children and physical abuse, sexual abuse, and neglect of children is more common than in the general population. Unfortunately, the response of child-serving systems often re-traumatizes the child.

2.1   The legislative and executive branches of the federal government should ensure Indian Child Welfare Act (ICWA) compliance and encourage tribal-state ICWA collaborations.

2.1.A   Within two years of the publication of this report, the Administration for Children and Families (ACF) in the Department of Health and Human Services (HHS), the Bureau of Indian Affairs (BIA) in the Department of the Interior (DOI), and tribes should develop a modernized unified data-collection system designed to collect Adoption and Foster Care Analysis and Reporting System (AFCARS) (ICWA and tribal dependency) data on all AI/AN children who are placed into foster care by their agency and share that data quarterly with tribes to allow tribes and the BIA to make informed decisions regarding AI/AN children.

2.1.B   The Secretaries of the Department of Interior (DOI) and Health and Human Services (HHS) should compel BIA and ACF to work together collaboratively to collect data regarding compliance with ICWA in state court systems. The ACF and BIA should work collaboratively to ensure state court compliance with ICWA.

2.1.C   The BIA should issue regulations (not simply update guidelines) and create an oversight board to review ICWA implementation and designate consequences of

noncompliance and/or incentives for compliance with ICWA to ensure the effective implementation of ICWA.

2.1.D The Department of Justice (DOJ) should create a position of Indian Child Welfare Specialist to provide advice to the Attorney General and DOJ staff on matters relative to AI/AN child welfare cases, to provide case support in cases before federal, tribal, and state courts, and to coordinate ICWA training for federal, tribal, and state judges; prosecutors; and other court personnel.

If AI/AN children today are to be provided with a reliable safety net, the letter and the spirit of ICWA must be enforced. ICWA provides critical legal protections for AI/AN children when intervention and treatment is deemed necessary by state child protection agencies. The most significant provisions seek to keep AI/AN children safely in their homes and provide AI/AN children with certain civil protections as members of their respective tribes.

The lack of accurate, relevant data on tribal children and families often results in AI/AN children being left out of discussions about policy development, resource allocation, and decision making at the federal level. Or, because of the lack of such data regarding AI/AN children, policy makers delay or decline to make decisions and resource allocations because they cannot "justify" the services. By increasing tribal capacity (through tribal child protection agencies in BIA and IHS) in the area of data collection, tribal engagement and federal responsiveness to AI/AN children's needs can be increased.

ICWA noncompliance is at least in part a result of minimal oversight of ICWA implementation and no enforcement mechanism. ICWA was enacted without providing sanctions for noncompliance, incentives for effective compliance, a data-collection requirement, and a mandate for an oversight committee or authority to monitor compliance. ICWA is the only federal child welfare law that does not include legislatively mandated oversight or periodic review.[9] These deficits in ICWA should be corrected.

The DOJ existing structure does not include a position that allows for investigation and research on Indian child welfare cases. The current environment is litigious and recent Indian child welfare cases have risen to the state and federal Supreme Courts. In addition to monitoring state compliance with ICWA included in other recommendations in this chapter, a position within the DOJ dedicated to supporting challenges to ICWA will improve child welfare outcomes and play a direct role in reducing trauma and violence experienced by AI/AN children in the child welfare system. Requirements for the position should include ICWA and family law experience. The position should be filled immediately.

2.2 The Bureau of Indian Affairs (BIA) in the Department of the Interior (DOI), the Administration for Children and Families (ACF) in the Department of Health and Human Services (HHS), and tribes, within one year of the publication of this report, should develop and submit a written plan to the White House Domestic Policy Council, to work collaboratively and efficiently to provide trauma-informed, culturally appropriate tribal child welfare services in Indian country.

When federal agencies fail to work together with tribes to confront problems in Indian country, the result is ineffective and inefficient systems. Child welfare services in Indian country are a good example of this inefficiency. Cooperation and collaboration among agencies that focus on tribal families and children must be thoughtfully planned and consistently delivered.

2.3 The Administration for Children and Families (ACF) in the Department of Health and Human Services (HHS), Bureau of Indian Affairs (BIA) in the Department of the Interior (DOI), and tribes should collectively identify child welfare best practices and produce an annual report on child welfare best practices in AI/AN communities that is easily accessible to tribal communities.

Tribal child protection and prevention teams need AI/AN-specific research about the intersection of domestic violence, trauma exposure, and child maltreatment in order to create and promote effective prevention strategies, interventions, treatment, and policy change. Tribal communities have traditional methods of practice-based evidence to deal with trauma and healing. These practices have been used for centuries, but are not acknowledged as "evidence-based" treatments. Although promising practices exist throughout tribal communities, we do not have enough information about the effectiveness of such programs and methods of implementation, which makes success hard to replicate.

2.4 **The Indian Health Service (IHS) in the Department of Health and Human Services (HHS), state public health services, and other state and federal agencies that provide pre- or postnatal services should provide culturally appropriate education and skills training for parents, foster parents, and caregivers of AI/AN children. Agencies should work with tribes to culturally adapt proven therapeutic models for their unique tribal communities (e.g., adaptation of home visitation service to include local cultural beliefs and values).**

Due to the prevalence of violence in AI/AN homes and communities and the influence of historical trauma, many AI/AN parents, foster parents, and prospective parents may need help developing traditional parenting skills. Caregivers may have experienced trauma as children or may continue to be victims of violence in their homes. Assistance for families experiencing violence or at risk for violence is most accessible when it is brought directly into the home.

2.5 **The Bureau of Indian Affairs (BIA) in the Department of the Interior (DOI), tribal social service agencies, and state social service agencies should have policies that permit removal of children from victims of domestic violence for "failure to protect" only as a last resort as long as the child is safe.**

Children are often removed from both parents when domestic violence occurs, even when one parent was also a victim of violence. Children who witness domestic violence have a greater need for stability and security; however when the child is removed from the nonoffending parent, it can produce the opposite effect.. To ensure stability and permanency for children in a home with domestic violence, children should remain with the non-offending parent (caregiver) whenever possible, as long as the child is safe.

2.6 **The Secretary of Health and Human Services (HHS) should increase and support access to culturally appropriate behavioral health and substance abuse prevention and treatment services in all AI/AN communities, especially the use of traditional healers and helpers identified by tribal communities.**

Substance abuse related to child abuse and neglect is more likely to be reported for AI/AN families. Treatment programs that work with AI/AN populations should incorporate AI/AN tribal customs and spiritual ceremonies, be trauma-informed, and be holistic. AI/AN people in recovery may have experienced multiple traumas in their lifetimes, suffer from historical and intergenerational trauma, and abuse alcohol and drugs as a way of coping with those traumas. Without treatment to heal from the underlying traumas, alcohol and drug abuse treatment may be ineffective.

Chapter 3—Promoting Well-Being for American Indian and Alaska Native Children in the Community

Violence in American Indian and Alaska Native (AI/AN) communities occurs at very high rates compared with non-AI/AN communities—higher for AI/AN people than for all other races. AI/AN children are exposed to many types of community-based violence, including simple assaults, violent threats, sexual assault, and homicide. Additionally, suicide, gang violence, sex and drug trafficking, and bullying are especially problematic for AI/AN youth. Coupling that rate of exposure with the high rate of homelessness makes AI/AN youth especially vulnerable to community violence. The recommendations in this chapter speak to increasing capacity and infrastructure in AI/AN communities to allow those communities to confront the impact of current and past violence and to prevent future violence.

3.1 **The White House Native American Affairs Office (see Recommendation 1.2) and executive branch agencies that are responsible for addressing the needs of AI/AN children, in consultation with tribes, should develop a strategy to braid (integrate) flexible funding to allow tribes to create comprehensive violence prevention, intervention, and treatment programs to serve the distinct needs of AI/AN children and families.**

3.1.A **The White House Native American Affairs Office, the U.S. Attorney General, the Secretaries of the Department of Interior (DOI) and Health and Human Services (HHS), and the heads of other agencies that provide funds that serve AI/AN children should annually consult with tribal governments to solicit recommendations on the**

mechanisms that would provide flexible funds for the assessment of local needs, and for the development and adaptation of promising practices that allow for the integration of the unique cultures and healing traditions of the local tribal community.

3.1.B The White House Native American Affairs Office and the U.S. Attorney General should work with the organizations that specialize in treatment and services for traumatized children, for example, National Child Traumatic Stress Network, to ensure that services for AI/AN children exposed to violence are trauma-informed.

3.1.C The White House Native American Affairs Office should coordinate the development and implementation of federal policy that mandates exposure to violence trauma screening and suicide screening be a part of services offered to AI/AN children during medical, juvenile justice, and/or social service intakes.

Although children exposed to violence in AI/AN communities are similar to all children exposed to violence, solutions to the exposure to traumatic events may vary greatly among the 566 distinct federally recognized tribes across the United States. Federal, tribal, and state agencies and organizations must collaborate to ensure that tribal communities are allowed the flexibility to implement solutions that work and are culturally and locally relevant to meet the challenges, the circumstances, and the unique characteristics of their children and communities.

Policies must be developed and implemented to ensure that screening for exposure to violence takes place in numerous settings and issues of confidentiality are resolved. Confidentiality issues will arise as children are screened by various child-serving organizations in the communities that serve them. The need for confidentiality must be balanced with the need for service providers to have information that will permit them to more effectively serve the child. The Advisory Committee urges federal, tribal, and state programs that collect these data to seek creative ways to monitor and use information for the benefit of the child rather than use confidentiality as an excuse to inappropriately refuse to share information.

3.2 The Department of Justice's National Institute of Justice (NIJ) and other Justice Department agencies with statutory research funding should set aside 10 percent of their annual research budgets for partnerships between tribes and research entities to develop, adapt, and validate trauma screens for use among AI/AN children and youth living in rural, tribal, and urban communities. Trauma screens should be tested and validated for use in schools, juvenile justice (law enforcement and courts), mental health, primary care, Defending Childhood Tribal Grantee programs, and social service agencies and should include measures of trauma history, trauma symptoms, recognizing trauma triggers, recognizing trauma reactions, and developing positive coping skills for both the child and the caregivers.

Early identification of exposure to violence, timely intervention and treatment, and especially prevention can protect a child from being trapped in a cycle of repeated exposure to violence.[10] Identification of children who have been traumatized by exposure to violence is the first step toward healing and recovery. Children must be screened in schools, clinics, social service agencies, juvenile justice facilities, wherever children are found. An AI/AN child's response to a trauma may be intensified because of the legacy of historical trauma. Tribal communities need assistance from research partnerships to develop, validate, and use instruments to screen for trauma symptoms and design an effective path forward for children.

3.3 The White House Native American Affairs Office and responsible federal agencies should provide AI/AN youth-serving organizations such as schools, Head Starts, daycares, foster care programs, and so forth with the resources needed to create and sustain safe places where AI/AN children exposed to violence can obtain services. Every youth-serving organization in tribal and urban Native communities should receive mandated trauma-informed training and have trauma-informed staff and consultants providing school-based trauma-informed treatment in bullying, suicide, and gang prevention/intervention.

Tribal child-serving systems and school staff are often unaware of the impact trauma has on the psychological and emotional health of their students. Schools that are trauma-informed can establish safe and nurturing environments where children can learn.

3.4 The Secretary of Housing and Urban Development (HUD) should designate and prioritize Native American Housing Assistance and Self-Determination Act (NAHSDA) funding for construction of facilities to serve AI/AN children exposed to violence and structures for positive youth activities. This will help tribal communities create positive environments such as shelters, housing, cultural facilities, recreational facilities, sport centers, and theaters through the Indian Community Development Block Grant Program and the Housing Assistance Programs.

The Advisory Committee repeatedly heard testimony about the need for safe houses for youth in tribal communities—safe settings for youth escaping violence and places where a youth's basic needs for safety, nutrition, mental health treatment, and education can be assessed and met. Safe houses may provide for their cultural and spiritual needs as well. Providing a safe place where violence-exposed youth can focus on healing is the first step toward helping a young person recover from trauma.

3.5 The White House Native American Affairs Office should work with the Congress and executive branch agencies in consultation with tribes to develop, promote, and fund youth-based afterschool programs for AI/AN youth. The programs must be culturally based and trauma-informed, must partner with parents/caregivers, and, when necessary, provide referrals to trauma-informed behavioral health providers. Where appropriate, local capacity should also be expanded through partnerships with America's volunteer organizations, for example, AmeriCorps.

Community-based and afterschool programs for youth that teach culture, prevention, and life skills will help AI/AN youth develop healthy lifestyles and values and strengthen their resiliency.

3.6 The White House Native American Affairs Office and the Secretary of Health and Human Services (HHS) should develop and implement a plan to expand access to Indian Health Service (IHS), tribal, and urban Indian centers to provide behavioral health

services to AI/AN children in schools. **This should include the deployment of behavioral health services providers to serve students in the school setting.**

Federal, tribal, state, and for-profit agencies that provide behavioral health services must cooperate to develop and deliver school-based services for AI/AN students. Federal agencies should work with public schools and Bureau of Indian Education (BIE)–funded schools to ensure that services are offered, preferably in the schools, to students attending BIE-funded schools. School-based services increase the availability and utilization of services and will increase safety in schools.

Chapter 4—Creating a Juvenile Justice System that Focuses on Prevention, Treatment, and Healing

Children entering the juvenile justice system are exposed to violence at staggeringly high rates. Many American Indian and Alaska Native (AI/AN) people believe that the Western criminal/juvenile justice system is inappropriate for children, particularly AI/AN children, as it is contrary to AI/AN values in raising children. The Advisory Committee concludes that the standard way juvenile justice has been administered by state jurisdictions is a failure and it re-traumatizes AI/AN children.

The Advisory Committee supports substantial reform of the juvenile justice systems impacting AI/AN youth. A reformed juvenile justice system should be tribally operated or strongly influenced by tribes within the local region.

4.1 Congress should authorize additional and adequate funding for tribal juvenile justice programs, a grossly underfunded area, in the form of block grants and self-governance compacts that would support the restructuring and maintenance of tribal juvenile justice systems.

4.1.A Congress should create an adequate tribal set-aside that allows access to all expanded federal funding that supports juvenile justice at an amount equal to the need in tribal communities. As an initial step towards the much larger commitment needed, Congress should

establish a minimum 10 percent tribal set-aside, as per the Violence Against Women Act (VAWA) tribal set aside, from funding for all Office of Juvenile Justice and Delinquency Prevention (OJJDP) funding making clear that the tribal set-aside is the minimum tribal funding and not in any way a cap on tribal funding. President Obama's annual budget request to Congress has included a 7 percent tribal set aside for the last few years. This is a very positive step and Congress should authorize this request immediately. However, the tribal set-aside should be increased to 10 percent in subsequent appropriations bills. Until Congress acts, the Department of Justice should establish this minimum 10 percent tribal set-aside administratively.

4.1.B   Federal funding for state juvenile justice programs should require that states engage in and support meaningful and consensual consultation with tribes on the design, content, and operation of juvenile justice programs to ensure that programming is imbued with cultural integrity to meet the needs of tribal youth.

4.1.C   Congress should direct the Department of Justice (DOJ) and the Department of Interior (DOI) to determine which agency should provide funding for both the construction and operation of jails and juvenile detention facilities in AI/AN communities, require consultation with tribes concerning selection process, ensure the trust responsibilities for these facilities and services are assured, and appropriate the necessary funds.

The funding tribes receive for juvenile justice programming must be adequate and stable. Currently, tribes need to rely on inadequate base funding from the BIA, thus forcing them to compete for grant funds to support the most basic components of a juvenile justice system. It is unacceptable for federal agencies to provide grant funding for a tribal program and limit the funding to three years, requiring tribes to re-compete or lose funding at the end of the grant period. Flexibility and stability in funding is important to allow local communities to utilize the funding in creative, impactful ways.

Programming offered in state juvenile justice systems is not meeting the needs of AI/AN youth and in some cases is harming these youth. Even those states with significant AI/AN populations fail to meaningfully consult with tribes about their juvenile justice systems to ensure that their programming is thoughtful and culturally based. One way to ensure that states with significant AI/AN populations involve the tribes in important decisions regarding AI/AN children is to tie federal funding to meaningful consultation with tribes.

Currently the DOJ and DOI have divided responsibilities to construct, operate, staff, and maintain jails and juvenile detention centers. This has resulted in dozens of facilities being constructed that are vacant or seriously underutilized because operating funds have not been provided. The split responsibility that exists now is not workable.

4.2 Federal, state, and private funding and technical assistance should be provided to tribes to develop or revise trauma-informed, culturally specific tribal codes to improve tribal juvenile justice systems.

Developing a tribal juvenile justice system requires developing tribal codes that fit the culture and community. Technical assistance should be provided to develop culturally appropriate, trauma-informed juvenile justice codes and systems.

4.3 Federal, tribal, and state justice systems should provide publicly funded legal representation to AI/AN children in the juvenile justice systems to protect their rights and minimize the harm that the juvenile justice system may cause them. The use of technology such as videoconferencing could make such representation available even in remote areas.

AI/AN youth need to be provided with counsel due to the impact of immaturity, the effects of exposure to violence and trauma, and caregivers who are no more likely to understand the system, rights, and process than the youth. Given the overrepresentation of AI/AN youth in state and federal justice systems and in secure confinement, it is critical that culturally competent, well-trained defense counsel be afforded to the youth at public expense in all federal, tribal, and state juvenile proceedings.

4.4 Federal, tribal, and state justice systems should only use detention of AI/AN youth when the youth is a danger to themselves or the community. It should be close to the child's community and provide trauma-informed, culturally appropriate, and individually tailored services, including reentry services. Alternatives to detention such as "safe houses" should be significantly developed in AI/AN urban and rural communities.

The use of juvenile detention is not effective as a deterrent to delinquent behavior, risky behavior, or truancy and should only be used when there is clear evidence that the youth is a danger to themselves or the community.

4.5 Federal, tribal, and state justice systems and service providers should make culturally appropriate trauma-informed screening, assessment, and care the standard in juvenile justice systems. The Indian Health Service (IHS) in the Department of Health and Human Services (HHS) and tribal and urban Indian behavioral health service providers must receive periodic training in culturally adapted trauma-informed interventions and cultural competency to provide appropriate services to AI/AN children and their families.

Behavioral health services for AI/AN youth may be handled by different agencies with different priorities. Youth in the juvenile justice system are typically not a priority to those community-based agencies. Culturally appropriate, trauma-informed screening and care must become the standard in all juvenile justice systems that impact AI/AN youth if the system is to treat children as sacred and promote wellness and resilience.

4.6 Congress should amend the Indian Child Welfare Act (ICWA) to provide that when a state court initiates any delinquency proceeding involving an Indian child for acts that took place on the reservation, all of the notice, intervention, and transfer provisions of ICWA will apply. For all other Indian children involved in state delinquency proceedings, ICWA should be amended to require notice to the tribe and a right to intervene. As a first step, the Department of Justice (DOJ) should establish a demonstration pilot project that would provide funding for three states to provide ICWA-type notification to tribes within their state whenever the state court initiates a delinquency proceeding against a child from that tribe which includes a plan to evaluate the results with an eye toward scaling it up for all AI/AN communities.

States have jurisdiction over AI/AN children when a violation occurs outside of Indian country, or within Indian country in PL-280 states or states that have a settlement act or other similar federal legislation. An overarching concern voiced at hearings conducted by the Advisory Committee was that states are not required to notify the tribe or involve the tribe in a juvenile delinquency proceeding. That concern is exacerbated because states generally do not provide the cultural support necessary for Native youth's rehabilitation and reentry into the tribal community.

4.7   Congress should amend the Federal Education Rights and Privacy Act (FERPA) to allow tribes to access their members' school attendance, performance, and disciplinary records.

FERPA[11] generally allows federal, state, and local education agencies the ability to access student records and other personally identifiable information kept by state public schools without the advance consent of the parents; it does not afford the same access to tribes. Tribes need this access in order to be informed enough to intervene early and respond to the red flags raised by truancy and disciplinary problems in schools as it pertains to AI/AN children exposed to violence.

Chapter 5—Empowering Alaska Tribes, Removing Barriers, and Providing Resources

Problems with children exposed to violence in American Indian and Alaska Native (AI/AN) communities are severe across the United States—but they are systemically worse in Alaska. Issues related to Alaska Native children exposed to violence are different for a variety of reasons including regional vastness and geographical isolation, extreme weather, exorbitant transportation costs, lack of economic opportunity and access to resources, a lack of respect for Alaska tribal sovereignty, and a lack of understanding and respect for Alaska Native history and culture, all of which have contributed to high levels of recurring violence. Alaska Tribes are best positioned to effectively address these problems so long as the current barriers are removed and Alaska Tribes are empowered to protect Alaska Native children.

5.1 The federal government should promptly implement all five recommendations in Chapter 2 (Reforming Justice for Alaska Natives: The Time Is Now) of the Indian Law and Order Commission's 2013 Final Report, A Roadmap for Making Native America Safer, and assess the cost of implementation. This will remove the barriers that currently inhibit the ability of Alaska Native Tribes to exercise criminal jurisdiction and utilize criminal remedies when confronting the highest rates of violent crime in the country.

5.1.A *(Indian Law and Order Commission Recommendation 2.1)*: **Congress should overturn the U.S. Supreme Court's decision in** *Alaska v. Native Village of Venetie Tribal Government*, **by amending the Alaska Native Claims Settlement Act (ANCSA) to provide that former reservation lands acquired in fee by Alaska Native villages and other lands transferred in fee to Native villages pursuant to ANCSA are Indian country.**

5.1.B *(Indian Law and Order Commission Recommendation 2.2)*: **Congress and the President should amend the definitions of Indian country to clarify (or affirm) that Native allotments and Native-owned town sites in Alaska are Indian country.**

5.1.C *(Indian Law and Order Commission Recommendation 2.3)*: **Congress should amend the Alaska Native Claims Settlement Act to allow a transfer of lands from Regional Corporations to Tribal governments; to allow transferred lands to be put into trust and included within the definition of Indian country in the Federal criminal code; to allow Alaska Native Tribes to put tribally owned fee simple land similarly into trust; and to channel more resources directly to Alaska Native Tribal**

governments for the provision of governmental services in those communities.

5.1.D *(Indian Law and Order Commission Recommendation 2.4)*: Congress should repeal Section 910 of Title IX of the Violence Against Women Reauthorization Act of 2013 (VAWA Amendments), and thereby permit Alaska Native communities and their courts to address domestic violence and sexual assault committed by Tribal members and non-Natives, just as in the lower 48.

5.1.E *(Indian Law and Order Commission Recommendation 2.5)*: Congress should affirm the inherent criminal jurisdiction of Alaska Native Tribal governments over their members within the external boundaries of their villages.

The Advisory Committee agrees with each of the five Alaska-specific Indian Law and Order Commission (ILOC) recommendations and the Commission's rationale for each recommendation. Until and unless these barriers are removed, the state of Alaska will continue to assert that Alaska Tribes do not have any criminal jurisdiction and thereby continue to contend that Alaska Tribes are only empowered to utilize civil courts and civil remedies when confronting the highest rates of violent crime in the country. The Advisory Committee recommends that these five ILOC recommendations be enacted as soon as possible in order to ensure that Alaska Tribes are also empowered to exercise criminal jurisdiction and criminal remedies when confronting such incredibly high rates of violent crime.

5.2 **The Department of Justice (DOJ) and the Department of Interior (DOI) should provide recurring base funding for Alaska Tribes to develop and sustain both civil and criminal tribal court systems, assist in the provision of law enforcement and related services, and assist with intergovernmental agreements.**

5.2.A As a first step, the DOJ and the DOI should—within one year—conduct a current inventory and a needs/cost assessment of law enforcement, court, and related services for every Alaska Tribe.

5.2.B The DOJ and the DOI should provide the funding necessary to address the unmet need identified, and ensure that each Alaska Tribe has the annual base funding level necessary to provide and sustain an adequate level of law enforcement, tribal court, and related funding and services.

5.2.C Congress should enact legislation along the lines of the current bipartisan bill sponsored by both Alaska senators (S. 1474 to be titled Alaska Safe Families and Villages Act of 2014) that supports the development, enhancement, and sustainability of Alaska tribal courts including full faith and credit for Alaska tribal court acts and decrees and the establishment of specific Alaska tribal court base funding streams and grants to Alaska Native Tribes carrying out intergovernmental agreements with the state of Alaska.

5.2.D The federal government should work together with Alaska Tribes and the state of Alaska to improve coordination and collaboration on a broad range of public safety measures that cause Alaska Native children to be exposed to high rates of violence.

The development, enhancement, and sustainment of Alaska tribal courts, and truly cooperative relationships between the state of Alaska and Alaska Tribes, are required to reduce violent crime and protect Alaska Native children from exposure to violence. Village-based tribal courts are the culturally appropriate provider. Alaska tribal courts must be developed, enhanced, and sustained in order to effectively address issues concerning Alaska Native children exposed to violence.

5.3 The state of Alaska should prioritize law enforcement responses and related resources for Alaska Tribes, and recognize and collaborate with Alaska tribal courts.

5.3.A The state of Alaska should prioritize the state law enforcement response and resources for Alaska Tribes. At a minimum, there must be at least one law enforcement official onsite in each village.

5.3.B The state of Alaska should prioritize the provision of needed village-based services including village-based women's shelters (which allow children to stay with their mothers), child advocacy centers, and alcohol and drug treatment services.

5.3.C The state of Alaska should recognize and collaborate with Alaska tribal courts including following existing federal laws designed to protect Alaska Native children and families such as VAWA protection order authority, which requires states to recognize and enforce tribal protection orders that have been issued by tribal courts–including Alaska Native tribal courts–without first requiring a state court certification of the tribal protection order.

5.3.D The state of Alaska should enter into self-governance intergovernmental agreements with Alaska Tribes in order to provide more local tools and options to combat village public safety issues and address issues concerning Alaska Native children exposed to violence.

The state of Alaska must increase the level of protection in Alaska Tribes. Village-based services are needed in law enforcement and victim protection. Approximately 370 State Troopers have primary responsibility for law enforcement in rural Alaska, but have a full-time presence in less than half of the remote Alaska Tribes. Seventy-five villages lack any law enforcement at all.[12]

5.4 The Administration for Child and Families (ACF) in the Department of Health and Human Services (HHS) and the State of Alaska Office of Children's Services (OCS) should jointly respond to the extreme disproportionality of Alaska Native children in foster care by establishing a time-limited, outcome-focused task force to develop real-time, Native inclusive strategies to reduce disproportionality.

Issues of foster care disproportionality are huge problems for many tribes. Inadequate numbers of Native foster families to assure compliance with ICWA impacts most state child welfare agencies as well. But this problem takes on added dimensions and particular significance in Alaska—not only due to the high level of removals of Alaska Native children and the fact that it has been increasing at an alarming rate—but also due to many other factors including the remoteness of Alaska Tribes, Alaska's vast size, the exorbitant cost of transportation, the financial limitations of subsistence economy, the lack of village-based foster care options, the lack of village-based services and resources, the lack of tribal courts, and the historic refusal of the state of Alaska to collaborate with Alaska Tribes and, until recently to recognize that Alaska Tribes even exist.

5.5 The Department of Interior (DOI) and the State of Alaska should empower Alaska Tribes to manage their own subsistence hunting and fishing rights, remove the current barriers, and provide Alaska Tribes with the resources needed to effectively manage their own subsistence hunting and fishing.

Regulations that limit the ability of Alaska Natives to conduct traditional subsistence hunting and fishing are directly connected to violence in Alaska Tribes and the exposure of Alaska Native children to that violence. Violence is essentially nonexistent during the times in which the communities are engaging in traditional subsistence hunting and fishing activities, and violence spikes during times when Alaska Natives are unable to provide for their families. Beyond providing basic food, subsistence fishing and hunting has been essential to Alaska Native families' way of life for generations. Like language and cultural traditions, it has been passed down from one generation to the next and is an important means of reinforcing tribal values and traditions and binding families together in common spirit and activity. Interfering with these traditions erodes culture, family, a sense of purpose and ability to provide for one's own, and a sense of pride.

Notes

1. For purposes of this report, we use the term "tribe" to refer to federally recognized tribes from the Secretary of Interior's list. 79 Fed. Reg. 4,748 (Jan. 29, 2014), *available at* http://www.gpo.gov/fdsys/pkg/FR-2014-01-29/pdf/2014-01683.pdf.

2. Indian Law and Order Commission, *A Roadmap for Making Native America Safer: Report to the President and Congress of the United States* (November 2013): 154, available at: http://www.aisc.ucla.edu/iloc/report/index.html.

3. The Advisory Committee is the anchor of the AI/AN Task Force established in 2013 by the Attorney General. The Advisory Committee consists of nonfederal experts in the area of AI/AN children exposed to violence.

4. Listenbee, Robert L., Jr., et al., *Report of the Attorney General's National Task Force on Children Exposed to Violence*, Washington, D.C.: U.S. Department of Justice, Office of Juvenile Justice and Delinquency Prevention, December 2012.

5. Indian Law and Order Commission, *A Roadmap for Making Native America Safer: Report to the President and Congress of the United States* (November 2013), available at: http://www.aisc.ucla.edu/iloc/report/index.html.

6. The Native peoples of Alaska are commonly referred to as "Alaska Natives," and "Alaska Native Villages." For the purposes of this report, we will use the term "Alaska Tribe" to refer to federally recognized tribes in the State of Alaska. 79 Fed. Reg. 4,748 (Jan. 29, 2014), *available at* http://www.gpo.gov/fdsys/pkg/FR-2014-01-29/pdf/2014-01683.pdf.

7. The Violence Against Women Reauthorization Act of 2013, PL-113-4, 127 Stat. 54 (March 7, 2013).

8. See Chapter 11 (Funding) of Final Report—Law Enforcement and Criminal Justice under Public Law 280 available at: http://www.tribal-institute.org/download/pl280_study.pdf.

9. Written Testimony of Sarah Hicks Kastelic (Alutiiq), Hearing of the Task Force on American Indian/Alaska Native Children Exposed to Violence, Anchorage, AK, June 11, 2014 at 23, available at: http://www.justice.gov/defendingchildhood/4th-hearing/hearing4-briefing-binder.pdf.

10. Listenbee, Robert L., Jr., et al., *Report of the Attorney General's National Task Force on Children Exposed to Violence*, Washington, D.C.: U.S. Department of Justice, Office of Juvenile Justice and Delinquency Prevention (December 2012): 66.

11. 20 U.S.C. 1232(g).

12. S. Rep. No. 113-260, at 2 (2014), *to accompany* S. 1474, 113th Cong. 2d Sess. (2014).

CHAPTER 1

Building a Strong Foundation

The health and well-being of American Indian and Alaska Native (AI/AN) children is critical to the strength and future stability of tribes[1] and Indian families.[2] Yet, AI/AN children are exposed to multiple forms of violence at rates higher than any other race in the United States, resulting in increased rates of altered neurological development, poor physical and mental health, poor school performance, substance abuse, and overrepresentation in the juvenile justice system.[3] Violence, including intentional injuries, homicide, and suicide, accounts for 75 percent of deaths of AI/AN youth ages twelve to twenty.[4] These serious adversities often lead to toxic stress reactions and chronic and severe trauma. With the convergence of exceptionally high crime rates, jurisdictional limitations, vastly under-resourced programs, and poverty, service providers and policy makers should assume that *all* AI/AN children have been exposed to violence. However, while AI/AN children face rates of violence at epidemic levels, some tribes and urban Indian organizations have found innovative ways to incorporate tradition, exercise sovereignty, and develop resources to protect their children from harm. This chapter includes foundational recommendations for tribes, urban Indian service providers, and policy makers at the federal, tribal, and state levels to transform the unconscionable reality in which AI/AN children live. The Advisory Committee believes that these recommendations, once acted on, will be the key to creating lasting and positive change.

Overview of AI/AN Children Exposed to Violence

There is a dearth of data and statistics specific to AI/AN children's exposure to violence due to poor identification practices, a view that the population is too small to study, and a lack of solid methodological practices. However, a review of non-Native studies along with the somewhat limited data on AI/AN children sheds light on the impact of violence on AI/AN children.

Children Exposed to Violence Nationally

The best overview of children exposed to violence on a nationwide scale is provided in the 2012 Final Report of the Attorney General's National Task Force on Children Exposed to Violence:[5]

> *Exposure to violence is a national crisis that affects almost two in every three of our children nationwide. For AI/AN children, while we do not have statistics, all indications are that these numbers are even higher. According to the National Survey of Children's Exposure to Violence (NatSCEV), an*

estimated 46 million of the 76 million children currently residing in the United States are exposed to violence, crime, and abuse each year.

It is important to realize that, although exposure to violence in any form harms children, exposure to different forms of violence can have different effects. **Sexual abuse** *places children at high risk for serious and often chronic problems with health, PTSD and other mental health disorders, suicidality, eating disorders, sleep disorders, substance abuse, and sexuality and sexual behavior.*

Children exposed to **physical abuse** *also are at high risk for severe and often lifelong problems with physical health, PTSD and other mental health disorders, suicidality, eating disorders, substance abuse, and sexuality and sexual behavior.*

Children who have been exposed to **intimate partner violence** *in their families also are at high risk for severe and potentially lifelong problems with physical health, mental health, school and peer relationships, and disruptive behavior.*

Children who are exposed to **community violence** *in their neighborhoods or schools often see family members, peers, trusted adults, or strangers (both innocent bystanders and active participants in violent activities) being injured or even murdered. They may come to believe that violence is "normal."*

The picture becomes even more complex when children are exposed to **multiple types of violence***; these children are called "polyvictims." The toxic combination of exposure to family violence, child physical and sexual abuse, and exposure to community violence increases the risk and severity of posttraumatic injuries and health and mental health disorders for exposed children by at least twofold and up to tenfold. Polyvictimized children are at high risk for losing the fundamental capacities they need to develop normally and to become successful learners and productive adults.*

Poverty Increases Both Risk and Adverse Impact of Exposure to Violence
Children living in poverty are far more likely to be exposed to violence and psychological trauma, both at home and in the surrounding community. In many poor communities, particularly those that are isolated and the victims of historical trauma and racism as well as poverty, violence has become the norm for children growing up.

AI/AN Children Exposed to Violence

AI/AN children experience violence in many forms, including sexual abuse, physical abuse, domestic violence, child maltreatment, and community violence. As noted in the preceding text, *polyvictimized* children face significant barriers. Different forms of violence may have different negative impacts; but all forms can be

"I'm not confident I would be able to identify even one [Alaska] Native person who has not experienced or witnessed physical violence, or worse, as a child."
Andy Teuber, Chair of Alaska Native Tribal Health Consortium; President / CEO of KANA and President of Tangirnaq Native Village (aka Woody Island Tribal Council) Testimony before the Task Force on American Indian/ Alaska Native Children Exposed to Violence, Anchorage, AK, June 11, 2014

"When children grow up surrounded by violence they learn to see the world in two ways: as a victim of violence and a perpetrator of violence."
William A. Thorne Jr., Appellate Court Judge, Utah Court of Appeals (Retired). Testimony before the Task Force on American Indian/ Alaska Native Children Exposed to Violence, Phoenix, AZ, February 11, 2014

toxic and lead to serious mental, physical, and social disabilities. For instance one report noted that AI/AN juveniles experience post-traumatic stress disorder (PTSD) at a rate of *22 percent*. Sadly, this is the same rate as veterans returning from Iraq and Afghanistan, and triple the rate of the general population.[6]

Statistics indicate that overall violence in tribal communities is very high:

- Violent crime rates in Indian country are more than 2.5 times the national rate; some reservations face more than twenty times the national rate of violence.[7]
- Thirty-four percent of AI/AN women will be raped in their life-times; and AI/AN women are 2.5 times more likely to be raped or sexually assaulted than women in the United States in general.[8]
- Thirty-nine percent of AI/AN women will be subject to domestic violence.[9]

The rates of child abuse, suicide, victimization, and involvement in the criminal justice system are extremely high among AI/AN youth:

- A 2008 report by the Indian Country Child Trauma Center calcu-lated that Native youth are 2.5 times more likely to experience trauma when compared with their non-Native peers.[10]
- In a sample of AI/AN youth, an average of 4.1 lifetime traumas have been reported, with threat of injury and witnessing injury being the most common form of trauma exposure.[11]
- AI/AN youth also experience high rates of child abuse: 15.9 per one thousand compared to 10.7 for white youth.[12]
- Native American youth are twice as likely as white youth and three times as likely as other minority youth to commit suicide.[13] In 2005, suicide was the second leading cause of death for Native Americans ages ten to twenty-five.[14]
- Violence, including intentional injuries, homicide, and suicide, account for 75 percent of deaths for AI/AN youth ages twelve to twenty.[15]
- AI/AN youth have higher rates of mental health and substance use problems than other ethnic groups.[16]
- Native youth are overrepresented in both federal and state juvenile justice systems and disproportionately receive the most severe dispositions. For example, in state juvenile justice systems, AI/AN juveniles are disproportionately represented compared to white juveniles.[17] In 2010, AI/AN youth made up 367 of every one hundred thousand juveniles in residential

placement, compared with 127 of every one hundred thousand for white juveniles.[18] These rates, which are calculated based on the total percentage of AI/AN youth in the state system, are in fact even more egregious because they do not include the AI/AN youth involved in tribal juvenile justice systems.

Poverty is a significant risk factor that is intensified in Indian country. On the Pine Ridge Indian Reservation in South Dakota, for example, 70 percent of adults are unemployed, and substance abuse, homelessness, rape, violence, and child abuse are everyday occurrences—nearly all of the children on this reservation will experience or witness violence. Yet until a few years ago, the reservation had just eight police officers to respond to the needs of its 16,986 residents despite having a homicide rate more than five times the national average.[19]

Impact of Historical Trauma

Compounding these high rates of violence is historical trauma: a cumulative emotional and psychological wounding over the life span and across generations, emanating from massive group trauma.[20] AI/AN people have, for more than five hundred years, endured physical, emotional, social, and spiritual genocide from European and American colonialist policy.[21] This is a direct attack on the cultural fabric of a people and an assault on the essence of a community that has a lasting impact on an individual's psyche, spiritual/emotional core, and well-being.[22] Many Native practitioners, clinicians, researchers, and traditional healers have long recognized the impact of historical trauma on Native peoples. The term *historical trauma* can be used as framework to understand what happened in Native America and why the statistics relating to AI/AN well-being are so dismal.[23]

To understand AI/AN children's exposure to violence within the context of historical trauma, it is essential to understand the disparate treatment of AI/AN families and communities by federal and state governments, and the lingering effects that government policies and practices have on the AI/AN population, including:

- the removal and confinement of tribes to reservations from historic lands,
- the boarding school experience,
- the relocation of AI/AN peoples to major cities,
- specific attempts to assimilate AI/AN children, and
- the erosion of sovereignty that led to the diminishment of criminal jurisdiction.

"Poverty creates trauma and that leads to trauma behavior in children . . . this is not new information."
Abby Abinanti, Chief Judge, Yurok Tribal Court. Testimony before the Task Force on American Indian/ Alaska Native Children Exposed to Violence, Phoenix, AZ, February 11, 2014

"Cultural trauma has been defined as a direct attack on the cultural fabric of a people and its lasting impact that it has had on an individual's psyche, spiritual/emotional core and well-being as well as the assault on the essence of a community."
Deborah Painte, Director, Native American Training Institute. Testimony before the Task Force on American Indian/ Alaska Native Children Exposed to Violence, Bismarck, ND, December 9, 2013

"The outcome of these assimilation efforts is heightened risk factors for child maltreatment in AI/AN communities. These policies left generations of parents and grandparents who were subjected to prolonged institutionalization and who do not have positive models of family life and family discipline."

Sarah Hicks Kastelic, Deputy Director, National Indian Welfare Association. Testimony before the Task Force on American Indian/ Alaska Native Children Exposed to Violence, Bismarck, ND, December 9, 2013

The mass trauma experienced by Native people has been referred to as a "soul wound" that began with the colonization of the Americas; continued throughout the aftermath of the doctrines of discovery and manifest destiny; and culminated in the shattered social fabric and homelands of Indigenous populations in the Americas.

These practices continue today and have a significant and lingering impact on AI/AN children and families. Accordingly, although an exhaustive history of federal Indian policy and its impact is beyond the scope of this report, the report does contain references to these policies throughout. Please see the "Suggested Further Reading" in the appendix for additional information.

Connecting Sovereignty, Trust Obligations, and AI/AN Children Exposed to Violence

Currently, there are 566 federally recognized Indian tribes in the United States consisting of reservation and nonreservation tribes.[24] The diversity and uniqueness of AI/AN tribes cannot be overemphasized. Tribes have different resources, social and economic conditions, languages, and cultural and traditional practices. American Indians are dual citizens of both the United States and a federally recognized tribe. American Indians reside in all states; however, the majority of American Indians live in the western United States with Oklahoma having the highest American Indian population and California having the second highest. Approximately 71 percent of AI/AN people live in urban areas,[25] largely as a result of relocation policies in the 1950s. Urban Indian organizations exist around the nation, and they provide crucial services to urban AI/AN populations, to include health care, social services, and, in some areas, quality services for children exposed to violence.

Tribal governments are independent sovereign Nations with inherent authority recognized by the U.S. Constitution. At the time of European contact with North America, the tribes were sovereign by nature and conducted their own internal affairs.[26] Tribal sovereignty is a core principle in the federal-tribal government-to-government relationship. Tribes have inherent sovereignty to determine their form of tribal government, the power to determine membership, the power to legislate and tax, the power to administer justice, the power to exclude persons from tribal territory,[27] and all the powers of sovereignty not expressly divested by agreement or clear statement of Congress. However, both state and federal constraints impede tribes from exercising full authority and marshaling their full potential to address violence against children.

The concept of tribal sovereignty is woven through each and every issue affecting AI/AN children including the primacy of tribal governments in responding to violence experienced or witnessed by Indian children. The unique legal posture of tribes in relation to the federal government is deeply rooted in American law and history, and knowledge of this historical context is essential to understanding the issues regarding AI/AN children exposed to violence.

Additionally, the federal government has a special relationship known as the trust responsibility with Indian tribes. The trust responsibility encompasses an obligation to guarantee law and order in Indian country.[28] For example, in the Indian Child Welfare Act (ICWA), Congress formally declared that it is the policy of this nation to protect the best interests of Indian children and to promote the stability and security of Indian tribes and families by establishing minimum federal standards for the removal of Indian children from their families and the placement of such children in foster or adoptive homes that will reflect the unique values of Indian culture, and by providing for assistance to Indian tribes in the operation of child and family service programs.[29]

The federal trust responsibility encompasses a range of issues impacting AI/AN children exposed to violence, including:

- identifying, assessing, and treating AI/AN children exposed to violence, including recognizing tribally recognized, culturally based healing practices;
- expanding tribal self-governance policies;
- training professionals who come into contact with AI/AN children exposed to violence;
- impacting juvenile justice issues related to AI/AN children;
- funding tribal programs;
- mandating the cooperation of federal agencies regarding trauma-based practices for AI/AN children exposed to violence; and
- collecting data and sharing information in Indian country.

Native children and youth, like their ancestors, continue to be resilient in the face of extreme adversity. Maintaining cultural traditions is still a very important part of the everyday lives of American Indians. Children grow up learning the traditions of the tribe, practice them each day, and will someday teach them to their children.[30] This focus on tribal self-determination and the use of tradition to respond to the needs of AI/AN children exposed to violence is echoed throughout this report and the Advisory Committee recommendations.

> *"The exercise of tribal sovereignty means being able to actively and consciously participate in the creation of our own future. If our future is decided by others, we are really not sovereign. There is a direct relationship between sovereignty and our willingness to determine what our future will be."*
>
> Dr. Eddie Brown, Executive Director, American Indian Policy Institute

ADVISORY COMMITTEE VISION FOR AMERICAN INDIAN AND ALASKA NATIVE CHILDREN

The Advisory Committee envisions a future where Native children are raised in a supportive community that is rich in American Indian and Alaska Native cultures, where the primacy of tribal governments in responding to AI/AN children exposed to violence is respected, where AI/AN tribes are empowered with authority and resources to prevent AI/AN children from being exposed to violence and where AI/AN tribes have sufficient tools to respond to and heal their children.

Reaching this vision by changing broken systems that traumatize AI/AN children—rather than respecting their sacredness—is the focus of this report. How can the tribes lead us to this vision? How can the federal government and state governments support tribes in achieving this vision? This report examines the complex systems involved and provides foundational recommendations on changes that need to be made to restore Native children and Native communities to wholeness and balance.

Foundational Findings and Recommendations

1.1 **Leaders at the highest levels of the executive and legislative branches of the federal government should coordinate and implement the recommendations in this report consistent with three core principles–Empowering Tribes, Removing Barriers, and Providing Resources–identified by the Advisory Committee.**

Core Principle #1 (Empowering Tribes):
Tribal sovereignty includes the inherent authority to govern and protect the health, safety, and welfare of tribal citizens, especially children, within tribal lands. Tribes must be empowered with authority and resources to prevent AI/AN children from being exposed to violence and with sufficient tools for tribes to respond and heal their children. Tribes cannot thrive without the authority and resources to implement their own decisions for their children. There is a vital connection between inherent

tribal sovereignty and protecting AI/AN children. Federal and state governments must recognize and respect the primacy of tribal governments in responding to AI/AN children. In each Advisory Committee hearing and Listening Session, witnesses spoke bravely and boldly about the critical importance of inherent tribal sovereignty in addressing AI/AN children's exposure to violence and the need for effective and appropriate services for AI/AN children that reflect the cultural integrity of each individual tribe.

Core Principle #2 (Removing Barriers):
Federal and state governments must remove the restrictions and barriers—such as jurisdictional and resource limitations—that currently prevent AI/AN Nations from effectively exercising their inherent sovereign authority to stop AI/AN children from being exposed to violence, and provide sufficient tools for tribes to heal their children who have been exposed to violence.

Core Principle #3 (Providing Resources):
AI/AN Nations must be provided with the assistance, collaboration, and resources to build capacity to fully implement and sustain tribally controlled, trauma-informed prevention and treatment models and systems that will empower their individual communities to prevent their children from being exposed to violence along with sufficient tools to respond and heal their children who have been exposed to violence.

Working with the executive branch, Congress should take legislative action on the recommendations in this report, making these recommendations a bipartisan priority. The Advisory Committee recognizes that implementation of its recommendations will require the assistance of multiple Cabinet offices and federal, tribal, and state departments to shape and sustain a truly national response. Coordination and implementation of the recommendations in this report must not only be consistent with these three core principles, but it must also be consistent with the federal government's trust responsibility and the tribal consultation policies of the various affected federal agencies.

The Advisory Committee commends Congress and the administration for positive bipartisan steps taken in the last few years designed to reduce violence in Indian country including the

Tribal Law and Order Act (TLOA) of 2010,[31] the Indian Law and Order Commission[32] which was created through TLOA, and the 2013 Violence Against Women Act (VAWA) Reauthorization[33] which included very important provisions designed to restore full tribal criminal jurisdiction over all persons who commit domestic violence crimes in Indian country.[34] The Advisory Committee would also like to commend Congress for two important bipartisan bills that have been moving forward this Congress—(1) S. 1474 (*Alaska Safe Families and Villages Act of 2014*),[35] and (2) S. 1622[36] (*Alyce Spotted Bear and Walter Soboleff Commission on Native Children*). There is a long history of bipartisanship on Indian law and policy going back to the time when Richard Nixon announced that "[t]he time has come to break decisively with the past and to create conditions for a new era in which the Indian future is determined by Indian acts and Indian decisions."[37] The Advisory Committee trusts that the same bipartisan spirit will lead to prompt bipartisan implementation of the recommendations in this report.

1.2 The White House should establish—no later than May 2015—a permanent fully staffed Native American Affairs Office within the White House Domestic Policy Council. This new Native American Affairs Office should include a senior position specializing in AI/AN children exposed to violence. This office should be responsible for coordination across the executive branch of all services provided for the benefit and protection of AI/AN children and the office lead should report directly to the Director of the Domestic Policy Council as a Special Assistant to the President. The Native American Affairs Office should have overall executive branch responsibility for coordinating and implementing the recommendations in this report including conducting annual tribal consultations.

The Advisory Committee believes that a permanent fully staffed Native American Affairs Office of the level recommended— including a senior position specializing in AI/AN children exposed to violence—is required in order to comply with the federal government's trust responsibility and to effectively address the current inability of the federal government to serve the needs of AI/AN children exposed to violence. The Advisory Committee commends the Obama administration for its many positive steps to engage and empower the AI/AN community in recent years including the establishment of annual White House Tribal Nations Conferences and the restoration of the ability of AI/AN tribes to assert full criminal jurisdiction over all alleged perpetrators of domestic violence through Title IX of the Violence Against Women Act (VAWA) Reauthorization.[38]

The Advisory Committee also commends the administration for establishing two very important White House positions: (1) Special Assistant to the President on Native American Affairs, a position within the White House Domestic Policy Council; and (2) Associate Director of Intergovernmental Affairs and Tribal Liaison, a position within the Office of Intergovernmental Affairs. But both of these positions are currently only temporary one-person offices. The Advisory Committee strongly recommends building upon the success of these two vital White House positions in order to ensure effective implementation of the recommendations in this report. The current "Special Assistant to the President on Native American Affairs" (or their designee) should serve on an interim basis as the lead person to coordinate and implement the recommendations in this report. However, a permanent fully staffed White House Native American Affairs Office is required in order to effectively coordinate and implement the recommendations in this report. This Native American Affairs Office should have a minimum of three to five full-time senior staff members including a senior position specializing in AI/AN children exposed to violence.

This new White House Native American Affairs Office should conduct annual consultations with tribal governments that should—at a minimum—include discussion of:

- Administering tribal funds and programs;
- Enhancing the safety of AI/AN children exposed to violence in the home and in the community;
- Enhancing child protection services through trauma-informed practice;
- Enhancing research and evaluation to address the mental health needs that include tribal cultural interventions to promote tribal best practice;
- Enhancing substance abuse services for caregivers and youth that address the exposure to violence; and
- Evaluating the implementation status of the recommendations in this report.

The new White House Native American Affairs Office will provide the essential executive branch coordination and collaboration required to effectively implement the recommendations in this report. The current "stovepipe organizational structure" of federal agencies restricts the flow of information and cross-organizational communication. Stovepipes within the executive branch make essential collaboration extremely difficult. Stovepipes exist for many reasons that include (1) the structure of the federal budget; (2) turf protection by the various executive branch agencies; and (3) a lack of commitment among executive branch leadership to promote real collaboration. This lack of coordination across federal agencies creates great hardship for tribes that receive funding from multiple federal sources. Conflicting policies, procedures, and requirements for grants that have similar purposes and data systems make it very difficult for agencies to work together, but more importantly make it extremely difficult for tribes to effectively engage the federal bureaucracy.

The Advisory Committee knows that this is an extremely difficult issue to address quickly, but the current arrangement is ineffective and does not serve Native people. The new Native American Affairs Office within the Domestic Policy Council should coordinate programs across the executive branch, and develop and implement a plan to increase collaboration among agencies and breaking down stovepipes. This should include braided funding streams[39] to tribes, joint grant solicitations, and adoption of compatible data systems. If this office is not established and these recommendations are not implemented, then the federal government will continue to force tribes to squander precious resources to meet bureaucratic needs rather than to address the needs of children in their communities.

The Advisory Committee recommends that the Attorney General take the lead in the interagency coordination needed to fully staff the White House Native American Affairs Office. Until that office is at full capacity, the Attorney General should support existing White House staff to assure successful implementation of all the recommendations in this report.

1.3 Congress should restore the inherent authority of American Indian and Alaska Native (AI/AN) tribes to assert full criminal jurisdiction over all persons who commit crimes against AI/AN children in Indian country.

The framework for criminal jurisdiction in Indian country is institutionally complex[40] and divided among federal, tribal, and state governments. The question of jurisdiction depends upon whether the crime is committed in Indian country, whether the perpetrator is Indian or non-Indian, whether the victim is Indian or non-Indian, and what type of crime is committed.[41] The jurisdictional maze in Indian country was further complicated by the U.S. Supreme Court's decision in *Oliphant v. Suquamish Indian Tribe*, 435 U.S. 191 (1978), which held that federally recognized tribes do not possess the sovereign power to assert criminal jurisdiction over non-Indians. With the federal government declining to prosecute 76 percent of the crimes referred by tribal authorities, tribal leaders have struggled to find ways to keep Native citizens safe, especially when the perpetrators are non-Indian.[42]

The complex nature of the justice systems in Indian country has contributed to a crisis of violent crime on many Indian reservations that has persisted for decades. As the Indian Law and Order Commission (ILOC) observed, "When Congress and the Administration ask why the crime rate is so high in Indian country, they need look no further than the archaic system in place, in which federal and state authority displaces tribal authority and often makes tribal law enforcement meaningless."[43] Federal reports have consistently found that the divided system of justice in place on Indian reservations lacks coordination, accountability, and adequate and consistent funding. These shortfalls serve to foster violence and disrupt the peace and public safety of tribal communities. When tribal law enforcement and justice systems are supported rather than discouraged from taking primary responsibility over local justice the result is usually better, stronger, and faster justice than the non-Native counterparts.[44]

> "[C]riminal jurisdiction in Indian country is an indefensible morass of complex, conflicting, and illogical commands, layered in over decades via congressional policies and court decisions and without the consent of tribal nations."
>
> Indian Law and Order Commission
> Report to the President and Congress of the United States, ix, November 2013

General Summary of Criminal Jurisdiction on Indian Lands
(details vary by tribe and state)

From: Indian Law and Order Commission, *A Roadmap for Making Native America Safer: Report to the President and Congress of the United States* (November 2013): 7.

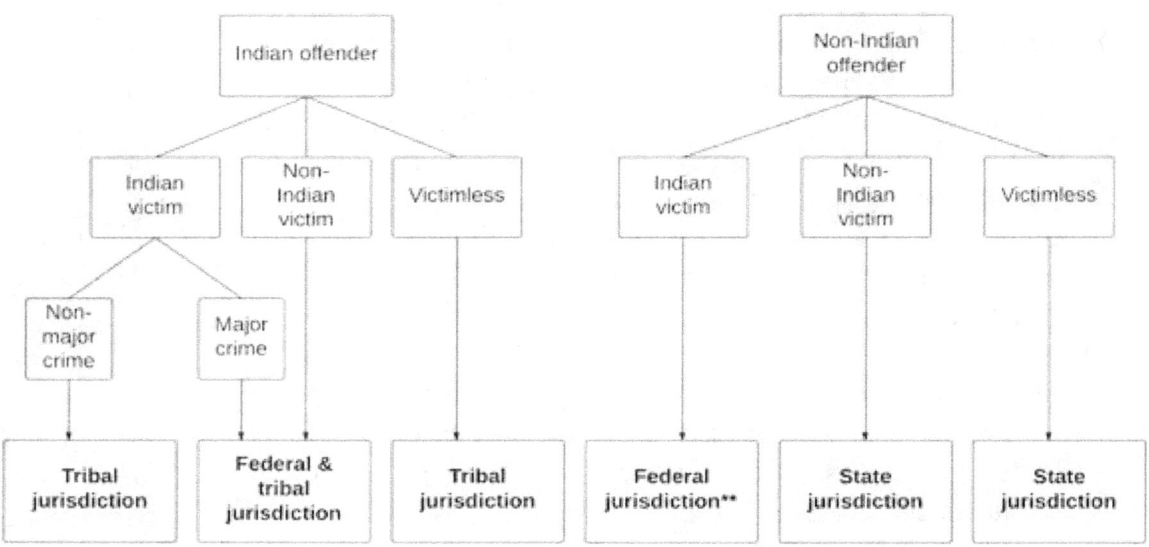

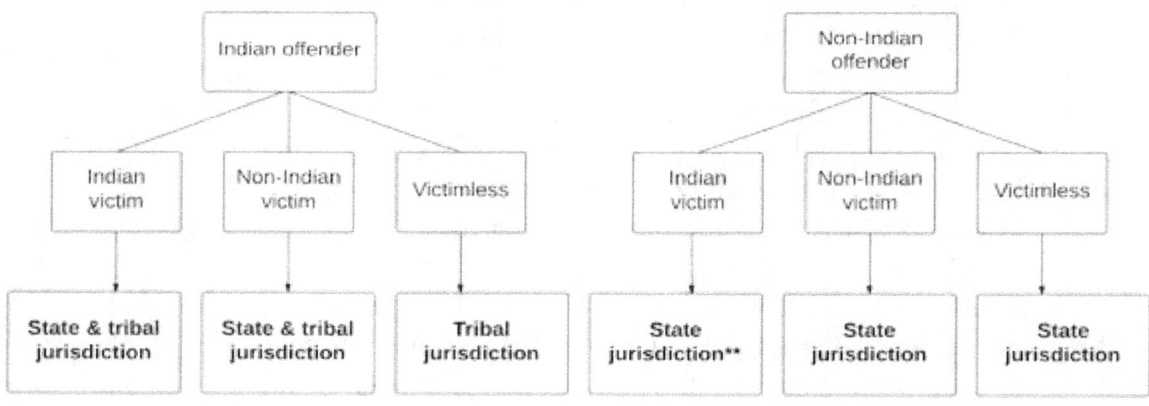

* Under the *Tribal Law and Order Act of 2010*, tribes can opt for added concurrent Federal jurisdiction, with Federal consent. Neither this tribe-by-tribe issue nor the various configurations of "Optional 280" status are shown in this chart.

** Under the *Violence Against Women Act Reauthorization of 2013* (VAWA), after 2015, tribes may exercise Special Domestic Violence Jurisdiction with the Federal government and with States for VAWA-defined domestic violence crimes.

Further impeding justice efforts in Indian country are the restraints placed directly on tribal justice systems. Although the U.S. Constitution does not apply to tribal courts,[45] Congress, through its plenary authority over tribes, enacted the Indian Civil Rights Act (ICRA).[46] ICRA further limits the power of tribal governments by requiring them to adhere to certain rights similar to, but not identical to the Bill of Rights protections. Among those limitations is a limit on a tribal court's criminal sentencing authority. Currently, ICRA limits a tribal court's criminal sentencing authority to just one year imprisonment and/or a $5,000 fine, regardless of the nature of the crime.[47] In 2010, in the Tribal Law and Order Act (TLOA),[48] Congress relaxed this sentencing restriction to three years imprisonment and/or a $15,000 fine, but only for those tribes that could provide certain additional, enumerated due process protections.[49] To date, only a handful of tribes have adopted this "enhanced sentencing."

In May 2013, Congress passed the VAWA.[50] In response to congressional findings that 34 percent of Native women will be raped in their lifetimes and 39 percent will be the victim of domestic violence,[51] Congress passed Title IX of VAWA, "Safety for Indian Women." Among its provisions, Congress amended the ICRA to authorize "special domestic violence criminal jurisdiction" to tribal courts over non-Indian offenders who (1) commit domestic violence, (2) commit dating violence, or (3) violate a protection order. This was the first time in the thirty-five years since the 1978 *Oliphant* decision that Congress authorized tribes to reassert tribal sovereign authority to prosecute non-Indian offenders who commit certain egregious crimes in Indian country. Unfortunately, despite numerous and horrific findings that non-Indians are committing sexual assault at high numbers in Indian country,[52] Title IX of VAWA did not extend special domestic violence criminal jurisdiction over non-Indians for the crime of sexual assault.

It is troubling that tribes have no criminal jurisdiction over non-Indians who commit heinous crimes of sexual and physical abuse of AI/AN children in Indian country. Congress has restored criminal jurisdiction over non-Indians who commit domestic violence, commit dating violence, and violate protection orders. Congress should now similarly restore the inherent authority of AI/AN tribes to assert full criminal jurisdiction over all persons who commit crimes against AI/AN children

in Indian country including both child sexual abuse and child physical abuse.

There are no statistics concerning the percentage of non-Indian perpetrators who commit crimes against AI/AN children on tribal land, but it is clear from what we do know that it is a very substantial problem. We know that 70 percent of violent crimes generally committed against AI/ANs involve an offender of a different race.[53] This statistic includes crimes against children twelve years of age and older. We also know that in domestic violence cases, 75 percent of the intimate victimizations and 25 percent of the family victimizations involve an offender of a different race.[54] Furthermore, national studies show that men who batter their companion also abuse their children in 49 to 70 percent of the cases.[55]

Furthermore, the Advisory Committee believes that Congress should fully implement the recommendations contained in chapter 1, "Jurisdiction: Bringing Clarity Out of Chaos," of the Indian Law and Order Commission's 2013 Final Report, *A Roadmap for Making Native America Safer*. The recommendations are summarized in the following text. More details, including the complete ILOC chapter 1 recommendations, are provided in the ILOC Executive Summary provided as an appendix to this report.

1. Any tribe that so chooses can opt out, fully or partially, of federal Indian country criminal jurisdiction and/or congressionally authorized state jurisdiction, except for federal laws of general application. Upon opting-out, Congress would immediately recognize the tribe's inherent criminal jurisdiction over all persons, Indian or non-Indian, within the exterior boundaries of the tribe's lands.
2. To implement tribes' opt-out authority, Congress should establish a new specialized federal circuit court, the U.S. Court of Indian Appeals, in order to provide a more cost-effective and familiarized forum, such as the U.S. Court of Appeals for the Federal Circuit, which hears matters involving intellectual property rights protection.
3. A tribe's opt-out authority includes the choice to return to partial or full federal or state criminal jurisdiction.
4. The opt-out authority should necessarily include opting out from the sentencing restrictions of ICRA.

Emphasis should be added to the first ILOC recommendation in the preceding text, with regard to tribes subject to congressionally authorized state jurisdiction, like Public Law 280 (PL-280), which authorized state criminal and civil jurisdiction and eliminated federal criminal jurisdiction for Indian country and major crimes in those six mandatory states.[56] There are multiple layers of concern over this piece of legislation. The tribal opposition to PL-280 has focused on the state's failure to provide law enforcement services and the encroachment on tribal sovereignty.[57] The states' opposition focuses on the failure of PL-280 to provide federal funding to the states for this additional jurisdiction amounting to an unfunded mandate on Indian lands that are not taxable. For tribes subject to PL-280,[58] effective investigations of child maltreatment crimes are compromised by the lack of clarity surrounding PL-280 and subsequent inconsistent interpretations of the law have contributed to another layer of confusion and complexity that could be resolved with clarifying legislation.[59]

The Advisory Committee also recommends implementation of four additional related ILOC recommendations (ILOC recommendations 4.2, 4.3, 4.4, and 5.2) that would allow tribal governments to more effectively protect AI/AN children exposed to violence. These four recommendations require federal and state courts (1) to inform the relevant tribal government when a tribal citizen is arrested or convicted of a crime; (2) to collaborate, if the tribal government so chooses, in choices involving corrections placement or community supervision; and (3) to inform the tribal government when that offender is slated for return to the community. More details concerning each of these four ILOC recommendations is provided in the ILOC Executive Summary provided as an appendix to this report.

The Advisory Committee wishes to emphasize the dire importance of the following recommendation:

1.4 Congress and the executive branch shall direct sufficient funds to AI/AN tribes to bring funding for tribal criminal and civil justice systems and tribal child protection systems into parity with the rest of the United States; and shall remove the barriers that currently impede the ability of AI/AN Nations to effectively address violence in their communities. *The Advisory Committee believes that treaties, existing law and trust responsibilities are not discretionary and demand this action.*

"We lack adequate resources and funding. Many times it feels like we are losing ground, losing our children."

Erma J. Vizenor, Chairwoman, White Earth Nation. Testimony before the Task Force on American Indian/ Alaska Native Children Exposed to Violence, Fort Lauderdale, FL, April 16, 2014

"Historically the responsibility of development of solutions has been given to other entities, such as state, federal, or private agencies, rather than tribal governments, resulting in interventions and outcomes that were not effective."

Brian Cladoosby, President, National Congress of American Indians. Testimony before the Task Force on American Indian/ Alaska Native Children Exposed to Violence, Fort Lauderdale, FL, April 16, 2014

To break the cycle of violence which grips Native communities the Advisory Committee believes that this nation must make the investment necessary to create an environment where AI/AN children, today and for generations to come, may thrive. This investment is not only the right thing to do, but is part of the legal obligation of this nation to those communities; an obligation which has never been adequately addressed. In order to more effectively address the needs of AI/AN children exposed to violence, substantial changes must be made in the methods by which AI/AN tribes are able to access federal funding and substantially increased levels of federal funding will be required.

In each Advisory Committee hearing and Listening Session, witnesses repeatedly expressed concern about the limited funding currently available for Indian country criminal and civil justice systems and child protection systems along with extreme frustration with the challenges involved in obtaining and utilizing the limited funding that is available.

Funding for child maltreatment prevention and child protection efforts is especially limited in Indian country.[60] Tribes recognize the importance of prevention and do incorporate limited child abuse prevention activities, despite little to no federal support.[61] Meanwhile, states receive proportionately more funding for prevention and child protection while tribes are not even eligible for the two major programs that fund these state programs— Title XX of the Social Services Block Grant and the Child Abuse Prevention and Treatment Act.[62]

The U.S. Department of the Interior (DOI) through the Bureau of Indian Affairs (BIA) provides limited funding for tribal court systems, but the funding level is far too low and the BIA has historically denied any tribal law enforcement and tribal court funding to tribes in jurisdictions—such as PL-280 jurisdictions[63]—where congressionally authorized concurrent state jurisdiction has been established. Furthermore, efforts to fund tribal justice systems such as the Indian Tribal Justice Act of 1993 (which authorized an additional $50 million per year in tribal court base funding) have repeatedly *authorized* increased tribal court funding, but the long promised funding has never materialized in the form of actual *appropriations*.[64]

Since the late 1990s,[65] the U.S. Department of Justice (DOJ) has also become a significant additional federal source of tribal justice funding.[66] Tribes have utilized DOJ grant funding to enhance various and diverse aspects of their tribal justice systems, from the enhancement of tribal codes, to the implementation of Juvenile Healing to Wellness Courts (tribal drug courts), to the design of unique tribal youth programs.[67] While these grants have offered immense support, they are a far cry from the consistent, tribally driven approach that is needed in Indian country. The Advisory Committee heard repeated frustration expressed concerning the competitive funding approach that the DOJ utilizes. Witnesses often describe it as a process in which you are forced to hope your neighboring tribe loses. The following are some of the most common concerns raised about this competitive federal funding process:

- Tribes most in need, often smaller tribes and those with the least amount of resources, are the least likely to be able to submit a "winning" grant application.
- Unlike their state and local governmental counterparts, tribes are forced to "compete" for core governmental funding, flying in the face of both tribal sovereignty and federal trust responsibility.
- Nonrenewable, short-term grants fail to allow for long-term planning, and often result in high turnover and the continuous shuttering of programs once the one-, two-, or three-year grant funding ends.
- Unlike current federal funding programs within the DOI and Department of Health and Human Services (HHS), DOJ single-issue pet projects reflect federal priorities and do not allow tribes to determine their own governmental priorities.

It is important to note that DOJ funding for tribal justice systems has been consistently decreasing in recent years. For example, when DOJ's main consolidated funding program—the Coordinated Tribal Assistance Solicitation (CTAS)—was introduced in FY 2010, a total of more than $126 million in DOJ grant funds were dispersed through CTAS. In the following four years, however, CTAS funding has consistently decreased by an approximate average of nearly 10 percent per year (see Coordinated Tribal Assistance Solicitation annual funding chart). In FY 2014, only $87 million was dispersed through CTAS.[69]

It is particularly troubling that the CTAS grant program with the closest direct connection to AI/AN children exposed to violence—the Office for Juvenile Justice and Delinquency Prevention (OJJDP) Tribal Youth Program (TYP)—has suffered the greatest decrease in funding levels. In the past four years, OJJDP TYP funding has plummeted from $25 million in FY 2010 down to only $5 million in FY 2014 (see TYP Annual Funding Chart).

"There are 566 recognized tribes in this country the winners of CTAS will have a start, but the losers way out-number the possible winners."
Abby Abinanti, Chief Judge, Yurok Tribal Court. Testimony before the Task Force on American Indian/ Alaska Native Children Exposed to Violence, Phoenix, AZ, February 11, 2014

Total Coordinated Tribal Assistance Solicitation (CTAS) Funding

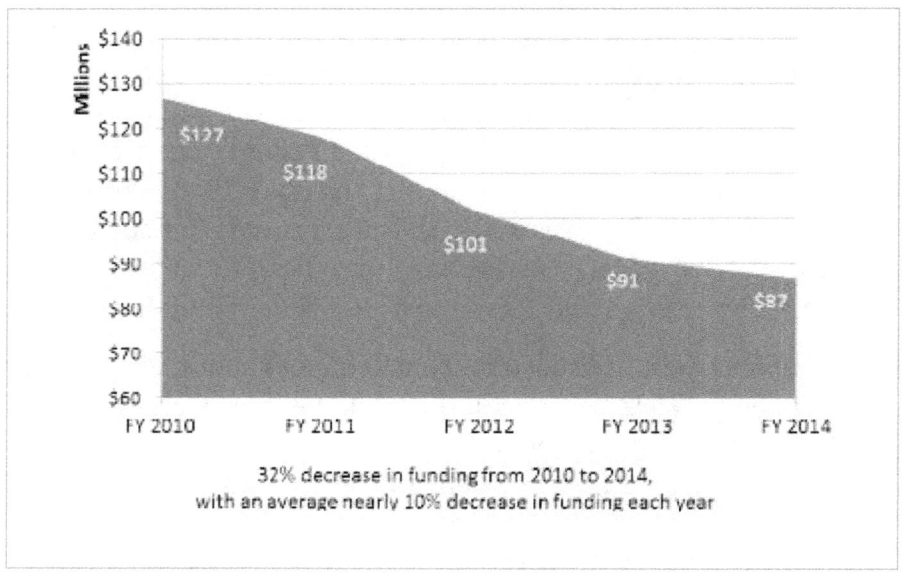

32% decrease in funding from 2010 to 2014,
with an average nearly 10% decrease in funding each year

Tribal Youth Program (TYP) Appropriations

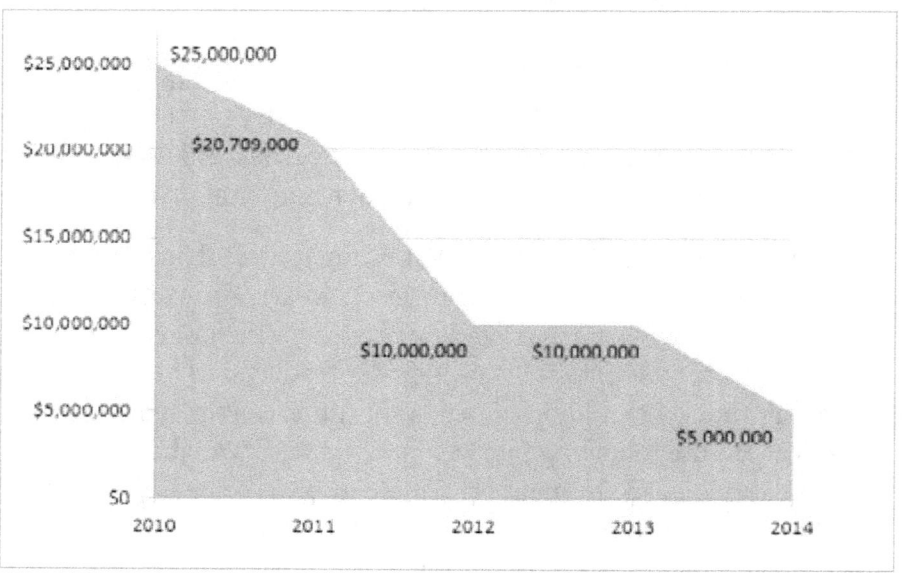

Tribes, like their state and local counterparts, deserve the benefit of reliability in their quest to build robust tribal justice systems that can adequately serve their youth. Base funding from pooled resources would offer tribes the reliability and flexibility that is needed. As both the ILOC Report[70] and the National Congress of American Indians (NCAI) FY 2015 Funding Request Report[71] note,

DOJ has already taken steps toward consolidated base funding through the creation of CTAS.[72] DOJ has also recently considered the possibility of base funding through formula grants with regard to the Office on Violence Against Women (OVW) Tribal Governments grant program.[73]

AI/AN children are generally served best when tribes have the opportunity to take ownership of the programs and resources that they provide. PL-93-638 contracts, self-governance compacts, and PL-102-477 funding agreements are all examples of successful federal programs that afford tribes the option to take over the management of federal funds. However, none of the programs currently applies to the DOJ.

1.4.A **Congress and the executive branch shall provide recurring *mandatory*, not discretionary, base funding for all tribal programs that impact AI/AN children exposed to violence including tribal criminal and civil justice systems and tribal child protection systems, and make it available on equal terms to all federally recognized tribes, whether their lands are under federal jurisdiction or congressionally authorized state jurisdiction.**

Part of the United States' trust responsibility to AI/AN Nations is the provision of basic governmental services in Indian country. Funding to fulfill this obligation, however, is currently provided in the *discretionary* portion of the federal budget despite the fact that the treaties that made promises to Indian tribes did not promise *"discretionary"* support and the trust responsibility is not *discretionary*. Because the spending is discretionary and not mandatory as it should be, public policies, like sequestration, are implemented and cut programs that clearly should not be cut.

The Advisory Committee heard repeated testimony concerning the vital need for ongoing reliable funding to meet the needs of AI/AN children exposed to violence. The disparate impact of sequestration in Indian country is but one example of why mandatory spending is necessary. The Advisory Committee heard repeated stories of critical tribal funding being cut across sectors—housing, law enforcement, health care, education—and how that negatively impacts children. Many of the recommendations in this report depend on new appropriations for vital programs that provide critical services and care to AI/AN children exposed to violence, but AI/AN communities cannot

"Villages and regions across the state are developing important and effective measures that need to be supported by the federal and state governments, not through temporary three or five year grants. I'll repeat that. Not through temporary three or five year grants; but ongoing, sustainable funding, allowing Native communities to take responsibility for the health/safety of their children, families and communities."

Gloria O'Neil, President/CEO, Cook Inlet Tribal Council, Inc. Testimony before the Task Force on American Indian/ Alaska Native Children Exposed to Violence, Anchorage, AK, June 11, 2014 depend upon the funding when it is repeatedly subject to cuts like the cuts that slashed the OJJDP TYP from $25 million per year to only $5 million per year in four short years.

Federal funding for these programs serving AI/AN children should be mandatory spending, not discretionary. This funding will guarantee direct benefits for AI/AN tribes. Funding should be awarded by formula as an open-ended entitlement grant, contingent upon AI/AN tribes submitting children exposed to violence plans for federal approval. Federal agencies administering these programs should submit yearly estimates of program expenditures as well as quarterly reports of estimated and actual program expenditures in support of the awarded funds. The funds should provide for, but not be limited to, monthly maintenance payments for the daily care and supervision of eligible AI/AN children; administrative costs to manage the program; training of staff and practitioners; recruitment of community representatives; and volunteers and costs related to the design, implementation, and operation of a national tribal-wide data collection system to support services to AI/AN children exposed to violence.

1.4.B Congress shall appropriate, not simply authorize, sufficient substantially increased funding to provide reliable tribal base funding for all tribal programs that impact AI/AN children exposed to violence. This includes tribal criminal and civil justice systems and tribal child protection systems. At a minimum, and as a helpful starting point, Congress shall enact the relevant funding level requests in the National Congress of American Indians (NCAI) Indian Country Budget Request for FY 2015.[74]

In order to more effectively address the needs of AI/AN children exposed to violence, substantially increased levels of federal funding will be required. For the past ten years, the National Congress of American Indians (NCAI) has published an annual Indian Country Budget Request Report developed in collaboration with tribal leaders, Native organizations, and tribal budget consultation bodies. The NCAI request provides a helpful starting point for the initial minimum levels of increased funding that will be needed. The NCAI annual budget requests are rooted in the attempt to honor the United States' trust responsibility, which includes providing basic governmental services in Indian country; honoring and fully supporting Indian self-determination; and elevating funding for Indian country governments and services to be equivalent to similarly situated non-Indian governments and services. The annual NCAI budget reports also provide insightful details concerning a wide range of federal programs required to implement these recommendations.

Because the formulation of the federal budget is a very complex process involving many players, it is essential as the recommendations in this report are implemented that:

- Each federal agency includes the requisite funding in its budget submissions;
- The Office of Management and Budget include the request in the President's Annual Budget Requests to the Congress;
- Both Houses of Congress appropriate sufficient recurring funds so that all tribes realize benefit; and
- Those funds are provided to tribes on a recurring basis.

> **1.4.C Congress shall authorize all federal agencies, beginning with the Department of Justice (DOJ), to enter into 638 self-determination and self-governance compacts with tribes to ensure that all tribal system funding, including both justice and child welfare, is subject to tribal management. Further, the Department of Health and Human Services (HHS) should fully utilize its current 638 self-determination and self-governance authority to the greatest extent feasible for flexible funding programs in Department of Health and Human Services (HHS) beyond the Indian Health Service (IHS) and seek additional legislative authority where needed.**

In 2000, PL-106-260 included a provision for designating HHS to conduct a study to determine the feasibility of a demonstration project extending tribal self-governance to HHS agencies other than the IHS. The HHS Feasibility Study, submitted to Congress in 2003,[75] determined that a demonstration project was feasible. Since that time, tribes identified the HHS self-governance expansion as a top priority and requested to work in collaboration with the department to identify how to develop the needed legislative language. However, up to this point, HHS has not moved forward on this action. The choice to self-govern represents for some tribes efficiency, accountability, and best practices in managing and

"If we really want to end childhood violence, we have to get out of the way of the people who have the solutions. It's our people. It's our culture. It's who we are that was ripped out of us and we're wounded and we're acting wounded and we're hurting each other, and it's a perpetual cycle that will not end until we are restored."

Elizabeth Medicine Crow, President/CEO, First Alaskan Institute. Testimony before the Task Force on American Indian/ Alaska Native Children Exposed to Violence, Anchorage, AK, June 12, 2014 operating tribal programs and administering federal funds at the local level. Expanding the option for self-governance translates to greater flexibility for tribes to provide critical social services within agencies such as the Administration on Aging, Administration on Children and Families, Substance Abuse and Mental Health Services Administration, and Health Resources and Services Administration. It is imperative that HHS work closely with tribes to strengthen current self-governance programs and advance initiatives that will streamline and improve HHS program delivery in Indian country. HHS should include not only the eleven programs[76] identified in the 2003 feasibility study, but also programs such as the direct Tribal Title IV-E foster care program established under the 2008 Fostering Connections Act.[77] The Advisory Committee agrees with the HHS Secretary's Tribal Advisory Committee, which recently sent HHS Secretary Burwell a Brief on Priority Issues[78] that indicated that HHS should (1) utilize current administrative authority to expand self-governance within HHS through demonstration projects; and (2) reconvene the Self-Governance Tribal Federal Workgroup in order to develop legislative language that would expand self-governance within HHS. Moreover, HHS should utilize its existing authority to provide the most flexible funding mechanisms currently available such as the block grant process HHS utilizes to provide Title IV-E funding for the territories.

While changes are underway to establish and implement the previous funding recommendations, Congress and the executive branch should implement the three following recommendations as interim steps as soon as possible.

1.4.D Congress shall end all grant-based and competitive Indian country criminal justice funding in the Department of Justice (DOJ) and instead establish a permanent, recurring base funding system for tribal law enforcement and justice services.

As soon as possible, Congress should end all grant-based and competitive Indian country criminal justice funding in the DOJ and instead pool these monies to establish a permanent, recurring base funding system for tribal law enforcement and justice services. Federal base funding for tribal justice systems should be made available on equal terms to all federally recognized tribes, whether their lands are under federal jurisdiction or congressionally authorized state jurisdiction.

1.4.E **Congress shall establish a much larger commitment than currently exists to fund tribal programs through the Department of Justice's Office of Justice Programs (OJP) and the Victims of Crime Act (VOCA) funding. As an initial step towards the much larger commitment needed, Congress shall establish a minimum 10 percent tribal set-aside, as per the Violence Against Women Act (VAWA) tribal set-aside, from funding for all discretionary Office of Justice Programs (OJP) and Victims of Crime Act (VOCA) funding making clear that the tribal set-aside is the minimum tribal funding and not in any way a cap on tribal funding. President Obama's annual budget request to Congress has included a 7 percent tribal set-aside for the last few years. This is a very positive step and Congress should authorize this request immediately. However, the set-aside should be increased to 10 percent in subsequent appropriation bills. Until Congress acts, the Department of Justice (DOJ) shall establish this minimum 10 percent tribal set-aside administratively.**

The 2012 National Task Force on Children Exposed to Violence determined that:

- AI/AN children have a significant degree of unmet needs for services and support to prevent and respond to the extreme levels of violence they experience;
- the federal government has a unique legal responsibility for the welfare of AI/AN children;
- the federal government also has a special relationship with Indian tribes based, at least in part, on its trust responsibility; and
- AI/AN communities confront additional burdens in meeting the needs of children exposed to violence.

After determining that AI/AN women face the highest levels of violence in the nation—along with the highest rates of unmet needs—Congress has set-aside a percentage of VAWA funding for tribal governments since VAWA's enactment in 1994. Since the 2005 VAWA Reauthorization, the tribal set-aside has been 10 percent. The Advisory Committee finds that the 10 percent VAWA tribal set-aside is a highly relevant precedent that should be applied to all discretionary OJP programs because that could potentially impact AI/AN children exposed to violence.

The same rationale applies to the VOCA funding that has served as a major funding source for states to provide services to victims of crime since its establishment in 1984. The vast majority of VOCA funds are distributed to the states. While tribes are eligible to apply to the state for funding, only a tiny percentage of VOCA funding has ever been distributed to tribes. Consequently, the Advisory Committee agrees with the NCAI[79] that Congress should specifically establish a 10 percent tribal set-aside of the overall full VOCA funding or at least a tribal set-aside in the range of at least $30 million annually similar to the Children's Justice Act fund for purposes of meeting the needs of AI/AN children who are victimized by or exposed to violence.

> **1.4.F** **The Departments of Justice (DOJ) and Department of Interior (DOI) should, within one year, conduct tribal consultations to determine the feasibility of implementing Indian Law and Order Commission (ILOC) Recommendation 3.8 to consolidate all DOI tribal criminal justice programs and all DOJ Indian country programs and services into a single "Indian country component" in the DOJ and report back to the President and AI/AN Nations on how tribes want to move forward on it.**

The Advisory Committee agrees with the Indian Law and Order Commission that the DOJ and the DOI (1) currently serve duplicative roles in funding, providing technical assistance and training, and providing direct services for tribal justice systems; and (2) these agencies often do not communicate well with each other, which results in substantial confusion and waste. While the Advisory Committee is in general agreement with the ILOC's Recommendation 3.8 to consolidate all DOI tribal criminal justice programs and all DOJ Indian country programs and services into a single DOJ "Indian country component," the Advisory Committee recommends that tribal consultation be conducted prior to making such a significant and far-reaching move.

1.5 The legislative branch of the federal government along with the executive branch, under the direction and oversight of the White House Native American Affairs Office, should provide adequate funding for and assistance with Indian country research and data collection.

Research and data collection are critical components of developing effective responses to AI/AN children exposed to violence.[80] Tribal governments, like every government, need the ability to track and access critical data involving their citizens across service areas and to accept the responsibility of gathering data. Tribal governments currently do not have adequate access to accurate, comprehensive data regarding key areas affecting AI/AN children exposed to violence, and frequently when data is gathered, it is not shared with tribes. Federal leadership is required to break down barriers that prevent the accurate collection of data relative to AI/AN children and the sharing of that data with tribes. Tribal governments must also find ways to improve their own data collection and sharing.

The collection of data on maltreatment of AI/AN children illustrates this problem. The current data collection system requires states to submit their child maltreatment data to the National Child Abuse and Neglect Data System (NCANDS). HHS uses the aggregate level data in its annual reports on the characteristics of child abuse and neglect. Unfortunately, this data does not include children within the tribal child welfare system. The federal requirements for reporting and investigating child abuse in Indian country require different action, and three different law enforcement agencies (federal, tribal, state) might be responding and collecting different or similar data. The policies of the three governments regarding confidentiality and sharing of information may impede the sharing of information.[81] It is critical to the understanding of child maltreatment of AI/AN children that data be collected on AI/AN children under federal, tribal, or state jurisdiction in a comprehensive data collection system.

Additionally, the BIA and IHS collect data about children exposed to violence pursuant to their role as a funder or service provider, but this data is not always readily available to tribes. Moreover, there is little coordination between the collections of different sources of data; thus, tribes lack the comprehensive information necessary to inform policy and practice.[82] Finally, most data collection methods are not based on indigenous ways and are not sensitive to cultural differences.

"[T]he statistics are dire, but we only have a third of the picture."
Theresa M. Pouley, Chief Judge, Tulalip Tribal Court. Testimony before the Task Force on American Indian/ Alaska Native Children Exposed to Violence, Phoenix, AZ, February 11, 2014

"There is little information on the risk factor for child maltreatment in AI/AN families. . . . This is problematic because national policy and child welfare practice focus on the prevention of child maltreatment and successful prevention programming requires an understanding of the culturally specific risk factors."
Sarah Hicks Kastelic, Deputy Director, National Indian Welfare Association. Testimony before the Task Force on American Indian/ Alaska Native Children Exposed to Violence, Bismarck, ND, December 9, 2013

"Most data collection methods are not based on indigenous ways of knowing."

Iris PrettyPaint, Native Aspirations Project Director, Kauffman and Associates, Inc. Testimony before the Task Force on American Indian/ Alaska Native Children Exposed to Violence, Fort Lauderdale, FL, April 16, 2014

Tribal Nations also need access to research initiatives to help develop effective prevention and intervention strategies for children exposed to violence. Currently, many tribal communities are developing and implementing culturally based prevention and intervention programs. However, most do not have the resources necessary to evaluate the effectiveness of these programs. Tribal leaders also have called for evaluations of research on the adaptation of evidence-based practices to meet cultural and linguistic needs. Tribes may deem some evidence-based programs culturally inappropriate for the families and children they service. Studies used to establish evidence-based practices almost never include AI/AN populations so the trustworthiness of these studies and their relevance to AI/AN populations is suspect.[83] Federal, state, and private funders have increasingly focused on projects that contain evidence-based (proven) practices.[84] Tribes and urban Indian organizations are increasingly finding themselves unable to successfully compete for grant funding, because of the lack of research on effective practices in AI/AN populations.

Collecting and sharing data on crime and AI/AN youth in the state juvenile justice systems and the federal system is problematic as well. Currently, there is almost no data about the serious problems that AI/AN youth experience in urban and rural communities such as drug trafficking, gang violence, human trafficking, bullying, etc. Research on AI/AN children has largely been limited to the prevalence of violence in the home and sexual abuse, but there is a dearth of studies on the use of traditional ways of healing. Research could provide unique solutions that could be helpful to the general population, as well as AI/AN children.

As a final comment regarding data collection for tribes, it should be noted that the National Incidence Study of Child Abuse and Neglect did not include AI/AN data because the sample was too small to be significant and because study methods did not lend themselves to such a small data set. Study methods utilized by federal agencies must be adjusted, for instance by oversampling, to ensure that AI/AN children can be either included in national reports or in supplementary reports.[85] Without inclusion in these major studies, AI/AN children who face elevated levels of maltreatment and high-risk factors are ignored, thus severely limiting the opportunities to create helpful policies and provide adequate funding to meet their needs.

1.6 The legislative and executive branches of the federal government should encourage tribal-state collaborations to meet the needs of AI/AN children exposed to violence.

The criminal justice, juvenile justice, and child welfare systems are too often ineffective, because tribes and states do not always act collaboratively. The failure to collaborate can result in unanswered calls for service to law enforcement, unprosecuted cases, juveniles languishing in detention far from their families, and child victims falling through the service cracks. In the juvenile justice system, it can lead to re-victimizing AI/AN children and contribute to their disproportionate involvement in the system and overrepresentation in juvenile detention facilities. The failure of tribes and states to collaborate in child welfare contributes to the unnecessary removal of AI/AN children from their families and communities, which often re-traumatizes children rather than healing them. The federal government should use its power and funds to encourage tribal-state collaborations.

Federal support and encouragement for intergovernmental agreements is mandated by TLOA. Currently, cross-jurisdictional agreements to deputize tribal and state officials and federal peace officers for the enforcement of federal criminal laws within Indian country show promise in some places, but are plagued with unconscionable administrative delays and impediments.[86] Historically, relationships between states and tribes have been poorly defined and frequently problematic, resulting [87] in protracted legal battles over jurisdiction.[88]

Collaboration between tribal and state court systems can produce great benefits. Some states and tribes have developed tribal and state court forums to deal with complex issues relative to ICWA compliance and criminal issues.[89] Local tribal and state courts, in some instances, have developed cooperative processes for civil commitment, protection order enforcement, adult and juvenile probation, joint drug courts, and cross-educational opportunities.[90] Local courts finding solutions to local problems is effective, but the collaboration must be much more widespread to produce a greater impact. The federal government should encourage state juvenile courts to develop collaborations with local tribes to enable involvement of the local tribe in the state proceedings when a tribal member is before the juvenile court.

Some state child welfare agencies cooperate with tribes in many ways, such as Title IV-E agreements.[91] Sharing resources is common in child

"State governments and tribal governments have far more in common than in conflict. Both types of government have a primary interest in protecting the health and welfare of their people. . . . As tribal and state governments gain resources and responsibilities, their capacity and incentive to cooperate increases."

Terry Cross, Executive Director, National Indian Child Welfare Association. Testimony before the Task Force on American Indian/ Alaska Native Children Exposed to Violence , Fort Lauderdale, FL, April 16, 2014 protection cases. Other states and tribes share training and educational opportunities. Some states share child welfare information with tribes. ICWA certainly encourages and requires collaboration. However, tribal governments need increased federal support to develop tribal-state agreements or protocols on child welfare and coordinated domestic violence programming. The federal government should improve the monitoring of tribal-state relations in the child welfare system and increase efforts to educate states about the benefits of tribal-state collaboration and strategies that work. The federal government should also incentivize state participation in efforts to improve service coordination and collaboration in child welfare and encourage development of cross-jurisdictional multidisciplinary teams to help in both criminal enforcement and child welfare matters. True collaborations require commitment and effort on all sides.

Finally, collaborations between state and urban Indian organizations can also prove to be effective. For example, the Denver Indian Family Resource Center (DIFRC) has provided in-home supportive services to the AI/AN population living in the front range and in and around Denver, Colorado. To help families meet their basic needs and provide safe homes for their children, DIFRC provides supportive services that include job search assistance, life skills education, housing assistance, and health advocacy.[92] At its Listening Session at Ain Dah Yung Center in Saint Paul,[93] Minnesota, the Advisory Committee also learned about effective collaborations between urban Indian organizations and state agencies.[94]

1.7 The federal government should provide training for AI/AN Nations and for the federal agencies serving AI/AN communities on the needs of AI/AN children exposed to violence. Federal employees assigned to work on issues pertaining to AI/AN communities should be required to obtain training on tribal sovereignty, working with tribal governments, and the impact of historical trauma and colonization on tribal Nations within the first sixty days of their job assignment.

Providing training and technical assistance to all service providers attending to the needs of AI/AN children is another fundamental obligation of the federal trust responsibility.

Professional education and training on the issues of children exposed to violence was underscored in the 2012 Children Exposed to Violence

Task Force Report including recognition of the critical role law enforcement played in responding to violence.[95] The ILOC Report emphasized the importance of training law enforcement personnel working in Indian country.[96] For example, law enforcement personnel may be the first responders to complaints of child abuse and neglect however, law enforcement training does not always include how to carefully interview an Indian child who has been the victim of abuse.[97] Inappropriate techniques can result in further trauma and possibly taint evidence needed for prosecution.[98] Training and technical assistance for tribal child protection personnel is critical as well.[99]

AI/AN communities struggle to ensure access to a qualified AI/AN workforce in the trauma treatment area.[100] Tribal and urban AI/AN professionals often have difficulty obtaining training that is tailored to the tribal community being served and oftentimes trainings are offered far from the tribal communities.[101]

Properly credentialed professionals that lack the cultural knowledge to identify and understand tribal familial needs face challenges in providing effective services.[102] Additionally, attracting and keeping credentialed professionals in rural areas, has proven difficult. However, there are resources available to AI/AN children in rural areas that are not being tapped. This includes interested and knowledgeable people within AI/AN communities who may be unlicensed, but either have the skills or are willing to develop the skills needed to support AI/AN children exposed to violence. Training community members and developing their skills can expand the workforce to provide services to families and children in need. Alaska's model of Community Health Aid is a useful example of this approach. The Community Health Aid model was initially developed by the IHS to combat the tuberculosis epidemic in Alaska.[103] It now enables a wide range of services including dental and behavior health services to be provided to people who would otherwise go without services. Training local people to provide services needed to treat trauma would be effective in rural areas that have difficulty attracting and retaining credentialed staff.

Federal agencies should require leadership, policy staff, program staff, and contractors that work with tribes or tribal programs that address children exposed to violence and independent grant reviewers who review grants submitted by tribes to receive training on sovereignty, culture, and history. Staff providing direct service or working specifically in a region should receive additional cultural and historical training specific to the community they serve.

"One of the main barriers both our youth and their families face are professionals who have the proper credentials required by the state but lack the cultural knowledge and ability or desire to even try to understand where our children and their families are coming from."

Darla Thiele, Director, Sunka Wakan Ah Ku Program. Testimony before the Task Force on American Indian/ Alaska Native Children Exposed to Violence, Bismarck, ND, December 9, 2014

AI/AN communities need an assessment of the current cultural-based training and technical assistance resources and recommendations for easily accessible online courses (such as Working Effectively with Tribal Governments[104]), improvements in current offerings, and recommendations for addressing the continued updating and monitoring of website and staff training. Tribal and urban AIAN organizations should be involved in the assessments.

Notes

1. Tribe – For purposes of this report, we use the term "tribe" to refer to federally recognized tribes from the Secretary of Interior's list. 79 Fed. Reg. 4,748 (Jan. 29, 2014), *available at* http://www.gpo.gov/fdsys/pkg/FR-2014-01-29/pdf/2014-01683.pdf.

2. Goodkind, J. R., et al., "Promoting Healing and Restoring Trust: Policy Recommendations for Improving Behavioral Health Care for American Indian/Alaska Native Adolescents," *American Journal of Community Psychology* 46 (2010): 386–94.

3. Carlson, B. E. "Children Exposed to Intimate Partner Violence: Research Findings and Implications for Intervention," *Trauma, Violence, and Abuse* 1(4) (2000): 321–42.

4. *Fast Facts: Native American Youth and Indian Country.* Center for Native American Youth at the Aspen Institute: 2. Available at: http://www.aspeninstitute.org/sites/default/files/content/upload/Native%20Youth%20Fast%20Facts%20Update_04-2014.pdf

5. Listenbee, Robert L., Jr., et al., *Report of the Attorney General's National Task Force on Children Exposed to Violence*, Washington, D.C.: U.S. Department of Justice, Office of Juvenile Justice and Delinquency Prevention, December 2012: 27–36.

6. Indian Law and Order Commission, *A Roadmap for Making Native America Safer: Report to the President and Congress of the United States* (November 2013): 154, available at: http://www.aisc.ucla.edu/iloc/report/index.html.

7. Arya, Neelum, and Rolnick, Addie, "A Tangled Web of Justice: American Indian and Alaska Native Youth in Federal, State, and Tribal Justice Systems," Washington, D.C.: *Campaign for Youth Justice Policy Brief* 1 (2008): n6.

8. BigFoot, Dolores Subia, et al., "Trauma Exposure in American Indian/Alaska Native Children," Indian Country Child Trauma Center (2008): 1–4, available at: http://www.theannainstitute.org/American%20Indians%20and%20Alaska%20Natives/Trauma%20Exposure%20in%20AIAN%20Children.pdf.

9. Congressional findings in the TLOA of 2010, PL-111-211, §202(a)(5) (2010).

10. Indian Law and Order Commission, *A Roadmap for Making Native America Safer: Report to the President and Congress of the United States* (November 2013): 151, available at: http://www.aisc.ucla.edu/iloc/report/index.html; *see also* BigFoot, Dolores Subia, et al., "Trauma Exposure in American Indian/Alaska Native Children," Indian Country Child Trauma Center (2008): 1–4, available at: http://www.theannainstitute.org/American%20Indians%20and%20Alaska%20Natives/Trauma%20Exposure%20in%20AIAN%20Children.pdf.

11. BigFoot, Dolores Subia, et al., "Trauma Exposure in American Indian/Alaska Native Children," Indian Country Child Trauma Center (2008): 1–4, available at: http://www.theannainstitute.org/American%20Indians%20and%20Alaska%20Natives/Trauma%20Exposure%20in%20AIAN%20Children.pdf.

12. Arya, Neelum, and Rolnick, Addie, "A Tangled Web of Justice: American Indian and Alaska Native Youth in Federal, State, and Tribal Justice Systems," Washington, D.C.: *Campaign for Youth Justice Policy Brief* 1 (2008): 5.

13. Ibid.

14. Ibid. *See also* U.S. Department of Health and Human Services, Centers for Disease Control and Prevention, National Center for Injury Prevention and Control, "Web Based Injury Statistics Query and Reporting System (WISQARS)." Retrieved May 4, 2008 from: http://www.cde.gov/ncipc/wisqars.

15. BigFoot, Dolores Subia, et al., "Trauma Exposure in American Indian/Alaska Native Children," Indian Country Child Trauma Center (2008): 1–4, available at: http://www.theannainstitute. org/American%20Indians%20and%20Alaska%20Natives/Trauma%20Exposure%20in%20AIAN%20 Children.pdf.

16. Ibid.

17. Indian Law and Order Commission, *A Roadmap for Making Native America Safer: Report to the President and Congress of the United States* (November 2013): 156, available at: http://www.aisc.ucla. edu/iloc/report/index.html.

18. Ibid., 157.

19. Listenbee, Robert L., Jr., et al., *Report of the Attorney General's National Task Force on Children Exposed to Violence*, Washington, D.C.: U.S. Department of Justice, Office of Juvenile Justice and Delinquency Prevention, December 2012: 35.

20. Yellow Horse Braveheart, Maria, *Historical Trauma*, available at: http://www.historicaltrauma. com/.

21. BigFoot, Dolores Subia, et al., "Trauma Exposure in American Indian/Alaska Native Children," Indian Country Child Trauma Center (2008): 1–4, available at: http://www.theannainstitute. org/American%20Indians%20and%20Alaska%20Natives/Trauma%20Exposure%20in%20AIAN%20 Children.pdf.

22. Written Testimony of Deborah Painte, Hearing of the Task Force on American Indian/Alaska Native Children Exposed to Violence, Bismarck, ND, December 9, 2013 at 2 (on file with Tribal Law and Policy Institute); *see also* Child Welfare Collaborative Group, National Child Traumatic Stress Network, and The California Social Work Education Center, *Child Welfare Trauma Training Toolkit: Trainer's Guide* (2nd ed.), Los Angeles, CA and Durham, NC: National Center for Child Traumatic Stress, 2013.

23. Written Testimony of Deborah Painte, Hearing of the Task Force on American Indian/Alaska Native Children Exposed to Violence, Bismarck, ND, December 9, 2013 at n6 (on file with Tribal Law and Policy Institute).

24. Indian Entities Recognized and Eligible to Receive Services from the U.S. Bureau of Indian Affairs, 79 *Federal Register*, 4,748 (January 29, 2014).

25. Urban Indian Health Institute, *Health Disparities in UIHO Service Areas*, available at: http:// www.uihi.org/wp-content/uploads/2013/04/UIHO_Fact-Sheet_2013-04-05.pdf.

26. Canby, William C., *American Indian Law, In a Nutshell*, West Publishing (2009): 72.

27. Newton, Nell Jessup, ed., *Cohen's Handbook of Federal Indian Law* § 4.01(2)(e), at 221 (2012).

28. Fletcher, Matthew L. M., "Statement of Matthew L. M. Fletcher before the Senate Committee on Indian Affairs—Oversight Hearing on Fulfilling the Federal Trust Responsibility: The Foundation of the Government-to-Government Relationship" (May 15, 2012), available at: http://papers.ssrn. com/sol3/papers.cfm?abstract_id=2060395.

29. Indian Child Welfare Act, PL-95-608, 92 Stat. 3069 (1978), codified as amended at 25 U.S.C. § 1902.

30. Beals, J., et al., "Prevalence of DSM-IV Disorders and Attendant Help-Seeking in 2 American Indian Reservation Populations," *Archives of General Psychiatry* 62 (2005).

31. Tribal Law and Order Act of 2010, PL-111-211, tit. II.

32. Indian Law and Order Commission, *A Roadmap for Making Native America Safer: Report to the President and Congress of the United States* (November 2013), available at: http://www.aisc.ucla.edu/ iloc/report/index.html.

33. VAWA of 2013, PL-113-4.

34. Ibid., tit. IX.

35. S. 1474, 113th Cong. 2d Sess. (2014). S. 1474 citation.

36. S. 1622, 113th Cong. 2d Sess. (2014).

37. Native American Rights Fund, *NARF Legal* Review, available at: http://www.narf.org/pubs/ rlr/nlr29-2.pdf.

38. The VAWA of 2013, PL-113-4, 127 Stat. 54 (March 7, 2013).

39. See the appendix for a definition of braided funding streams.

40. Newton, Nell Jessup, ed., *Cohen's Handbook of Federal Indian Law* § 9.01, at 737 (2012) ("The federal statutory scheme for Indian country criminal jurisdiction has been criticized in light of the increasing problems in public safety and criminal justice in Indian country."); *also see* Robert N. Clinton, *Criminal Jurisdiction over Indian Lands: A Journey through a Jurisdictional Maze*, 18 *Ariz. L. Rev.* 503 (1976): 535–6.

41. The General Crimes Act, 18 U.S.C. §1152; the Assimilative Crimes Act, 18 U.S.C. § 1; the Major Crimes Act, 18 U.S.C. §1153 (providing federal criminal jurisdiction over ten enumerated major crimes committed in Indian country that is exclusive of the states); and *Oliphant v. Suquamish Indian Tribe*, 435 U.S. 191 (holding that tribes lack criminal jurisdiction over non-Indian defendants).

42. S. Rep. No. 111-093, to *accompany* S. 797, 111th Cong. 1st Sess. (2009).

43. Indian Law and Order Commission, *A Roadmap for Making Native America Safer: Report to the President and Congress of the United States* (November 2013): ix, available at: http://www.aisc.ucla.edu/iloc/report/index.html.

44. Ibid., 17.

45. *Talton v. Mayes*, 163 U.S. 376 (1896) (holding that individual rights protections, which limit federal, and later state governments, do not apply to tribal governments).

46. ICRA of 1968, 25 U.S.C. §§ 1301–1304.

47. 25 U.S.C.§ 1302(a)(7)(B).

48. TLOA of 2010, PL-111-211, H.R. 725, 124 Stat. 2258 (July 29, 2010).

49. 25 U.S.C.§ 1302(a)(7)(C); § 1302(b)–(d). Additional due process protection requirements for tribes that choose to exercise this "enhanced sentencing" include (1) provide the defendant the right to effective assistance of counsel at least equal to that guaranteed by the U.S. Constitution; (2) provide indigent defendant the assistance of a defense attorney licensed to practice law by any jurisdiction in the United States, at the expense of the tribal government; (3) require that the presiding judge has sufficient legal training and is licensed to practice law by any jurisdiction in the United States; (4) make the criminal laws publicly available; and (5) maintain a record of the criminal proceeding.

50. VAWA of 2013, PL-113-4, 127 Stat. 54 (March 7, 2013).

51. Congressional findings in TLOA of 2010, PL-111-211, §202(a)(5) (2010).

52. "Alaska Native people in Anchorage were 9.7 times more likely to experience sexual assault than others living in the city." Amnesty International, *Maze of Injustice, The Failure to Protect Indigenous Women from Sexual Violence in the USA*, New York: Amnesty International USA (2007): 36.

53. Bureau of Justice Statistics, American Indians and Crime, 1992–2002, vi. Available at: http://www.bjs.gov/content/pub/pdf/aic02.pdf

54. Ibid., 8.

55. Bancroft, Lundy, and Silverman, Jay G., *The Batterer as Parent: Addressing the Impact of Domestic Violence on Family Dynamics*, Thousand Oaks, CA: Sage Publications (2002): 42–4.

56. For purposes of 18 USC §§ 1152 and 1153.

57. Written Testimony of Brian Cladoosby, Hearing of the Task Force on American Indian/Alaska Native Children Exposed to Violence, Fort Lauderdale, FL, April 16–17, 2014 at 22, available at: http://www.justice.gov/defendingchildhood/fl-briefingbinder.pdf.

58. PL-83-280, 18 U.S.C. § 1162 ("Each of the State or Territories listed in the following table shall have jurisdiction over offenses committed by or against Indians in the area of Indian country listed opposite the name of the State or Territory to the same extent that such State or Territory has jurisdiction over offense committed elsewhere within the State or Territory, and the criminal laws of such State or Territory shall have the same force and effect within such Indian country as they have elsewhere. . .").

59. Written Testimony of Sarah Hicks Kastelic, Hearing of the Task Force on American Indian/Alaska Native Children Exposed to Violence, Bismarck, ND, December 9, 2013 at 29, available at: http://www.justice.gov/defendingchildhood/nd-briefingbinder.pdf.

60. Ibid., 32.

61. Ibid., 33.

62. Ibid., 32–3.

63. See Chapter 11 (Funding) of Final Report—Law Enforcement and Criminal Justice under Public Law 280 available at: http://www.tribal-institute.org/download/pl280_study.pdf.

64. Ibid.

65. Testimony of Attorney General Janet Reno before S. Comm. on Indian Affairs, 105th Cong., available at: http://www.justice.gov/archive/otj/Congressional_Testimony/attgensiac.htm.

66. See, e.g., Indian Law and Order Commission, *A Roadmap for Making Native America Safer: Report to the President and Congress of the United States* (November 2013): 83, available at: http://www.aisc.ucla.edu/iloc/report/index.html (comparing the FY 2012 DOJ funding for tribal justice systems of $316 million with the FY 2012 DOI funding for tribal law enforcement and justice programming at $346 million).

67. U.S. Department of Justice, "Coordinated Tribal Assistance Solicitation Awards," available at: http://www.justice.gov/tribal/grants.

68. CTAS (Coordinated Tribal Assistance Solicitation).

69. Ibid.

70. Indian Law and Order Commission, *A Roadmap for Making Native America Safer: Report to the President and Congress of the United States* (November 2013), available at: http://www.aisc.ucla.edu/iloc/report/index.html.

71. National Congress of American Indians, *Fiscal Year 2015 Indian Country Budget Request: An Honorable Budget for Indian Country: Equitable Funding for Tribes*, Washington, D.C. (January 2014): 29, available at: http://www.ncai.org/NCAI_2014_Budget_Request.pdf.

72. Indian Law and Order Commission, *A Roadmap for Making Native America Safer: Report to the President and Congress of the United States* (November 2013): 85, available at: http://www.aisc.ucla.edu/iloc/report/index.html; National Congress of American Indians, *Fiscal Year 2015 Indian Country Budget Request: An Honorable Budget for Indian Country: Equitable Funding for Tribes*, Washington, D.C.: 30 (January 2014) available at: http://www.ncai.org/NCAI_2014_Budget_Request.pdf.

73. National Congress of American Indians, *Fiscal Year 2015 Indian Country Budget Request: An Honorable Budget for Indian Country: Equitable Funding for Tribes*, Washington, D.C.: 30 (January 2014) available at: http://www.ncai.org/NCAI_2014_Budget_Request.pdf.

74. Ibid.

75. "Tribal Self-Governance Demonstration Feasibility Study," Washington, D.C.: U.S. Department of Health and Human Services, Office of the Assistant Secretary for Planning and Evaluation (March 2003), available at: www.bbna.com/tgs/self-gov-stdy.htm.

76. The eleven programs identified in the 2003 feasibility study were Administration on Aging (Grants for Native Americans); Administration for Children and Families (Tribal Temporary Assistance for Needy Families), Low Income Home Energy Assistance, Community Services Block Grant, Child Care and Development Fund, Native Employment Works, Head Start, Child Welfare Services, Promoting Safe and Stable Families, and Family Violence Prevention: Grants for Battered Women's Shelters); and Substance Abuse and Mental Health Services Administration (Target Capacity Expansion).

77. Fostering Connections to Success and Increasing Adoptions Act of 2008, PL-110-351, available at: http://www.nrc4tribes.org/files/Tab%207_1%20FC%20legislation%20-%20Public_Law_110-351.pdf.

78. Letter from Rex Lee Jim, Chairman, Secretary's Tribal Advisory Committee to Secretary Sylvia Mathews Burwell, Department of Health and Human Services, regarding Secretary's Tribal Advisory Committee Brief on Priority Issues (July 21, 2014) (on file with the Tribal Law and Policy Institute).

79. National Congress of American Indians, The National Congress of American Indians Resolution #ANC-14-048; Support for a Dedicated Tribal Set-Aside in the Victims of Crime Act Fund, available at: http://www.ncai.org/attachments/Resolution_setxfZPHiQTTzySUNFbXPG-MQbWeImEpTlwnDJOrYdpnOLIJlyiU_ANC-14-048.pdf.

80. Listenbee, Robert L., Jr., et al., *Report of the Attorney General's National Task Force on Children Exposed to Violence*, Washington, D.C.: U.S. Department of Justice, Office of Juvenile Justice and Delinquency Prevention (December 2012): 42; and Indian Law and Order Commission, *A Roadmap for Making Native America Safer: Report to the President and Congress of the United States* (November 2013): 109, available at: http://www.aisc.ucla.edu/iloc/report/index.html.

81. Written Testimony of Sarah Hicks Kastelic, Hearing of the Task Force on American Indian/Alaska Native Children Exposed to Violence, Bismarck, ND, December 9, 2013 at 35, available at: http://www.justice.gov/defendingchildhood/nd-briefingbinder.pdf.

82. Ibid.

83. Written Testimony of Iris PrettyPaint, Hearing of the Task Force on American Indian/Alaska Native Children Exposed to Violence, Fort Lauderdale, FL, April 16–17, 2014 at 157, available at: http://www.justice.gov/defendingchildhood/fl-briefingbinder.pdf.

84. Written Testimony of Sarah Hicks Kastelic, Hearing of the Task Force on American Indian/Alaska Native Children Exposed to Violence, Bismarck, ND, December 9, 2013 at 36, available at: http://www.justice.gov/defendingchildhood/nd-briefingbinder.pdf.

85. Ibid., 50.

86. Indian Law and Order Commission, *A Roadmap for Making Native America Safer: Report to the President and Congress of the United States* (November 2013): 101, available at: http://www.aisc.ucla.edu/iloc/report/index.html.

87. Written Testimony of Terry Cross, Hearing of the Task Force on American Indian/Alaska Native Children Exposed to Violence, Fort Lauderdale, FL, April 16–17, 2014, at 79, available at: http://www.justice.gov/defendingchildhood/nd-briefingbinder.pdf. Citing Earle, K. A. *Child Abuse and Neglect: An Examination of American Indian Data*, Seattle, WA: Case Family Programs, 2000.

88. Written Testimony of Terry Cross, Hearing of the Task Force on American Indian/Alaska Native Children Exposed to Violence, Fort Lauderdale, FL, April 16–17, 2014, at 79, available at: http://www.justice.gov/defendingchildhood/nd-briefingbinder.pdf. Citing Hicks, S., and Dossett, J., *Principled Devolution,* Washington, D.C.: Working Paper, National Congress of American Indians (2000); and Johnson, S., Kaufmann, J., Dossett, J., and Hicks, S., *Government to Government: Understanding State and Tribal Governments*, Denver, CO: National Conference of State Legislatures, 2000.

89. *See e.g.,* the Walking on Common Ground website, an online resource part of the Walking on Common Ground initiative. The initiative, established in 1988, promotes and facilitates federal, tribal, and state collaboration, and includes the development of a series of tribal court-state court forums. Available at: http://www.walkingoncommonground.org/index.cfm.

90. *See e.g.,* Goldberg, Carole, and Champagne, Duane, *Promising Strategies: Tribal and State Court Relations*, West Hollywood, CA: Tribal Law and Policy Institute, March 2013 (detailing ten different collaborative innovations between states and tribes from across the country).

91. Tribal-State Title IV-E agreements describe how ICWA will be implemented and address services related to out-of-home placements for AI/AN children in foster care. They can also specify the process for tribal notification when the state receives a referral for an Indian child; the roles of state or tribal law enforcement; the roles of the BIA, state, and tribal courts; process for transfers of jurisdiction; and procedures for establishing eligibility for Title IV-E agreements. To learn more, see: http://nrc4tribes.org/Direct-Tribal-Title-IV-E-Funding.cfm.

92. The DIFRC programs include family preservation, family reunification, Indian child welfare advocacy, healthy living, and behavioral health programs. See: http://difrc.org/.

93. Urban Listening Session of the Task Force on American Indian/Alaska Native Children Exposed to Violence, Minneapolis, MN, May 20–21, 2014. See: http://adycenter.org/.

94. Ain Dah Yung Center has family preservation programs where they work with the state child protection services, mental health programs working with Ramsey County, ICWA compliance program, and other programs that are collaborative. See http://adycenter.org/programs.

95. Listenbee, Robert L., Jr. et al., *Report of the Attorney General's National Task Force on Children Exposed to Violence*, Washington, D.C.: U.S. Department of Justice, Office of Juvenile Justice and Delinquency Prevention (December 2012): 10, 12, 14, 19, and 20.

96. Indian Law and Order Commission, *A Roadmap for Making Native America Safer: Report to the President and Congress of the United States* (November 2013): 107, available at: http://www.aisc.ucla.edu/iloc/report/index.html.

97. Written Testimony of Sarah Hicks Kastelic, Hearing of the Task Force on American Indian/Alaska Native Children Exposed to Violence, Bismarck, ND, December 9, 2013 at 31, available at: http://www.justice.gov/defendingchildhood/nd-briefingbinder.pdf.

98. Ibid.

99. Ibid., 30.

100. Ibid., 36.

101. Ibid.

102. Written Testimony of Darla Thiele, Hearing of the Task Force on American Indian/Alaska Native Children Exposed to Violence, Bismarck, ND, December 9, 2013 at 147, available at: http://www.justice.gov/defendingchildhood/nd-briefingbinder.pdf.

103. Testimony of Andy Teuber, Hearing of the Task Force on American Indian/Alaska Native Children Exposed to Violence, Anchorage AK, June 11, 2014 at 12, available at: http://www.justice.gov/defendingchildhood/4th-hearing/AlaskaPanel1.pdf.

104. Advisory Council on Historic Presentation's Native American Program, "Working Effectively with Tribal Governments" (2008). This is a free online training curriculum, developed to aid federal employees in their work with tribal governments. The curriculum includes a historical overview of federal Indian policy, as well as cultural factors, and has been adapted from the Environment Protection Agency's original curriculum to be government-wide. Available at: http://tribal.golearnportal.org/.

CHAPTER 2

Promoting Well-Being for American Indian and Alaska Native Children in the Home

Every single day, a majority of American Indian and Alaska Native (AI/AN) children are exposed to violence within the walls of their own homes. This exposure not only contradicts traditional understandings that children are to be protected and viewed as sacred, but it leaves hundreds of children traumatized and struggling to cope over the course of their lifetime. Despite leadership from tribal governments, parents, and families, domestic violence in the homes of AI/AN children and physical abuse, sexual abuse, and neglect of children is more common than in the general population. The Attorney General's National Taskforce on Children Exposed to Violence noted in its report:

> Children who have been exposed to intimate partner violence in their families also are at high risk for severe and potentially life-long problems with physical health, mental health, school and peer relationships, and disruptive behavior. Children who witness or live with intimate partner violence are often burdened by a sense of loss or by profound guilt because they believe that they should have somehow intervened or prevented the violence—or, tragically, that they actually caused the violence.[1]

Generally, children living with batterers are at a much greater risk of being physically and sexually assaulted. National studies show that men who batter their companion also abuse their children in 49 to 70 percent of the cases.[2] Child abuse investigations reveal violence against the mother in 28 to 59 percent of the cases.[3]

A recent study supported by DOJ's Office on Violence Against Women (OVW) examines the co-occurrence of domestic violence and child maltreatment in Indian country and provides insight into key challenges specific to Native communities.[4] The Advisory Committee heard testimony that substantiated many of the findings in the report, including the following:

- Native children are often removed from their mother for "failure to protect" or because the mother lacks resources to support the child. Rather than working with the mother to resolve the problems, children are removed too frequently, and few services are provided to help the mother regain custody of her children. Children experience not only the trauma of exposure to domestic violence, but the additional trauma of removal from the non-abusing parent's care and their community.
- The lack of domestic violence shelters, transitional housing, and permanent housing are an ongoing problem on reservations. Mothers who leave their abusers often lose their

children because they cannot find safe housing or shelter on or near reservations.

- Collaboration across agencies is weak at best. Many domestic violence programs don't look at the children as victims and do not provide services. Many child protection agencies don't understand the dynamics of power and control in domestic violence and wrongly view the victim as responsible. Some tribal communities have multidisciplinary teams to address domestic violence and child abuse but individual agencies often lack understanding of each other's purpose and function within the system. Domestic violence training is needed for child protection workers, law enforcement officers, and court systems. Domestic violence advocates need training regarding the impact of domestic violence on children. Because tribal communities often lack a sufficient number of law enforcement officers, victims often share the concern that protection orders will not be enforced, or that law enforcement will not respond appropriately.

- Due to a lack of funding—or to siloed funding streams—domestic violence agencies often cannot use funding for treatment and services for children.

- Child protection case plans often focus on the non-abusing parent, usually the mother, even though she may have done nothing to abuse or neglect her children. Even when domestic violence is the key reason for intervention by child protection, the victim may be held responsible rather than the batterer. Case plans' unrealistic requirements may also setup the non-abusing parent for failure.

- Too often Native communities fail to hold batterers accountable and even allow them to participate in sacred ceremonies.

- Victims of domestic violence often need treatment for alcohol and drugs that is not available in the community. Furthermore, victims do not have access to safe places for their children when participating in treatment.

- Tribes have inadequate social service departments (and in some cases none) to handle the number and complexity of child abuse and domestic violence cases of child maltreatment.

- Culture, tradition, and values are often missing in many tribal social service agencies. Western ideas and practices take priority over traditional ways. Social service models that incorporate Native values and traditions are critically needed. Close family connections between clients and service providers in small

"Many families suffer from generations of violence, substance abuse, and dysfunction. The tribal alcohol treatment program estimates that 96 percent of families on the reservations are impacted by the alcohol and 90 percent of adults have had personal experience with family violence."

Lisa Thompson-Heth, Executive Director, Wiconi-Wawokiya, Inc. Testimony before the Task Force on American Indian/Alaska Native Children Exposed to Violence, Bismarck, ND, December 9, 2013. Citing the 2010 Crow Creek Community Assessment.

"Not only are we seeing children who are currently being abused, but we are seeing children whose parents and grandparents were victims of sexual abuse and familial abuse. The cycle continues and we are witnessing the generations of trauma every day in the eyes of our youngest and most precious resource, our children."

Elsie Boudreau, Social Worker and Director, Alaska Native Unity with Alaska CARES and Alaska Native Justice Center. Testimony before the Task Force on American Indian/ Alaska Native Children Exposed to Violence, Anchorage, AK, June 12, 2014

Native communities can impact decision making. In small communities professionals may also have several jobs and wear several different hats, creating potential professional conflicts.

Unfortunately, children who witness domestic violence in their homes are also more likely to be victimized. Biological parents and parental figures perpetrate 32 to 39.7 percent of all sexual assaults against children. The vast majority of these sex offenders are fathers or father figures.[5] Other family members are responsible for 11.3 to 22.4 percent of the child sexual abuse.[6] Official crime reporting data indicate that 27 percent of all reported sex offenders are family members and 49 percent of offenders of victims under age six and 42 percent of offenders of victims between ages six and eleven are family members.[7] The greatest risk for child sexual abuse comes within a family structure at the hands of a male family member, possibly another child (30–50 percent of offenders of children are children under the age of eighteen). Studies have demonstrated that exposure to family members that batter is one of the strongest indicators of the risk of sexual abuse.[8]

Additionally, we know that one in every three AI/AN women is sexually assaulted, often in childhood.[9] In 2001, the Health Director of the Oglala Sioux Tribe estimated that between 95 and 98 percent of the tribal population had experienced sexual abuse as children.[10] In 2013, 39 percent of the children seen in child advocacy centers in Alaska were Alaska Native.[11]

Sexual abuse can have a devastating impact on a child. The Attorney General's National Taskforce on Children Exposed to Violence stated in their report:

> **Sexual abuse** places children at high risk for serious and often chronic problems with health, PTSD and other mental health disorders, suicidality, eating disorders, sleep disorders, substance abuse, and distortions about problems with sexuality and appropriate sexual behavior. Sexually abused children often become hyper-vigilant about future sexual violation and experience a sense of betrayal that breaks down the innate trust they feel for adults who should care for and protect them. Females may become vulnerable to predators and exploitive adults or older peers who re-victimize them, which can lead them to have difficulty caring for and protecting their own children.[12]

Traditional tribal child-rearing practices and beliefs allowed a natural system of child protection to flourish. AI/AN beliefs reinforced that all things had a spiritual nature that demanded respect, especially children.[13] Not only were children respected, but they were taught to respect others. Extraordinary patience and tolerance marked the methods that were used to teach Indian children self-discipline.[14] At the heart of this traditional system were beliefs, traditions, and customs involving extended family with clearly delineated roles and responsibilities. Child-rearing responsibilities were often divided between extended family and community members.[15] In this way, the protection of children in the tribe was the responsibility of all people in the community. The safety net for Native children that protected them from abuse and neglect was formed by traditional beliefs and child rearing practices.

If AI/AN children today are to be provided with a reliable safety net, the letter and the spirit of ICWA must be enforced. As a law, ICWA provides critical legal protections for AI/AN children when intervention and treatment is deemed necessary by state child protection agencies. The most significant provisions of ICWA seek to keep AI/AN children safely in their homes and provide AI/AN children with certain civil protections as members of their respective tribe.

Unfortunately, many states do not comply with the letter or spirit of ICWA. AI/AN children are far more likely to become a part of the child welfare system because of unsubstantiated allegations of neglect. Of all AI/AN cases of maltreatment, 79.4 percent are neglect, 10.6 percent are physical abuse, and 5.2 percent are sexual abuse.[16] Cultural bias, racism, and a misunderstanding of poverty reflected in legal definitions and workers' decisions to substantiate allegations of neglect make AI/AN families susceptible to biased treatment in child welfare systems.[17]

This chapter examines AI/AN children's exposure to domestic violence and child maltreatment in the home and the infrastructure that continues to re-traumatize children and separate them from their families and larger tribal communities. Implementation of the recommendations in this chapter will reestablish effective systems throughout tribal communities that will heal and return honor and dignity to children who experience violence in the home and support the infrastructure that will allow tribes to be more effective in protecting their child populations.

"I am in a corner and my body is being touched and groped. How do I say 'stop'? I close my eyes and my tears begin to flow. I go to a faraway place with my mind, a safe place, a happy place, a place where I don't have to feel what my body is experiencing. After it's over, I am lifeless, and I begin to come back to my body once again."

Lenny Hayes, Mental Health Therapist and survivor of child sexual abuse. Testimony before the Task Force on American Indian/ Alaska Native Children Exposed to Violence, Bismarck, ND, December 9, 2013

ADVISORY COMMITTEE VISION FOR WELL-BEING IN THE HOME

The Advisory Committee envisions AI/AN homes where children are nurtured and supported and encouraged to thrive. The Advisory Committee pictures a child welfare system that appreciates that AI/AN children develop identity and connection within their tribal community (clan, band, extended family) and that identity and connection will lead to a child's resiliency, wellness, and overall well-being. The Advisory Committee sees a system that develops supportive culturally appropriate responses to violence in the home while focusing on prevention and early intervention in families. Child welfare and domestic violence programs should be trauma-informed and educated on the most effective treatments for addressing victims of trauma and the healing process, including traditional healing methods.

The Advisory Committee imagines a tribal community that can respond to violence in the home in a knowledgeable manner with the data and information they need to make informed decisions; that has the option of responding in state proceedings, as states comply with ICWA; that has the resources to respond; and that has the ability to respond in a multidisciplinary and multi-departmental approach.

Findings and Recommendations

2.1 The legislative and executive branches of the federal government should ensure Indian Child Welfare Act (ICWA) compliance and encourage tribal-state ICWA collaborations.

2.1.A Within two years of the publication of this report, the Administration for Children and Families (ACF) in the Department of Health and Human Services (HHS), the Bureau of Indian Affairs (BIA) in the Department of the Interior (DOI), and tribes should develop a modernized unified data-collection system designed to collect Adoption and Foster Care Analysis and Reporting System (AFCARS) (ICWA and tribal dependency) data on all AI/AN children who are placed into foster care by their agency and share that data quarterly with tribes to allow tribes and the BIA to make informed decisions regarding AI/AN children.

2.1.B The Secretaries of the Department of Interior (DOI) and Health and Human Services (HHS) should compel BIA and ACF to work together collaboratively to collect data regarding compliance with ICWA in state court systems. The ACF and BIA should work collaboratively to ensure state court compliance with ICWA.

2.1.C The BIA should issue regulations (not simply update guidelines) and create an oversight board to review ICWA implementation and designate consequences of noncompliance and/or incentives for compliance with ICWA to ensure the effective implementation of ICWA.

2.1.D The Department of Justice (DOJ) should create a position of Indian Child Welfare Specialist to provide advice to the Attorney General and DOJ staff on matters relative to AI/AN child welfare cases, to provide case support in cases before federal, tribal, and state courts, and to coordinate ICWA training for federal, tribal, and state judges; prosecutors; and other court personnel.

"It is essential to remember that because of the historic treatment of AI/AN peoples, removal of AI/AN children from their homes, families, and communities is itself a form of violence—one form of trauma that far too many AI/AN children still face today. ICWA ensures that only when necessary for their safety are AI/AN children exposed to this additional layer of violence in the aftermath of abuse or neglect."

Terry Cross, Executive Director, National Indian Child Welfare Association. Written testimony before the Task Force on American Indian/Alaska Native Children Exposed to Violence, Fort Lauderdale, FL, April 16, 2014

Currently the BIA and tribes have no reliable data regarding AI/AN children in foster care.[18] Gathering and analyzing such data would allow for appropriate guidance in decision making for directing services to meet the needs of the most vulnerable children, those in foster care. As more tribal agencies strive to become Title IV-E agencies,[19] they need assistance to develop effective systems to collect information. Like any government, tribes must be able to track critical data involving their citizens across different service areas (federal, tribal, and state). Currently, tribes lack the capacity to collect, analyze, and report data.

The lack of accurate, relevant data on tribal children and families means that AI/AN children are often "invisible" during discussions about policy development, resource allocation discussion, and decision making at the federal level. Or, because of the lack of such data regarding AI/AN children, policy makers delay or decline to make decision and resource allocations because they cannot "justify" the services. By increasing tribal capacity (through tribal child protection agencies, BIA, and IHS) in the area of data collection, we can increase tribal engagement and federal responsiveness to AI/AN children's needs. It is not a simple task to engage the various agencies providing child protective services in Indian country, but it is critical to making well-informed decisions.

What limited data we do have indicates that nationally, AI/AN children make up a slightly higher percentage of substantiated reports of abuse or neglect than their percentage of the general population. AI/AN children were 7,770 of the 666,924 substantiated reports of children physically abused, sexually abused, and neglected in 2012.[20] AI/AN children made up 1.2 percent of all substantiated reports of maltreatment and made up 1 percent of the total child population in the United States in 2012.[21] These statistics represent information gathered through the National Child Abuse and Neglect Data System (NCANDS), a federally sponsored data system, supported by the Child Abuse Prevention and Treatment Act (CAPTA).[22] NCANDS, through the Children's Bureau,[23] collects and analyzes data on child abuse and neglect annually. Data is submitted by the fifty states, the District of Columbia, and Puerto Rico. All states that receive federal funds from the CAPTA Basic State Grant program must provide the data required by the act to the extent practicable.[24] **Tribes and tribal consortia are not eligible for the Basic State Grant program and therefore are not required to and do not provide data to the NCANDS system for children and families they serve. The data underlying these statistics represent only those AI/AN children who are screened through state child protective service programs.** In 2000, a study found that approximately 61 percent of all AI/AN child maltreatment data is reported.[25] The majority of the children accounted for by NCANDS are children living in urban areas or off reservation. Tribal programs, BIA or IHS programs, or tribal consortia are often the primary service providers for AI/AN children and families; however, they are not required to report child abuse and neglect data to states. That leaves out a significant portion of the AI/AN population that has unmet needs.

Although BIA regional offices, IHS, and other agencies may collect data on the prevalence of child maltreatment in the tribal communities with which they work, this data is not kept consistently nor is the cumulative data available either regionally or nationally. NCANDS does not include AI/AN children who come to the attention of and are served by tribal child welfare systems.[26] We thus can only look at incomplete statistical data, a common concern with AI/AN statistical information.

AFCARS collects case-level information on children in foster care and those who have been adopted with Title IV-E agency involvement through the Children's Bureau. Again, this provides information primarily on AI/AN children in urban and rural areas outside of Indian country, although a few tribal agencies are Title IV-E and would be included. Currently, the agency and the tribes have no reliable data regarding their children in foster care to guide them. As more tribal agencies strive to become Title IV-E agencies, they need assistance to develop effective systems to collect information. Like any government, tribes need the ability to track, analyze, and report critical data involving their citizens across different service areas (federal, tribal, and state). When ICWA is followed, the goals of safety, permanency, child well-being, and family well-being can be met more successfully.[27] A decrease in ICWA compliance has resulted in an increase in foster care and adoption rates for AI/AN children.[28] There is recent research documenting noncompliance with most key provision of ICWA, including:

- Failure to identify AI/AN children and ensure they are receiving the protections of the law.[29]
- Inadequate or lack of notice to tribes and family members.[30]
- Placement of children outside the placement preferences without good cause or in a more restrictive setting than necessary.[31]

ICWA noncompliance is likely a result of minimal oversight of ICWA implementation and no enforcement mechanism.[32] ICWA was enacted without providing sanctions for noncompliance, incentives for effective compliance, a data collection requirement, or a mandate for an oversight committee or authority to monitor compliance. ICWA is the only federal child welfare law that does not include legislatively mandated oversight or periodic review.[33] These deficits in ICWA should be corrected.

The DOJ existing structure does not include a position that allows for investigation and research on Indian child welfare cases. The current environment is litigious and recent Indian child welfare cases have risen to the state and federal Supreme Courts. In addition to monitoring state compliance with ICWA included in other recommendations in this chapter, a position within the DOJ dedicated to supporting challenges to ICWA will improve child welfare outcomes and play a direct role in reducing trauma and violence experienced by AI/AN children in the child welfare system.

Requirements for the position should include ICWA and family law experience. The position should be filled immediately.

▪ **2.2   The Bureau of Indian Affairs (BIA) in the Department of Interior, the Administration for Children and Families (ACF) in the Department of Health and Human Services (HHS), and tribes, within one year of the publication of this report, should develop and submit a written plan to the White House Domestic Policy Council, to work collaboratively and efficiently to provide trauma-informed, culturally appropriate tribal child welfare services in Indian country.**

When federal agencies fail to work together with tribes to confront problems in Indian country, ineffective and inefficient systems result. Child welfare services in Indian country are a good example of this inefficiency. At present, it seems to take a public health crisis before agencies respond by collaboratively sharing expertise and resources, and even then it is problematic. The Spirit Lake Nation experienced a very public crisis in their child welfare system caused by the murder of a child in 2013.[34] Their tribal chairman testified before the Advisory Committee on the ineffectiveness of the federal response to their crisis and the frustration with the process.[35] Cooperation and collaboration among agencies that focus on tribal families and children must be thoughtfully planned and consistently delivered.

Trauma-informed must become the standard of care for children in Indian country. This approach would allow service providers to effectively identify, assess, and treat children and their families injured by, or exposed to, violence and other traumatic events. This means service providers who understand the impact of exposure to violence and trauma; recognize when an individual has been exposed and is in need of help; and respond by helping in ways that reflect awareness of trauma's adverse impacts and consistently support the person's recovery. This means child welfare service providers who understand the culture of trauma as well as the culture of the tribes they serve. This means a combination of culturally appropriate and traditional healing services that complement, augment, or supplement appropriate mainstream services for families.

2.3 The Administration for Children and Families (ACF) in the Department of Health and Human Services (HHS), Bureau of Indian Affairs (BIA) in the Department of Interior (DOI), and tribes should collectively identify child welfare best practices and produce an annual report on child welfare best practices in AI/AN communities that is easily accessible to tribal communities.

Tribal child protection and prevention teams need Indian country–specific research about the intersection of domestic violence, trauma exposure to violence, and child maltreatment in order to create and promote effective prevention strategies, interventions, treatment, and policy change. Although promising practices exist throughout tribal communities, we do not have enough information about the effectiveness of such programs and methods of implementation, which makes success hard to replicate. Tribal communities have traditional methods of practice based evidence to deal with trauma and healing. These practices have been used for centuries, but are not acknowledged as "evidence-based treatments." There is limited information on the cultural interventions and assessments that are being used with AI/AN children. This is largely due to the fact that tribal communities lack the resources or professional skill necessary to establish evidence-based practices or to create cultural adaptations to evidence-based practice.

Many AI/AN people recognize that emotional and psychological well-being cannot be separated from spiritual well-being.[36] There is growing evidence that Native youth who are culturally and spiritually engaged are more resilient than their peers.[37] Research has revealed that 34 percent of Native adolescents and 49 percent of adults preferred to seek mental or substance abuse services from a cultural or spiritual healer.[38] In other research, American Indian caregivers preferred cultural treatments (e.g., sweat lodge, prayer) for their children and found the traditional based ceremonies more effective than standard or typical behavioral health treatment.[39] The integration of traditional healing practices into mental health prevention and treatment for Native children and youth is essential.

The shared goal of all practitioners working with traumatized children is to help that child regain the developmental momentum that was derailed by witnessing or experiencing violence. Across cultures and traditions there are commonalities in trauma interventions that promote healing and well-being. They include:

- Helping a child learn to respond realistically to threat;
- Restoring safety and well-being in intimate relationships;
- Learning the difference between reliving a traumatic event and remembering it; and
- Putting traumatic events in perspective as only part of one's life experience.

There is much to gain from integrating different intervention techniques that are tailored to the cultural, contextual, and individual characteristics and needs of the child and the family. This challenge has particular urgency in light of the wide range of cultural differences found within discrete ethnic and racial groups such as AI/AN peoples. Different tribes have their own highly evolved healing practices that were developed in response to specific circumstances and their place in this world.

Adaptation of standard treatment and intervention involves a process of developing enhancements where the intervener(s) is deeply respectful of the cultural values of the child and family, strives to learn about the traditional healing practices of participating cultural groups, and successfully builds on the foundation of traditional teachings and practices to blend with evidence-based interventions.

Some evidenced-based practices have been effectively enhanced for use in AI/AN communities. Cultural adaptations of evidence-based treatments with AI/AN clients have been conducted with Trauma-Focused Cognitive Behavioral Therapy (TF-CBT)[40] and Parent-Child Interaction Therapy (PCIT).[41] These initiatives used the Learning Collaborative model recommended by the National Child Traumatic Stress Network (NCTSN) to create an approach to community inclusion in which dialogue and reciprocal learning were used as the vehicle for cultural translation, replacing the hierarchical adherence training model that tends to characterize dissemination of evidence-based practices. This transactional, circular training plan is viewed by many as consistent with the holistic worldview of AI/AN peoples. This process produced a culturally congruent treatment framework titled the Honoring Children series, which the developers consider a translation, transformation, and enhancement of the evidence-based treatments involved. A similar process is currently underway as part of an NCTSN learning community to translate the principles of Child-Parent Psychotherapy[42] into intervention modalities that are congruent with AI/AN cultural and spiritual values and practices. At the core of these initiatives is the understanding that incorporating the spiritual values and healing practices of the AI/AN communities must be at the core of efforts to adapt evidence-based interventions for these populations.[43]

The NCTSN Trauma-Informed Child Welfare Training Toolkit has been adapted for training state child welfare workers working with minority populations. The initial adaptation included more information on ICWA and suggestions for adapting training for tribal populations that include case studies of AI/AN children. The NCTSN's National Native Children's Trauma Center (NNCTC) has partnered with BIA child welfare workers to expand the adaptation of the toolkit to include modules on the impact of historical and intergenerational trauma for AI/AN families, include Code of Federal Regulations and tribal codes, and reframe Secondary Traumatic Stress (STS) to better describe STS from a tribal perspective.

Adaptation of the Child Welfare toolkit involved an implementation process to support trauma-informed child welfare practice. The process has included the development of trauma-informed Family Group Decision Making for use with AI/AN families, the development of trauma screening for AI/AN children and their caregivers that incorporates evaluating access to tribal cultural and spiritual healing, referrals that include trauma-informed services from mental health and substance abuse, and the effective approaches child protection workers have utilized to better serve the children and families in their rural reservation communities.

Regularly sharing practices that work in AI/AN communities for healing trauma-impacted children and adults and for preventing violence and child maltreatment will allow AI/AN communities to develop and sustain contemporary programs informed by traditional values. If appropriate, these programs can be publicized and shared with other tribal Nations to ensure that effective practices are utilized.

2.4 The Indian Health Service (IHS) in the Department of Health and Human Services (HHS), state public health services, and other state and federal agencies that provide pre- or postnatal services should provide culturally appropriate education and skills training for parents, foster parents, and caregivers of AI/AN children. Agencies should work with tribes to culturally adapt proven therapeutic models for their unique tribal communities (e.g., adaptation of home visitation service to include local cultural beliefs and values).

"But more must be done to ensure tribal communities are encouraged to use these time tested healing strategies when appropriate. And I say this because there has been a push and this is not to belittle them, but I think that to expand and enhance services, we need to be going beyond evidence-based practices and evidence-based treatment. We need to be able to also bring our cultural healing into our formal service array. We must also be cautious and mindful of the cultural hegemony that is implicit in the mental health field so that we will not inadvertently continue cultural traumatization that has been inflicted against our Native populations, which has led to the erosion of natural protective factors which are language, our spiritual beliefs, ceremonies, practices, roles, and values."

Deborah Painte, Director, Native American Training Institute. Testimony before the Task Force on American Indian/Alaska Native Children Exposed to Violence, Bismarck, ND, December 9, 2013

"Recognition of practices that are effective in AI/AN communities is vital, as so many governmental grants and private foundations only fund evidence-based practices. Many evidence-based practices are not effective in tribal communities. Anytime in Indian country we want to submit something that's productive, that works, that produces results, unless it's evidence based, my friends, my relatives, it gets shoved to the side.· These practice-based initiatives must be looked at and respected and funded because they do work, they are working."

Jesse Taken Alive, Councilman, Standing Rock Tribal Council. Testimony before the Task Force on American Indian/ Alaska Native Children Exposed to Violence, Bismarck, ND, December 9, 2013

Due to the prevalence of violence in AI/AN homes and communities and the influence of historical trauma, many AI/AN parents, foster parents, and prospective parents may need help developing traditional parenting skills. Caregivers may have experienced trauma as children or may continue to be victims of violence in their homes. Assistance for families experiencing violence or at risk for violence is most accessible when it is brought directly into the home. Home visitation programs bring para-professionals or professionals, such as nurses, social workers, family educators, and mental health professionals, into the home to meet regularly to help parents and children develop ways of communicating together, managing the basic routines that are essential to daily family life and healthy growth, and participating in medical and mental health treatment. Certain home visitation programs show considerable promise in reducing child abuse and promoting healthy development of children in families.[44] Starting early and working with families over the long term has proven to be an effective strategy.

State and federal agencies should ensure that in-home services to caregivers of all AI/AN children, including parents, foster parents, and other caregivers are culturally appropriate. Training local tribal members to work with caregivers and foster parents in developing trauma-informed, nurturing, culturally appropriate parenting and coping skills is an effective and cost-efficient practice. Because of the high incidence of violence in the AI/AN community and the impact of historical trauma, home services should be provided to all caregivers of AI/AN children.

Particular attention to home visitation should be provided for children in foster care and other out-of-home placements. It is highly likely that these children have already experienced multiple traumas. Home services should ensure that foster children are safe and are receiving the help they need to recover from trauma and that their foster parents are properly trained. Certification of foster families must require that foster families are trauma-informed and trained in both trauma and culture to deal with the complex problems of AI/AN foster children.

Home visitation programs such as the Safe Care, Parents as Teachers, and Family Spirit programs appear to be a step in the right direction. Home visitation programs are designed for AI/AN mothers and their children and promote mothers' parenting, coping, and problem-solving skills to address demographic challenges, family-of-origin problems, and personal stressors. The

Family Spirit curriculum incorporates traditional tribal teachings into sixty-three independent lessons on prenatal care, child development, toddler care, life skills, and healthy living. Building on this program and others that provide home visitation to meet the needs of families in AI/AN communities in a culturally responsive and trauma-informed way is vital. The Safe Care curriculum addresses the dynamics of child abuse and domestic violence and provides referrals to services available in the community. More home visitation programs could include a specific child maltreatment focus and not primarily child interaction enhancements.

2.5 The Bureau of Indian Affairs (BIA) in the Department of Interior (DOI), tribal social service agencies, and state social service agencies should have policies that permit removal of children from victims of domestic violence for "failure to protect" only as a last resort as long as the child is safe.

Children are often removed from both parents when domestic violence occurs, even when one parent was also a victim of the violence. Children who witness domestic violence have a greater need for stability and security; however, removal from the non-offending parent can produce the opposite effect. To ensure stability and permanency for children in a home with domestic violence, children should remain with the non-offending parent (caregiver) whenever possible, as long as the child is safe and future risk is minimized. Protecting, supporting, and assisting the non-offending parent will provide increased safety and security for the child.

Currently child protection systems in Indian country and in urban areas frequently hold the victim (usually the mother) accountable for domestic violence in the home. This standard typically requires the victim to be active in treatment or lose her children.[45] Although most of the Native communities' child protection agencies interviewed for the report, *Responses to the Co-Occurrence of Child Maltreatment and Domestic Violence in Indian Country: Repairing the Harm and Protecting Children and Mothers*,[46] did not track domestic violence reports unless it was the original reason for a child protection intervention, social workers indicated that a high percentage of women in the child protection system are victims of domestic violence. For this reason, it is imperative that federal, tribal, and state leadership address this issue.

"We also have to start earlier. We have to reach out at a very early age. We know that programs like the Nurse Family Partnership work and that those programs go into the home. We could train lay people and our own community, grandmothers and aunties, to teach young people how to be parents again, because that was lost when our grandmothers were beaten and that was how they taught the next generation to be parents."

Sarah Jumping Eagle, Pediatrician. Testimony before the Task Force on American Indian/Alaska Native Children Exposed to Violence, Bismarck, ND, December 9, 2013

"We are all no doubt familiar with the high rates of domestic violence and sexual assault against Native women, and we forget sometimes that most Native women are also mothers, and grandmothers, and aunties. When children see their mother being abused, it is a traumatic event. I have seen systems that sanction victims for allowing their children to witness this trauma. I hope that the committee will recommend that such laws and policies be highly scrutinized, because they can cause yet an additional layer of trauma for both mother and child. No child should have to witness domestic violence, period. However, the responsibility for that exposure lies with the perpetrator; not the victim."

Sarah Deer, Law Professor, William Mitchell College of Law. Testimony before the Task Force on American Indian/Alaska Native Children Exposed to Violence, Bismarck, ND, December 7, 2013

The system must recognize that the batterer is the problem. In some communities, there is a tradition of referring every victim of domestic violence to mental health services, reinforcing the notion that the victim is the problem.[47] Consistently, the mother is the one who is required to follow the case plan. The mother should not be singled out unless there is specific identifiable abuse attributed to the mother, not failure to protect.[48]

Caring for a child's well-being requires much more than keeping a child physically safe. One must also recognize the tremendous emotional, psychological, and spiritual trauma caused by removing a child from a parent, and the absolute necessity of providing opportunities for rebuilding trust and healing. Judge William Thorne Jr., who has worked in both state and tribal justice systems, addressed the importance of well-being in his testimony before the Advisory Committee:

> For several decades now, we've talked in terms of federal legislation that talks about safety being the paramount value, safety being the utmost value. I think that's wrong. Safety is necessary, but safety is a subset of well-being. If we truly believe that safety was the paramount value, we would put our kids in plastic bubbles. No one would touch them. No one would communicate with them. No one would harm them. But that can't be what we do. Instead, I would propose that well-being is the paramount value. And safety is a subset of that. Safety is a part of that. Safety's necessary, but it's not sufficient. It's not enough by itself.

> Our goal should—instead of just simply suppressing conduct, should be to heal the victims. I mean, in my 34 years as a judge I've seen second, third, fourth generation kids coming out of foster care. And they're coming out of foster care because we didn't do a good job of healing them. We took them away from their families. We removed them from the harms that they were exposed to. But we didn't heal them. It's very much like saying, "Just in case." Well, when you check into a hospital, you don't expect them to amputate your leg just in case. When you have an eye infection, you don't expect them to take the eye just in case. When we take children from their families and we take children away from their communities just in case, what we've really done is set up the next generation of children to come through the system.

> I think what we have is a direct result of a hundred years of the boarding-school philosophy, then translated into removal philosophy, and then the predominant notion in this country of removing children as a way of intervening and solving problems

when the family has problems. We take them away, but we don't heal them. So that when they become parents themselves, they are not equipped. For good reason most of us parent the way we were parented, including the fact that some things happened to us that we swore would never, ever happen to our own kids. But I still hear my father's voice come out of my mouth sometimes. And that's scary. We parent as we were parented. Well, when we put kids in boarding schools, where do they learn to parent? When we put kids in foster care, where do they learn to parent? How do they learn to cope with the struggles when they've never seen an adult struggle with problems and overcome them?

William Thorne Jr., Appellate Court Judge, Utah Court of Appeals, retired. Testimony before the Task Force on American Indian/Alaska Native Children Exposed to Violence, Phoenix, AZ, February 11, 2014

Data on substantiated reports of maltreatment collected in 2013 by HHS's Children's Bureau in the Office of the Administration for Children and Families was analyzed by the National Indian Child Welfare Association.[49] The analysis indicated that neglect is more often substantiated for AI/AN children and physical abuse is less often substantiated for AI/AN children, than for all children. Knowing that a child may be subject to more than one type of maltreatment the following data are notable: [50]

- Of all maltreatment victims, 89.3 percent of AI/AN children were involved in the child welfare system because of a disposition of neglect compared to 78.3 percent of all children nationwide.
- Of all maltreatment victims, 15.6 percent of AI/AN children were involved in the child welfare system because of a disposition of physical abuse compared to 18.3 percent of all children nationwide.
- Of all maltreatment victims, 5.6 percent of AI/AN children were involved in the child welfare system because of a disposition of sexual abuse compared to 9.3 percent of all children nationwide.

This data demonstrates that AI/AN children and families are more likely to be involved in the child welfare system because of neglect and less likely to be involved because of physical or sexual abuse. These findings refute presumptions about AI/AN families and communities that are found in the media and elsewhere and they highlight AI/AN families' unique needs for appropriate child maltreatment interventions. Even though the primary reason for child welfare involvement is neglect, AI/AN children are dispro-portionately removed from their homes and placed in foster care.

Although neglect can pose a serious risk to children's well-being, of all the types of child maltreatment, neglect is best suited to in-home services that safely avoid the trauma of removal.[51] In-home services are, however, often either unavailable or unused. Instead AI/AN children are frequently placed outside their homes in foster care.

2.6 The Secretary of Health and Human Services (HHS) should increase and support access to culturally appropriate behavioral health and substance abuse prevention and treatment services in all AI/AN communities, especially the use of traditional healers and helpers identified by tribal communities.

Substance abuse related to child abuse and neglect is more likely to be reported for AI/AN families. NCANDS data gathered in child protection cases in 2013 indicated that alcohol abuse was an issue for a caregiver in 30 percent of the AI/AN child victim cases of substantiated maltreatment, compared to 28.5 percent of child victims nationwide. In 24.5 percent of the AI/AN child victim cases of substantiated maltreatment a parent had a drug abuse problem compared to 20 percent of child victims nationwide.[52] Alcohol and drug abuse was also more likely in cases in which maltreatment was reported, but not substantiated. Alcohol abuse by a caregiver was indicated in 14 percent of the AI/AN child nonvictims (unsubstantiated abuse), compare to 4.9 percent of children nationwide. Of AI/AN child nonvictims, 11.7 percent had a parent with a drug abuse problem, compared to 8.4 percent of children nationwide.[53]

This data substantiates the dramatic need for culturally appropriate substance abuse programs and the relationship between alcohol and drug abuse and child maltreatment. Although the data primarily applies to urban Indians, Alaska Natives, and PL-280 reservations, the need for culturally appropriate and accessible substance abuse programs was also described in the study on the co-occurrence of domestic violence and child maltreatment in Indian country.[54] The report indicated that many women in Indian country who were involved with child protection and identified as domestic violence victims also had alcohol and drug abuse problems.[55] Unfortunately, it indicated that women in need of substance abuse treatment often had to leave the community to access services, which presented a significant problem with the care of their children while they were away for treatment. Developing greater accessibility to culturally appropriate substance abuse treatment for all AI/AN caregivers could substantially decrease the number of children exposed to domestic violence and child maltreatment.

Treatment programs that work with AI/AN populations should incorporate AI/AN tribal customs and spiritual ceremonies, and be trauma-informed holistic. AI/AN people in recovery may have experienced multiple traumas in their lifetime, suffer from historical and intergenerational trauma, and may abuse alcohol and drugs as a way of coping with those traumas. Without treatment to heal from the underlying traumas, alcohol and drug abuse treatment may be ineffective and victim blaming. Many AI/AN people may need a more holistic healing process. Thus, it is important to accurately assess and meet each individual's needs.

Increasing access requires increasing funding. Federal funding to agencies such as IHS has historically been grossly inadequate. The funding must be increased to meet the need.

"Drug abuse is rampant, not only on the White Earth Reservation, but other reservations as well. I have been informed that 80 percent of the Indian babies born at the Bemidji Hospital have drugs in their bodies at birth. Have withdrawals that require specialized care at hospitals in Fargo, North Dakota. I cannot forget hearing about the baby who has damaged hands from clinching during withdrawals. Babies born victims. The violence of drugs. The Bemidji Hospital serves White Earth, Leech Lake, and Red Lake Tribes, the three largest tribes in Minnesota."

Erma Vizenor, Chairwoman, White Earth Nation. Testimony before the Task Force on American Indian/Alaska Native Children Exposed to Violence, Fort Lauderdale, FL, April 16, 2014

Notes

1. Listenbee, Robert L., Jr., et al., *Report of the Attorney General's National Task Force on Children Exposed to Violence*, Washington, D.C.: U.S. Department of Justice, Office of Juvenile Justice and Delinquency Prevention (December 2012): 32.

2. Bancroft, Lundy, and Silverman, Jay G., *The Batterer as Parent: Addressing the Impact of Domestic Violence on Family Dynamics,* Thousand Oaks, CA: Sage Publications, 2002: 42–4.

3. Carter, Janet, "Domestic Violence, Child Abuse, and Youth Violence: Strategies for Prevention and Early Intervention," Family Violence Prevention Fund: available at: http://www.mincava.umn.edu/link/documents/fvpf2/fvpf2.shtml.

4. White Eagle, Maureen, Clairmont, Bonnie, and Hunter, Lonna, "Responses to the Co-Occurrence of Domestic Violence and Child Maltreatment in Indian Country: Repairing the Harm and Protecting Children and Mothers," Tribal Law and Policy Institute (December 2011).

5. Child Abuse Solutions, "Fact Sheet Child Sexual Abuse in Custody Disputes," available at http://www.childabusesolutions.com/page_07.html. Citing Greenfield, L., *Child Victimizers: Violent Offenders and Their Victims*, Washington, D.C.: U. S. Department of Justice, Bureau of Justice Statistics and Office of Juvenile Justice and Delinquency Prevention (March 1996): 10.

6. Greenfield, L., *Child Victimizers: Violent Offenders and Their Victims*, Washington, D.C.: U. S. Department of Justice, Bureau of Justice Statistics and Office of Juvenile Justice and Delinquency Prevention (March 1996): 10.

7. Snyder, Howard, *Sexual Assault of Young Children as Reported to Law Enforcement: Victim, Incident, and Offender Characteristics*, National Center for Juvenile Justice (July 2000).

8. Bancroft, Lundy, and Silverman, Jay G., *The Batterer as Parent: Addressing the Impact of Domestic Violence on Family Dynamics,* Thousand Oaks, CA: Sage Publications, 2002: 43.

9. Amnesty International USA, *Maze of Injustice: The Failure to Protect Indigenous Women from Sexual Violence in the United States*, New York: Amnesty International Publications, 2007: 2.

10. Written Testimony of Barbara Bettelyoun, Hearing of the Task Force on American Indian/Alaska Native Children Exposed to Violence, Bismarck, ND, December 9, 2013 at 67, available at: http://www.justice.gov/defendingchildhood/nd-briefingbinder.pdf

11. Written Testimony of Elsie Boudreau, Hearing of the Task Force on American Indian/Alaska Native Children Exposed to Violence, Anchorage, AK, June 12, 2014 at 145, available at http://www.justice.gov/defendingchildhood/4th-hearing/hearing4-briefing-binder.pdf.

12. Listenbee, Robert L., Jr., et al., *Report of the Attorney General's National Task Force on Children Exposed to Violence*, Washington, D.C.: U.S. Department of Justice, Office of Juvenile Justice and Delinquency Prevention (December 2012): 30.

13. Cross, T. A., Earle, K. A., and Simmons, D., "Child Abuse and Neglect in Indian Country: Policy Issues," *Families in Society: The Journal of Contemporary Human Services* 81(1) (2000): 49.

14. Ibid.

15. Ibid.

16. Bragg, Lien, *Child Protection in Families Experiencing Domestic Violence*, available at: https://www.childwelfare.gov/pubs/usermanuals/domesticviolence/index.cfm. Note the earlier statistics in this chapter for 2013 were based on rates for each child and not each case.

17. Written Testimony of Terry Cross, Hearing of the Task Force on American Indian/Alaska Native Children Exposed to Violence, Fort Lauderdale, FL, April 16, 2014 at 65, available at: http://www.justice.gov/defendingchildhood/fl-briefingbinder.pdf.

18. Currently 8,344 AI/AN children are in state foster care placement. See Written Testimony of Sarah Hicks Kastelic (Alutiiq), Hearing of the Task Force on American Indian/Alaska Native Children Exposed to Violence, Anchorage, AK, June 11, 2014 at 23, available at: http://www.justice.gov/defendingchildhood/4th-hearing/hearing4-briefing-binder.pdf, citing U.S. DHHS, Administration on Children, Youth and Families. Child Maltreatment 2003 Washington, D.C.

19. The state/tribal Title IV-E agency administers or supervises the administration of the State/Tribal Child Welfare Services Plan under subpart 1 of Title IV-B of the act.

20. Written Testimony of Sarah Hicks Kastelic (Alutiiq), Hearing of the Task Force on American Indian/Alaska Native Children Exposed to Violence, Anchorage, AK, June 11, 2014 at 23, available at: http://www.justice.gov/defendingchildhood/4th-hearing/hearing4-briefing-binder.pdf, citing U.S. Department of Health and Human Services, Administration for Children and Families, Administration on children, Youth and Families, Children's Bureau, *Child Maltreatment 2012,* December

2013. Available at: http://www.acf.hhs.gov/programs/cb/resource/child-maltreatment-2012, accessed September 12, 2014.

21. Written Testimony of Sarah Hicks Kastelic (Alutiiq), Hearing of the Task Force on American Indian/Alaska Native Children Exposed to Violence, Anchorage, AK, June 11, 2014 at 23, available at: http://www.justice.gov/defendingchildhood/4th-hearing/hearing4-briefing-binder.pdf, citing Summers, Woods, and Donovan, 2013.

22. Child Abuse Prevention and Treatment Act, 42 U.S.C. 5101 et seq.; 42 U.S.C. 5116 et seq.

23. The **Children's Bureau** is a federal agency focused on improving the lives of children and families through programs that reduce child abuse and neglect, increase the number of adoptions, and strengthen foster care. The **Children's Bureau** is headed by an Associate Commissioner who advises the Administration on Children, Youth and Families' Commissioner on matters related to child welfare.

24. U.S. Department of Health and Human Services, Administration for Children and Families, Administration on Children, Youth and Families, Children's Bureau, *Child Maltreatment 2012*, available at: http://www.acf.hhs.gov/sites/default/files/cb/cm2012.pdf.

25. Earle, K. A., *Child Abuse and Neglect: An Examination of American Indian Data*, Casey Family Programs; National Indian Child Welfare Association (2000).

26. Written Testimony of Sarah Hicks Kastelic (Alutiiq), Hearing of the Task Force on American Indian/Alaska Native Children Exposed to Violence, Anchorage, AK, June 11, 2014 at 23, available at: http://www.justice.gov/defendingchildhood/4th-hearing/hearing4-briefing-binder.pdf.

27. Ibid., citing Limb, Chance, and Brown, 2004.

28. Ibid., citing Crofoot and Harris, 2012.

29. Ibid., citing Jones, Gillette, Painte, and Paulson, 2000; Bellonger and Rubio, 2004.

30. Ibid., citing Brown, Limb, Munoz, and Clifford, 2002; Bellonger and Rubio, 2004; and Wazak, 2010.

31. Ibid., citing Jones et al. 2000; Bellonger and Rubio, 2004; Carter 2009.

32. Ibid.

33. Ibid.

34. The tragic murder and sexual abuse of children lead to an examination of the child welfare system in the Spirit Lake Nation. For months it was a top story in the state newspapers and also resulted in coverage by the *New York Times*: http://www.nytimes.com/2012/07/08/us/child-welfare-dangers-seen-on-spirit-lake-reservation.html?pagewanted=all&_r=0, available at http://www.nytimes.com/2012/07/08/us/child-welfare-dangers-seen-on-spirit-lake-reservation.html?pagewanted=all&_r=0.

35. Testimony of Leander McDonald, Hearing of the Task Force on American Indian/Alaska Native Children Exposed to Violence, Bismarck, ND, December 9, 2013 at 10–22, available at:http://www.justice.gov/defendingchildhood/1st-hearing/panel2.pdf.

36. Gone, J. P., and Alcantara, C., "Identifying Effective Mental Health Interventions for American Indians and Alaska Natives: A Review of the Literature," *Cultural Diversity and Ethnic Minority Psychology* 13(4) (2007): 356–63.

37. Grey, N., and Nye P. S., "American Indian and Alaska Native Substance Abuse: Co-Morbidity and Cultural Issues," *American Indian and Alaska Native Mental Health Research* 10(2) (2001): 67–82; Rieckmann, T. R., Wadsworth, M. E., and Deyhle, D., "Cultural Identity, Explanatory Style, and Depression in Navajo Adolescents," *Cultural Diversity and Ethnic Minority Psychology* 10(4) (2004): 365–82; Spicer, P., Novins, D. K., Mitchell, C. M., and Beals, J., "Aboriginal Social Organization, Contemporary Experience and American Indian Adolescent Alcohol Use," *Quarterly Journal of Studies on Alcohol* 64(4) (2003): 450–57; Yoder, K. A., Whitbeck, L. B., Hoyt, D. R., and LaFromboise, T., "Suicide Ideation among American Indian Youths," *Archives of Suicide Research* 10(2) (2006): 177–90.

38. Beals, J., Manson, S. M., Whitesell, N. R., Spicer, P., Novins, D. K., Mitchel, C. M., et al., "Prevalence of DSM-IV Disorders and Attendant Help-Seeking in 2 American Indian Reservation Populations," *Archives of General Psychiatry* 62 (2005): 99–108.

39. Walls, M. L., Johnson, K. D., Whitbeck, L. B., and Hoyt, D. R., "Mental Health and Substance Abuse Services Preferences among American Indian People of the Northern Midwest," *Community Mental Health Journal* 42(6) (2006): 521–35.

40. BigFoot, D., and Schmidt, S., "Honoring Children, Mending the Circle: Cultural Adaptation of Trauma-Focused Cognitive-Behavioral Therapy for American Indian and Alaska Native Children," *Journal of Clinical Psychology* 66(8) (2010): 847–56.

41. BigFoot, D., Funderburk, B., Novins, K., and Spicer, P., "Evidence-Based Practice and Early Childhood Intervention in American Indian and Alaska Native Communities," *Zero to Three* 32(4) (2011).

42. Lieberman, A. F., and Van Horn, P., "Toward Evidence-Based Treatment: Child-Parent Psychotherapy with Preschoolers Exposed to Marital Violence," *J Am Acad Child Adolesc Psychiatry* 44(12) (2005): 1241–8.

43. Ibid.

44. Supplee, Lauren, and Adirim, Terry, "Evidence-Based Home Visiting to Enhance Child Health and Child Development and to Support Families," American Psychological Association (July 2012) available at: http://www.apa.org/pi/families/resources/newsletter/2012/07/home-visiting.aspx.

45. White Eagle, Maureen, Clairmont, Bonnie, and Hunter, Lonna, "Responses to the Co-Occurrence of Child Maltreatment and Domestic Violence in Indian Country: Repairing the Harm and Protecting Children and Mothers," West Hollywood, CA: Tribal Law and Policy Institute (December 2011): 1.

46. White Eagle, Maureen, Clairmont, Bonnie, and Hunter, Lonna, "Responses to the Co-Occurrence of Child Maltreatment and Domestic Violence in Indian Country: Repairing the Harm and Protecting Children and Mothers," West Hollywood, CA: Tribal Law and Policy Institute (December 2011).

47. Ibid., 6.

48. Ibid.

49. This data is somewhat limited as tribal agencies are not required to submit data and the data describes only those AI/AN children who are screened by state child protective services programs. This would include some PL-280 affected tribes, Alaska Natives, and some tribes that have agreements with the state agencies

50. National Indian Child Welfare Association (NICWA) Memorandum to Ric Brodrick, Member of the Task Force on American Indian/Alaska Native Children Exposed to Violence, regarding analysis of data retrieved by the Children's Bureau from the National Child Abuse and Neglect Data System (September 12, 2014) (on file with the Tribal Law and Policy Institute).

51. Written Testimony of Terry Cross, Hearing of the Task Force on American Indian/Alaska Native Children Exposed to Violence, Fort Lauderdale, FL, April 16, 2014 at 65, available at: http://www.justice.gov/defendingchildhood/fl-briefingbinder.pdf.

52. National Indian Child Welfare Association (NICWA) Memorandum to Ric Brodrick, Member of the Task Force on American Indian/Alaska Native Children Exposed to Violence, regarding analysis of data retrieved by the Children's Bureau from the National Child Abuse and Neglect Data System (September 12, 2014) (on file with the Tribal Law and Policy Institute).

53. Ibid.

54. White Eagle, Maureen, Clairmont, Bonnie, and Hunter, Lonna, "Responses to the Co-Occurrence of Child Maltreatment and Domestic Violence in Indian Country: Repairing the Harm and Protecting Children and Mothers," West Hollywood, CA: Tribal Law and Policy Institute (December 2011): 3.

55. National Indian Child Welfare Association (NICWA) Memorandum to Ric Brodrick, Member of the Task Force on American Indian/Alaska Native Children Exposed to Violence, regarding analysis of data retrieved by the Children's Bureau from the National Child Abuse and Neglect Data System (September 12, 2014) (on file with the Tribal Law and Policy Institute).

Promoting Well-Being for American Indian and Alaska Native Children in the Community

"So in creating a community of caring, we must work harder to increase our students' feelings of belonging in the school and their connectedness to cultural identity."

Matthew Taylor, Associate Director, National Native Children's Trauma Center Testimony before the Task Force on American Indian/ Alaska Native Children Exposed to Violence, Fort Lauderdale, FL, April 17, 2014

Violence in American Indian and Alaska Native (AI/AN) communities occurs at very high rates compared with non-AI/AN communities—higher for AI/AN than all other races.[1] And violence, including intentional injuries, homicide, and suicide, accounts for 75 percent of deaths of AI/AN youth ages twelve through twenty.[2] Unfortunately, Indian children cannot escape the violence that surrounds them.

Repeated exposure to childhood violence has a staggering lifelong impact on an individual's health and well-being. The Adverse Childhood Experiences (ACE) Study demonstrated that persons who experience four or more childhood adversities have a four- to twelvefold increased risk for alcoholism, drug use, depression, and suicide attempt when compared to those that had experienced none.[3] This study, coupled with data that show American Indians and Alaska Natives have a fivefold higher risk of being exposed to four or more adverse childhood events,[4] underscores the overwhelming impact of exposure to violence in AI/AN communities.

Children engulfed by this level of community violence often struggle with rebuilding trust, finding meaning in life apart from desires for safety and justice, finding realistic ways to protect themselves and their loved ones from danger and dealing with feelings of guilt, shame, powerlessness, and doubt. Additionally, when children experience ongoing violence in their communities, it may become an accepted condition of life. They may learn to think of recurring danger, fear, injury, and death as normal. Instead of celebrating life, too often they must mourn losses. This may confuse them in figuring out how to navigate life. These children wait nervously or helplessly for the next explosion of violence in their neighborhood or school, or they mourn the all-too-common deaths or devastated lives of families, friends, and community members. At some point, these children may feel the need to fight back against actual or potential perpetrators, causing them to have difficulty acting appropriately on those feelings. Unfortunately, a number of these children become perpetrators in adolescence and adulthood.

AI/AN children live in communities that are markedly diverse culturally, demographically, and geographically. Many AI/AN children are not eligible for tribal membership and some have lost their heritage and identity, but they live in tribal communities, have suffered the same traumas, and need services. Some are in extremely remote settings like many Alaska Native villages or at the bottom of the Grand Canyon; others are in rural, sparsely populated areas like the reservations located in the Great Plains and the mountainous west; and still others are close to or within large metropolitan areas. In 1952, the federal government created the Urban Relocation Program, which encouraged American Indians to leave reservations and move to cities such as Chicago, Denver, and Los Angeles. The intent of the relocation program was to provide better jobs and upward economic mobility. AI/AN people were lured by the hope of a better life, but for most that promise was not realized and life circumstances deteriorated. Since that time, AI/AN people have continued to migrate to cities in search of opportunities not available on reservations. Today, approximately 64 percent[5] to 78 percent[6] of American Indians and Alaska Natives live in urban areas. Los Angeles County is home to the largest urban American Indian population—more than 160,000.[7] Chicago, Seattle, Phoenix, Denver, Minneapolis, Anchorage, and other cities all have large AI/AN populations.

AI/AN communities may differ substantially in culture and geography; however, one common feature of nearly all of these communities is a shared history of destructive federal policies intended to assimilate Indian people into the American way of life. These federal policies included forced relocation, forced removal of their children to be educated in boarding schools, and prohibition of spiritual and cultural practices. What tribes describe as having the most negative impact was the forced removal of Indian children from home and placement in boarding schools far from their families and communities. The removal of generations of children over time has disrupted once well-established and venerable parenting practices. To this day, historical trauma continues to intensify contemporary traumatic experiences for Native children and families. Contemporary society creates numerous contexts for exposure to violence by AI/AN children including those who witness domestic violence, those who are victims of child abuse and neglect, and those whose caregivers are debilitated by substance abuse and addiction while living in households that struggle with multigenerational and pervasive poverty. All of these factors contribute to the extraordinarily high rates of violence in tribal communities.[8]

AI/AN communities confront many forms of community violence. AI/AN children are exposed to many types of violence in their communities, including simple assaults, violent threats, sexual assault, and homicide. AI/AN children and teens are 2.4 times

"We are strong believers that we have the answers to our problems and change must come from within. The plans developed through this process must have the full support of tribal leadership and we must recognize the role that our unique cultures play in addressing this issue within this contemporary society."
Leander Russell McDonald, Chairman, Spirit Lake Tribe. Testimony before the Task Force on American Indian/ Alaska Native Children Exposed to Violence, Bismarck, ND, December 9, 2013

more likely to die from guns than Caucasian children and teens.[9] Additionally, suicide, gang violence, sex and drug trafficking, and bullying are especially problematic for AI/AN youth. Coupling those factors with the high rate of homelessness makes AI/AN youth especially vulnerable to community violence.

Suicide. Some youth see suicide as a viable option to escape exposure to violence. The sheer number of AI/AN youth taking their own lives is staggering—more than three times the national average, and up to ten times the national average on some reservations.[10] Suicide is the second leading cause of death among AI/AN youth ages ten through twenty-four.[11] For Alaska Native youth, from 2003 to 2006, the suicide rate was 51.4 per one hundred thousand compared to 16.9 per one hundred thousand in non–Alaska Native populations, with considerable variation in the suicide rates of Natives from different regions of the state of Alaska and different Native ethnic groups.[12] AI/AN children and teens had the highest rate of gun suicides, nearly twice as high as Caucasian children and teens.[13]

In 2011, the Office of the Inspector General (OIG) of HHS found "the need for behavioral health services far outstrips capacity, especially in rural reservation communities."[14] IHS confirmed that of the 630 participating facilities that participated in the OIG evaluation, "18 percent did not provide behavioral health services and 39 percent of facilities are 'severely impacted' by staff shortages." IHS is woefully unprepared to provide services to AI/AN patients who present with near epidemic levels of PTSD, anxiety, depression, substance abuse, and suicide attempts."

Gang Violence and Sex and Drug Trafficking. The influence of criminal street gangs is a national problem that also impacts tribal communities. Tribal communities have witnessed firsthand the impact of gang subculture in both rural and urban communities. A 2000 survey in Indian country found that 23 percent of Indian country respondents had active youth gangs in their communities.[15] This was a key problem in the urban Indian community of Little Earth of United Tribes (Minneapolis), which the Advisory Committee visited for a Listening Session. Native gang members from Little Earth travel back and forth from urban areas to rural Indian communities, causing disruptions in both arenas.

Gangs in AI/AN communities are increasingly involved in both sex-trafficking and drug-trafficking activities. The Minnesota

Indian Women's Resource Center, working with AI/AN women and girls victimized by sex trafficking, found that Mexican gangs in their area specifically target Native girls and that 85 percent of the women and girls trafficked in Minneapolis were Native.[16] This happens because the traffickers can represent Native girls as many different ethnicities, thus enhancing their "marketability."[17]

Many of the drug-related issues tribal communities face today are associated with a street gang influence. The oil boom in North Dakota and Montana has also brought an increase in non-Indian gang activity, sales of illicit drugs, and trafficking of Native children and women. Arizona tribes, particularly those close to the Mexican border, have experienced similar challenges with gangs.

AI/AN youth are also using illicit drugs at alarming rates. American Indian students (grades 8–10) annual use of heroin and OxyContin was about two to three times higher than national averages in 2009–12.[18] In 2009–12, 56.2 percent of American Indian eighth graders and 61.4 percent of tenth graders had used marijuana, compared to 16.4 percent of eighth graders and 33.4 percent of tenth graders in a national survey (Monitoring the Future).[19]

School Violence and Bullying. According to the IHS's 2011 *American Indian/Alaska Native Behavioral Health Briefing Book*, 27.5 percent of Native youth in grades six through twelve experience bullying compared to 20.1 percent of students nationwide. Furthermore, 30.9 percent of Native students report engaging in bullying behavior compared to 18.8 percent nationally. AI/AN students report injuries with weapons and fights on schools grounds at a higher rate than any other ethnic group. In 2004, 22 percent of AI/AN high school students reported being threatened or injured with a weapon on school grounds in the previous twelve months compared to 11 percent of African American, 9 percent of Hispanic, and 8 percent of Caucasian students. Because most schools have a heightened concern about student safety, many use suspension as a means of addressing behavior issues. AI/AN students currently experience suspension and expulsion rates second only to African American students.[20]

In the early twentieth century, the United States began turning to the states to provide education to AI/AN children with passage of the Johnson-O'Malley Act of 1934.[21] The Johnson-O'Malley Act authorized the federal government to contract with states to provide education of American Indian children. It provides

"When a young teenager is encouraged to be a gang member by his family from a very young age, and has watched gang activities and substance abuse his entire life, it is unrealistic to expect him to remain unaffected."
Sheri Fremont, Director, Family Advocacy Center, Salt River. Testimony before the Task Force on American Indian/Alaska Native Children Exposed to Violence, Phoenix, AZ, February 11, 2014

"Over the years, we've seen an influx of young, Alaska Native victims from rural Alaska, who are coerced and vulnerable to predators. Typical cases from rural Alaska look a little bit different. They usually include that they are lured to Anchorage by family members or boyfriends. This is referred to as 'tundra pimping.'"
Diana Bline, Director of Program Services, Covenant House Alaska. Testimony before the Task Force on American Indian/Alaska Native Children Exposed to Violence, Anchorage, AK, June 12, 2014

"I recently had a situation where mom was subject to a child petition because she wasn't sending her child to school. And everyone's saying, 'Send the child to school. Send the child to school.' Started talking to that mom, what was going on at school? The child was being bullied. Extremely, to the extent that the child was curled up in the fetal position at night begging his mom not to send him to school. The reaction of the court was he has to be in school."

Shannon Smith, Executive Director/Attorney, Indian Child Welfare Act Law Center. Testimony before the Task Force on American Indian/ Alaska Native Children Exposed to Violence, Fort Lauderdale, FL, April 17, 2014

education support for AI/AN children attending non-BIA, nontribal school systems. This program should be adapted to prevent violence exposure in schools. The Advisory Committee urges the Secretary of the Department of Interior (DOI) to fill the Johnson O'Malley Director's position, update the student count, and adapt the program's services in support of the prevention of school suspensions, school violence, and bullying.

Vulnerability Due to Homelessness. Homelessness may be caused by a need to escape violence in the home, and homeless youth become easy targets of violent crime in the community. In Minnesota, where the Advisory Committee conducted a Listening Session, it was reported that AI/AN youth make up 20 percent of homeless youth ages twelve through seventeen, although they make up only 1 percent of the general population. In a Listening Session held by the Advisory Committee in Bethel, Alaska, the principal of the Bethel High School testified about youths leaving home in middle school to avoid the violence in their homes and "couch surfing" (moving from relatives' to friends' homes) for a safe place to stay. Similarly, the director of a homeless youth program in Anchorage told the Advisory Committee that many of the youth served may have left home to escape violence. Unfortunately, this left them vulnerable to violence on the streets because they were now isolated from the protection of their community.

The cycle of violence that now grips AI/AN communities was years in the making and largely due to failed federal policies. Breaking the cycle of violence will require cooperation at the federal, tribal, and state level as well as the investment of significant new resources. Until additional resources are provided, reallocation of existing resources could provide needed assistance in the short term. For the past several years the President has requested a 7 percent set-aside from DOJ/OJP's discretionary grant and reimbursement programs for flexible tribal justice assistance grants, which is more than double the enacted funding level for these programs in FY 2014. The 7 percent set-aside would allow OJP to increase flexibility in awarding funds, streamline reporting requirements, help tribes respond to the diverse criminal justice and public safety needs in Indian country today, help tribes identify their most important criminal justice priorities, and foster development of innovative, evidence-based approaches. This set-aside would replace line-item appropriations for OJP's traditional tribal justice assistance programs—the Tribal Justice Infrastructure: Tribal Courts, Indian

Alcohol and Substance Abuse, Tribal Civil and Criminal Legal Assistance, and Tribal Youth Programs. The Advisory Committee urges the Congress to approve this set-aside so that the Attorney General may dedicate these funds to addressing the needs of AI/AN children exposed to violence.

Whether AI/AN children are in rural or urban communities, feelings of belonging and connectedness to their culture and family are critical to their development of identity and resilience.[22] It is important to be inclusive in the provision of services for AI/AN children exposed to violence. The AI/AN community must be committed to wellness, recovery from trauma, and prevention of violence. Although we address the issues of community violence and violence in the home separately in this report, it should be noted that they are oftentimes interrelated and intertwined.

Addressing community violence requires action in several broad and specific areas. Fixing the jurisdictional quagmire that currently ensnares AI/AN communities and strengthening tribal sovereignty and self-determination are addressed in the recommendations contained in Chapter 1 of this report. Reform of the juvenile justice system is addressed in Chapter 4. The recommendations in this chapter speak to increasing capacity and infrastructure in AI/AN communities to allow those communities to confront the impact of current and past violence and to prevent future violence.

"As a magnet city, Anchorage's homeless youth population is 45 percent greater than the entire rest of the state. With high rates of abuse, paired with harsh weather conditions, our youth are at extreme risk for sexual abuse, prostitution and exploitation."

Diana Bline, Director of Program Services, Covenant House Alaska. Testimony before the Task Force on American Indian/Alaska Native Children Exposed to Violence, Anchorage, AK, June 12, 2014

ADVISORY COMMITTEE VISION FOR WELL-BEING IN THE COMMUNITY

The Advisory Committee envisions Native communities that are supportive and offer a nurturing environment for children—communities that build on Native traditions and values, are free from violence, and can restore the well-being of children and adults impacted by exposure to violence.

The Advisory Committee believes that children can find safety, identity, and connection within their tribal community (clan, band, extended family). Government agencies and tribes have a responsibility to provide for the welfare of their children and to share culture, traditions, language, history, and teachings with their children. This responsibility exists whether the children are residing on a reservation, in Alaska Native villages, or in an urban area.

Developing and maintaining communities where children can thrive includes having a clear understanding of the impact that witnessing and experiencing violence has on children. Community leaders and members, social service providers, and families must be able to identify the children impacted by violence in the community, and ensure culturally appropriate and trauma-informed services are available to treat and prevent violence. Schools and youth-serving agencies should be trauma-informed and have the resources to respond appropriately.

Findings and Recommendations

3.1 The White House Native American Affairs Office (see Recommendation 1.2) and executive branch agencies that are responsible for addressing the needs of AI/AN children, in consultation with tribes, should develop a strategy to braid (integrate) flexible funding to allow tribes to create comprehensive violence prevention, intervention, and treatment programs to serve the distinct needs of AI/AN children and families.

3.1.A The White House Native American Affairs Office, the U.S. Attorney General, the Secretaries of the Department of Interior (DOI) and Health and Human Services (HHS), and heads of other agencies that provide funds that serve AI/AN children should annually consult with tribal governments to solicit recommendations on the mechanisms that would provide flexible funds for the assessment of local needs, and for the development and adaptation of promising practices that allow for the integration of the unique cultures and healing traditions of the local tribal community.

3.1.B   The White House Native American Affairs Office and the U.S. Attorney General should work with the organizations that specialize in treatment and services for traumatized children, for example, National Child Traumatic Stress Network, to ensure that services for AI/AN children exposed to violence are trauma-informed.

3.1.C   The White House Native American Affairs Office should coordinate the development and implementation of federal policy that mandates exposure to violence trauma screening and suicide screening be a part of services offered to AI/AN children during medical, juvenile justice, and/or social service intakes.

Although children exposed to violence in AI/AN communities may be similar to all children exposed to violence, effective solutions to the effects of such exposure may vary greatly among the 566 distinct federally recognized tribes across the United States. Federal, tribal, and state agencies and organizations must collaborate to ensure that tribal communities have the flexibility to integrate solutions that work and are culturally and locally relevant to meet the challenges, circumstances, and unique characteristics of their children and communities.

Currently, federal and state grants implementing standard federal or state solutions are not always effective in AI/AN communities. During one of the Advisory Committee's Listening Sessions, the principal of Bethel Regional High School in Bethel, Alaska, provided a good example of this challenge. Bethel Regional High School received funding to reduce alcohol use among high school students. The grant funding was contingent on Bethel Regional High School's commitment to utilizing one of the endorsed curricula that was not culturally or geographically appropriate. One requirement of the approach was to display health or relevant statistics on billboards in a targeted community; however that public display of information approach was neither helpful nor respectful of local culture in Bethel. The funding, while allowing for some productive local activities, was too restrictive. Ultimately it became impossible to meet the requirement of the grant. The ineffective curriculum was abandoned, no billboards ever went up, and the helpful activities that were identified could not be sustained and simply ended with the expiration of the three-year grant.

Policies must be developed and implemented to ensure that screening for exposure to violence takes place in numerous settings and issues of confidentiality are resolved. Confidentiality issues will arise as children are screened by various child-serving organizations in the communities that serve them. The need for confidentiality must be balanced with the need for service providers to have information that will permit them to more effectively serve the child. The Advisory Committee urges federal, tribal, and state programs that collect these data to seek creative ways to monitor and use information for the benefit of the child rather than use confidentiality as an excuse to inappropriately refuse to share information. Similarly, federal agencies that collect and aggregate data on services provided to American Indian and Alaska Natives are urged to share those data with their federal partners and tribes.

The need for data sharing and monitoring in serving children is demonstrated in a program developed by the Tribal Department of Education of the Coeur d'Alene Tribe. The Coeur d'Alene Tribe was plagued with youth issues such as high drop-out rates, suicide, and substance abuse. The Tribal Department of Education began to gather and analyze data, which indicated that the issues seemed to begin in grades six through eight. The tribe developed a youth-at-risk tracking program known as the Strengthening the Spirit Program, an Educational Pipeline. There are more than seven hundred Coeur d'Alene children in the educational pipeline. The children range in ages from birth through PhD students and remain in the pipeline until graduation and sometimes beyond. The students receive a plethora of services and have access to multiple resources. The Strengthening the Spirit Program is community based, and various organizations come together to collaborate and focus on tribal youth, sharing data and information. As a result of this program, the tribe reports no drop-outs, no gangs, and no suicides.

3.2 **The Department of Justice's National Institute of Justice (NIJ) and other Justice Department agencies with statutory research funding should set-aside 10 percent of their annual research budgets for partnerships between tribes and research entities to develop, adapt, and validate trauma screens for use among AI/AN children and youth living in rural, tribal and urban communities. Trauma screens should be tested and validated for use in schools, juvenile justice (law enforcement and courts), mental health, primary care, Defending Childhood Tribal Grantee programs, and social service agencies and should include measures of trauma history, trauma symptoms, recognizing trauma triggers, recognizing trauma reactions, and developing positive coping skills for both the child and the caregivers.**

Identification of children who have been traumatized by exposure to violence is the first step toward healing and recovery. Children must be screened in schools, clinics, social service agencies, juvenile justice facilities, wherever children are found. Tribal communities need assistance from research partnerships to develop, validate, and use instruments to screen for trauma symptoms and design an effective path forward for children.

3.3 **The White House Native American Affairs Office and responsible federal agencies should provide AI/AN youth-serving organizations such as schools, Head Starts, daycares, foster care programs, and so forth with the resources needed to create and sustain safe places where AI/AN children exposed to violence can obtain services. Every youth-serving organization in tribal and urban Indian communities should receive mandated trauma-informed training and have trauma-informed staff and consultants providing school-based trauma-informed treatment in bullying, suicide, and gang prevention/intervention.**

The vast majority of AI/AN students attend public schools on and off tribal lands. There are also federally and tribally operated schools through the Bureau of Indian Education (BIE) at the DOI. BIE schools are in sixty-two tribal communities and operate 183 elementary, secondary, and residential schools. Of these 183 schools, 126 are tribally controlled.[23] Strategies for prevention,

"While we are truly grateful for any help no matter how small, I must, in all honesty, say that the funding we receive from DOJ has been a drop of relief in a very large bucket of need. Department of Justice grant objectives often do not fit our tribal priorities at the time and there is little flexibility either in the grant competition or administration to bend federal priorities toward our actual local tribal priorities. It feels like we are told we must push a square federal peg in a round tribal hole."

Richard J. Peterson, President, Central Council Tlingit and Haida Tribes of Alaska. Testimony before the Task Force on American Indian/ Alaska Native Children Exposed to Violence, Anchorage, AK, June 11, 2014 intervention, and healing should focus where children can be found (e.g., in schools, preschools, and daycare programs).

AI/AN children who have experienced chronic trauma have poor educational outcomes. One of the coping skills these children might use is vigilance (staying awake while the abuser is awake), which means they are unable to get the sleep they need. These children are protecting themselves but are oftentimes unable to attend school regularly. Truancy very often results in retention at grade level or not graduating from high school. While they are unconsciously trying to manage symptoms of trauma, these students may also engage in disruptive and inappropriate classroom behaviors that may lead to discipline problems, a special education assessment and an inappropriate special education diagnosis. Children spend the majority of their childhood in schools. Unfortunately, just more than 50 percent of AI/AN students actually graduate from high school, compared to nearly 80 percent for the non-Native population nationally.[24] This low graduation rate can be tied to exposure to violence.[25] In addition, AI/AN students are the highest percentage of all groups to report injuries with weapons and fights on schools grounds.[26] Schools must become trauma-informed and incorporate trauma-informed care to support students. Schools too often use expulsion or suspension to discipline for behaviors that are the result of the students' history of and ongoing exposure to trauma. School staff are often unaware of the impact trauma has on the psychological and emotional health of their students. Schools that are trauma-informed can establish safe and nurturing environments where children can learn.

Federal, tribal, and state agencies that provide medical care, social services, education, and juvenile justice services for AI/AN children and families must be required to screen for trauma history and trauma symptoms. Staff working in tribal child-serving systems must undergo training and education to understand the impact trauma has on children. These agencies must work with trauma experts like the National Child Traumatic Stress Network (NCTSN) so that they understand and use best practices for screening and treating AI/AN children living in rural and urban settings. Personnel working in Indian Head Start (i.e., early childhood professionals) and schools serving AI/AN children must also be trained to identify trauma symptoms and child behaviors resulting from exposure to violence. They must understand the use of trauma-informed, culturally relevant trauma-screening tools and be required to screen so that cooperative strategies can be developed to help the child and family.

3.4 The Secretary of Housing and Urban Development (HUD) should designate and prioritize Native American Housing Assistance and Self-Determination Act (NAHSDA) funding for construction of facilities to serve AI/AN children exposed to violence and structures for positive youth activities. This will help tribal communities create positive environments such as shelters, housing, cultural facilities, recreational facilities, sport centers, and theaters through the Indian Community Development Block Grant Program and the Housing Assistance Programs.

The Advisory Committee repeatedly heard testimony about the need for safe houses for youth in tribal communities. Safe houses provide secure and safe settings for youth escaping violence. They are places where a youth's basic needs for safety, nutrition, mental health treatment, and education can be assessed and met. Safe houses may provide for their cultural and spiritual needs as well. Providing a safe place where violence-exposed youth can focus on healing is the first step toward helping a young person recover from trauma.

The Advisory Committee heard testimony from the Lummi Safe House Manager stating, "In our safe house, there's no penalty systems, we take care of our kids, we love our kids, we see them as kids when they walk in the door, we do not see them as that troubled kid or that one that just came from detention. Or even if they're on a runaway status, which means they came from who knows where, the cops bring them in and sign them in at the door and we take care of them."[27] Under current authority, BIA, IHS, and tribes are authorized to use available resources to establish and operate emergency shelters or halfway houses for Indian youth with alcohol or substance abuse problems.[28] They should exercise that authority to establish safe houses.

AI/AN youth also need access to facilities for positive youth development. The Advisory Committee heard young people testify repeatedly that having "nothing to do" contributes to high-risk behavior and poor choices by AI/AN youth. Facilities that provide alternatives for youth and support positive youth development should be tailored to the needs and interests of local youth; for example, for youth from the Great Plains, basketball often provides motivation for positive choices and success.

"Our rates of forcible rape, high school dating and sexual violence, infant homicide, and suicide are significantly higher than national averages. Thirteen percent of our suicides are children and nearly 40 percent are Alaska Native or American Indian. In 2012, someone was worried enough to make a report to child protection for nearly one out of ten Alaskan children, and 4 percent of our pregnant women in our PRAMS data source admit to being victims of intimate partner violence during their recent pregnancy."

Cathy Baldwin-Johnson, Medical Director, Alaska CARES. Testimony before the Task Force on American Indian/ Alaska Native Children Exposed to Violence, Anchorage, AK, June 12, 2014

3.5 The White House Native American Affairs Office should work with the Congress and executive branch agencies in consultation with tribes to develop, promote, and fund youth-based afterschool programs for AI/AN youth. The programs must be culturally based and trauma-informed, must partner with parents/caregivers, and, when necessary, provide referrals to trauma-informed behavioral health providers. Where appropriate, local capacity should also be expanded through partnerships with America's volunteer organizations, for example, AmeriCorp.

There are a number of successful community-based or afterschool programs for youth that teach culture and prevention along with life skills. For example, the Akimel O'odham/Pee-Posh Youth Council focuses on leadership development, responsibility to community, and involvement in cultural activities. In a Listening Session with the Advisory Committee in Sacaton, Arizona, these youth described the challenges their community faces and the solutions the young people are seeking.

3.6 The White House Native American Affairs Office and the Secretary of Health and Human Services (HHS) should develop and implement a plan to expand access to Indian Health Service (IHS), tribal, and urban Indian centers to provide behavioral health services to AI/AN children in schools. This should include the deployment of behavioral health services providers to serve students in the school setting.

Schools (K–12) have become the de facto mental health providers in America. Schools are often the first to identify the mental and behavioral health needs of their students. They provide mental health services to their AI/AN students with commitment and creativity. Many districts hire a mental health counselor, or contract with a for-profit company that places a provider, like Altacare, in schools and bills private insurance and Medicaid.

The IHS and tribes should work with schools to ensure that school-based health services are available in all schools with significant AI/AN student populations so that all students are ready to learn. Tribes should consider collocating tribal support services in or near BIE schools. To be helpful to AI/AN children, clinical services must be culturally sensitive. Professionals providing services must be trauma-informed and culturally informed. They must be knowledgeable and respectful of the local customs and healing practices.

Federal, tribal, state, and for-profit agencies that provide behavioral health services must cooperate to develop and deliver school-based services for AI/AN students. Federal agencies should work with public schools and BIE-funded schools to ensure that services are offered, preferably in the schools, to students attending BIE-funded schools. School-based services increase the availability and utilization by students and will increase the safety in schools.

Notes

1. Perry, Steven, "American Indians and Crime: A BJS Statistical Profile 1992-2002," Washington, D.C.: U.S. Department of Justice, Bureau of Justice Statistics (December 2004): 5.

2. Center for Native American Youth at the Aspen Institute, "Fast Facts: Native American Youth and Indian Country," available at: http://www.aspeninstitute.org/sites/default/files/content/upload/Native%20Youth%20Fast%20Facts%20Update_04-2014.pdf.

3. Felitti V. J., Anda R. F., Nordenberg D., et.al., "Relationship of Childhood Abuse and Household Dysfunction to Many of the Leading Causes of Death in Adults: The Adverse Childhood Experiences (ACE) Study," *American Journal of Preventative Medicine* 14(4) (1998).

4. Koss M. P., Yuan N. P., Dightman D., et al., "Adverse Childhood Exposures and Alcohol Dependence among Seven Native American Tribes," *American Journal of Preventative Medicine* 25(3) (October 2003): 238–44.

5. Indian Law and Order Commission, *A Roadmap for Making Native America Safer: Report to the President and Congress of the United States* (November 2013): 149, available at: http://www.aisc.ucla.edu/iloc/report/index.html. Citing Arya, Neelum, and Rolnick, Addie, "A Tangled Web of Justice: American Indian and Alaska Native Youth in Federal, State, and Tribal Justice Systems," *Campaign for Youth Justice Policy Brief* 5 (2008): 4.

6. Norris, Tina, Vines, Paula L., and Hoeffel, Elizabeth M., "The American Indian and Alaska Native Population: 2010," *2010 Census Briefs, U.S. Census* (January 2012). The percentage of AI/AN populations that live on/off Indian land varies substantially depending upon who self-identifies as AI/AN. The 2010 Census self-identifies, and includes individuals of more than one race. The 2010 Census defined "American Indian or Alaska Native" as a person having origins in any of the original peoples of North and South America (including Central America) and who maintains tribal affiliation or community attachment. This is much broader than those who may be members of a tribe.

7. Ong, Paul M., and Ong, Jonathan D., "The Status of American Indians/Alaska Natives in Los Angeles: American Indian Population Change at the Dawn of the 21st Century," *Los Angeles Urban Indian Roundtable Policy Brief* 1, UCLA American Indian Studies Center (November 2012).

8. Written Testimony of Deborah Painte, Hearing of the Task Force on American Indian/Alaska Native Children Exposed to Violence, Bismarck, ND, December 9, 2013 at supplement, available at: http://www.justice.gov/defendingchildhood/aian-hearings.html.

9. Children's Defense Fund, "Protect Children, Not Guns, Overview," available at http://www.childrensdefense.org/child-research-data-publications/data/state-data-repository/protect-children-not-guns-key-facts-2013.pdf.

10. Suicide Prevention Resource Center, "Suicide among Racial/Ethnic Populations in the U.S.: American Indians/Alaska Natives," Waltham, MA: Education Development Center, 2013. See also, Mullany, B., Barlow, A., Goklish, N., et al., "Toward Understanding Suicide among Youths: Results from the White Mountain Apache Tribally Mandated Suicide Surveillance System, 2001–2006," *American Journal of Public Health* 99(10) (October 1999): 1840–8.

11. Suicide Prevention Resource Center, "Suicide among Racial/Ethnic Populations in the U.S.: American Indians/Alaska Natives," Waltham, MA: Education Development Center, 2013.

12. Craig, J., and Hull-Jilly, D., "Characteristics of Suicide among Alaska Native and Alaska Non-Native People, 2003–2008," *State of Alaska Epidemiology Bulletin* 15(1) (July 2012).

13. Children's Defense Fund, "Protect Children, Not Guns, Overview," available at http://www.childrensdefense.org/child-research-data-publications/data/state-data-repository/protect-children-not-guns-key-facts-2013.pdf.

14. Levinson, Daniel, "Access to Mental Health Services at Indian Health Service and Tribal Facilities," Department of Health and Human Services, Office of Inspector General (September 2011).

15. Major, Aline K., Egley Jr., Arlen, Howell, James C., et al., "Youth Gangs in Indian Country," *OJJDP Juvenile Justice Bulletin*, U.S. Department of Justice, Office of Juvenile Justice and Delinquency Prevention (March 2004): 4.

16. Park, Patina Interim Director of the Minnesota Indian Women's Resource Center, Urban Listening Session on May 20, 2014, Summary, 9.

17. Park, Patina Interim Director of the Minnesota Indian Women's Resource Center, Testimony before the Task Force on American Indian/Alaska Native Children Exposed to Violence, Minneapolis, MN, Urban Listening Session, May 20, 2014.

18. Volkow, Nora, "Substance Abuse in American Indian Youth Is Worse Than We Thought," *Nora's Blog,* National Institute on Drug Abuse (September 2014), available at: http://www.drugabuse.gov/about-nida/noras-blog/2014/09/substance-use-in-american-indian-youth-worse-than-we-thought.

19. Ibid.

20. "Status and Trends in the Education of American Indians and Alaska Natives," U.S. Department of Education, National Center for Education Statistics (August 2005), available at: http://nces.ed.gov/pubs2005/nativetrends/ind_3_2.asp.

21. 48 Stat. 596 (codified as amended at 25 U.S.C. § 455 (2000)).

22. Strand, J. A., and Peacock, R., "Resource Guide for Cultural Resilience," *Tribal College Journal of American Indian Higher Education* 14(4) (2003).

23. Written Testimony of the Native Indian Education Association, submitted to the Attorney General's Advisory Committee on American Indian/Alaska Native Children Exposed to Violence (July 2014) (on file with the Tribal Law and Policy Institute).

24. Ibid.

25. Ibid.

26. Trujillo, Octaviana V., and Alston, Denise A., *A Report on the Status of American Indians and Alaska Natives in Education: Historical Legacy to Cultural Empowerment*, Washington, D.C.: National Education Association, 2005: 2.

27. Jessie Deardorff, Manager, Lummi Safe House, Testimony before the Attorney General's Advisory Committee on American Indian/Alaska Native Children Exposed to Violence, Phoenix, AZ, February 11, 2014.

28. 25 U.S.C. § 2433a.

CHAPTER 4

Creating a Juvenile Justice System that Focuses on Prevention, Treatment, and Healing

"We are here today talking about our young people, sacred people. And the sacredness is not acknowledged, not recognized by the American legal system. It simply isn't. That's why we say that the ancient laws, the ancient principles, the ancient practices, have to be acknowledged by the governments. And I talk not only of the federal government, the state governments, but our own Indian Nations. They have to acknowledge that sacredness."

Justice Herb Yazzie, Chief Justice, Navajo Nation Supreme Court. Testimony before the Task Force on American Indian/Alaska Native Children Exposed to Violence, Phoenix, AZ, February 11, 2014

Children entering the juvenile justice system are exposed to violence at staggeringly high rates. We know that this exposure has a number of negative effects including changes in neurological development, decreased physical and mental health, decreased school performance, and increases in risky behaviors such as substance abuse and delinquent behavior.[1] Of children who enter the juvenile justice system, the prevalence of trauma symptoms due to violence exposure is estimated at 73 to 95 percent.[2] Research has shown that a majority of youth detained in juvenile detention centers have been exposed to violence, whether it is exposure to direct violence as a victim (e.g., physical or sexual abuse) or witnessing violence (e.g., domestic violence, gang shootings). Unfortunately, the research on how exposure to violence intersects with the juvenile justice system has been slow to inform juvenile justice system practice.[3]

The slow application of knowledge about the intersection of the prevalence of youth exposure to violence and the juvenile justice system response is very likely one of the reasons the Western model of juvenile justice used for so long by state, federal, and many tribal jurisdictions does not work.

Many American Indian and Alaska Native (AI/AN) people believe that the Western criminal/juvenile justice system is inappropriate for children, particularly AI/AN children, as it is contrary to AI/AN values in raising children. As Justice Herb Yazzie said in testimony: "I would be blunt in saying that the American criminal justice system is inappropriate to be applied to young people. . . . You do not apply criminal concepts to young kids. . . . So I encourage you to seek ways to break the application of criminal law concepts to young people." This concern raised during testimony points to trends in the 1990s away from a juvenile justice system focused on rehabilitation and toward the overuse of secure detention and formal processing of cases in state court systems. As evidence of this concern, a review of the results of twenty-nine randomized controlled trials found no evidence that formal delinquency processing had any positive effect on juvenile crime control, and in fact this review discovered that most of these randomized controlled trials found formal processing actually increases delinquency.[4] The inescapable conclusion is that the standard approach to juvenile justice in state jurisdictions is a failure.

Testimony at public hearings and site visits conducted by the Advisory Committee established that these formal processing systems are often relied upon by tribal juvenile justice systems as well. This is a disturbing trend, when funding for tribal juvenile justice systems is so disproportionately smaller than that for state systems. This failure is compounded for tribal communities that lack the taxation authority and funding streams available to states. The Indian Law and Order Commission arrived at the same conclusion in its recent report as it entitled its chapter on juvenile justice: "Juvenile Justice: Failing the Next Generation."

Over the history of the federal and tribal relationship, federal law and policies have systematically impeded the sovereignty and governing ability of tribes to meaningfully and positively impact the lives of tribal children. The federal boarding school policies at one time resulted in nearly half of all AI/AN children being in residential boarding schools, sometimes hundreds or even thousands of miles away from their families where many experienced physical and sexual trauma, and loss of role models of effective parenting.[5] Likewise, the allotment acts passed by the U.S. Congress were an attempt to assimilate the American Indian into the dominant culture,[6] but instead had the effect of conveying almost 100 million acres of Indian reservation lands into ownership by non-Indians.[7] Later, in 1953, Congress passed PL-280[8] resulting in states being delegated criminal and limited civil jurisdiction over Indians located on reservations. PL-280 and the Allotment acts have created a patchwork of non-Indian and Indian landownership on most reservations, and a patchwork of criminal federal, tribal, and state jurisdiction over Indians who reside on these reservations or trust lands. AI/AN children accused of delinquent acts or truancy are at risk of becoming involved in the courts of one or more of the juvenile justice systems of these three sovereign entities.

This complex jurisdictional system has a dramatic effect on the ability of tribes to react to the needs of their youth. The juvenile systems impacting AI/AN youth, whether federal, tribal, or state, are all failing these children and creating more harm to them, while not reducing juvenile crime and truancy. This finding was reinforced at the Advisory Committee's Juvenile Justice Hearing in Arizona, and at other hearings and Listening Sessions.

This chapter provides a vision for what an effective AI/AN juvenile justice system would look like, reviews findings from hearings, and discusses concrete recommendations. Our hope is that these recommendations lead us to a more effective, tribally driven juvenile justice system for AI/AN youth.

"Now, sadly, we know that the road to involvement in the juvenile justice system is often paved with experiences of victimization and trauma."

Kevin Washburn, Assistant Secretary for Indian Affairs, U.S. Department of Interior. Testimony before the Task Force on American Indian/ Alaska Native Children Exposed to Violence, Phoenix, AZ, February 11, 2014

"When I got out, there was all this negative around me and no positive. I hung out with my friends because I didn't have a home to go to. My mother was in the hospital and my father moved. I didn't know where my brothers were. It was pretty hard. I wished I was back in the detention center.

Now I am homeless. I'm living with my grandma temporarily. I plan to go to college in the fall in New Mexico. I'm not sure what to major in. I like cosmetology so if college doesn't work out, I will go to cosmetology school. I still cut my wrists, but I have the desire to stop. I want to make something of my life."

Temetria Young, 18 years old. Testimony before the Task Force on American Indian/ Alaska Native Children Exposed to Violence, Phoenix, AZ, February 11, 2014

Three different jurisdictional systems impact AI/AN youth involved in the juvenile justice system: federal, tribal, and/or state. The confusing criminal jurisdictional framework, which is designed for adults, has a significant and oftentimes harmful impact on youth. Depending upon where a delinquent act takes place, the race of the victim, the seriousness of the act, and whether PL-280 or a similar-styled law applies, one or more of the three systems could have jurisdiction over the juvenile. While this jurisdictional maze is problematic for adults, it is far more disastrous for youth caught in the systems and does not allow for notification of their tribes, which might not realize the extent of their youth's involvement in the state or federal juvenile justice systems.

Many tribal communities have no tribal juvenile court system or juvenile code, and oftentimes lack the supporting service delivery system necessary to meet the specific needs of their youth who come in contact with the juvenile justice system. Due to the fact that tribes do not have a tax base, these systems are largely dependent on federal authorizations and appropriation. Tribes in PL-280 states and Alaska Tribes[9] generally receive little to no funding for court services overall, and much less for handling the unique needs posed by juvenile justice cases specifically.

If a tribe is one of the fortunate few to have successful economic enterprises acting as tax base surrogates that can be used to support juvenile justice system infrastructure and staffing, there is still a significant lack of training in best practices to better the lives of juveniles. A few tribes that have funding through successful economic ventures have developed juvenile justice systems that provide services and support to the youth that enter their systems, with strong focus on prevention and rehabilitation in their communities. However, the Advisory Committee also saw, in these examples, a heavy reliance on detention, even in cases of status offenses such as curfew violations. These detention centers were also much more akin to adult correctional facilities than to a place where these children would feel safe and have their needs addressed. While the Advisory Committee understands that this is a very common practice in state and federal jurisdictions, we believe that a tribe's continued common use of detention for children having such extreme rates of exposure to violence is another infliction of violence on these children. As such, there must be strong support for community-based, culturally specific alternatives to detention for AI/AN children.

Over and over again the Advisory Committee heard testimony to the effect that: "We have the answers." "The answers lie within our people, within the communities." "We as Indian people hold the healing ability to heal our communities though our cultural ways."[10] Tribal culture and tribal and family connections play an important role in responding to the effects of exposure to violence through the development of resiliency. The current system does not support that local participation and develop the capacity of the local community. It does not support local practices that work, but rather supports evidence-based practices that worked in Europe or some non-Indian community, not in Indian country, Alaska Native villages or urban Indian communities.[11]

The Advisory Committee supports substantial reform of the juvenile justice systems impacting AI/AN youth. A reformed juvenile justice system should be tribally operated or strongly influenced by tribes within the local region. It is a system:

- Where tribes, parents, and families know where their children are and believe they are safe and in good care.
- Where youth are appropriately screened, and services are trauma-informed.
- Where tribal-specific or culturally based traditional healing, understanding, and practices are interwoven with all therapeutic services available for children and their families.
- Where federal, tribal, and state systems coordinate and cooperate ensuring that their AI/AN youths' needs are being met in a seamless and accountable method.
- Where a variety of diversion and reentry programs involving the tribal or local community are available.
- Where there is less reliance on the use of family methods that disrupt families, and where detention and removal from home are utilized as a last resort when there is no other recourse to protect the child or community.
- Where, when detention is necessary to protect public safety youth are placed close to home and family with adequate and effective services.
- Where juvenile justice codes reflect an understanding of children's exposure to violence and reflect local cultural values, and status offenses are treated differently from other juvenile offenses.
- Where successes are tracked so that other nontribal justice systems feel confident in referring Native children to their system and services.

"One of the barriers, both our youth and their families face, are professionals. They come and they have proper credentials that are required by the state, but they lack the cultural knowledge and ability or even desire to understand where our children and their families are coming from in their history and their lives."

Darla Thiele, Director, Sunka Wakan Ah Ku Program. Testimony before the Task Force on American Indian/ Alaska Native Children Exposed to Violence, Bismarck, ND, December 9, 2013

"We must expand our notion of healing and therapeutic interventions to go beyond those from the Western world and once again look to traditional ceremonies, practices, beliefs and rituals that served us throughout time immemorial. . . . So I caution against the sole use of Evidence Based Practices (EBP) alone, as the only direction, but a holistic and comprehensive approach must be taken that integrates the best of both worlds."

Deborah Painte. Testimony before the Advisory Committee, Bismarck, ND, December 9, 2013

ADVISORY COMMITTEE VISION FOR JUVENILE JUSTICE REFORM

The Advisory Committee envisions a reformed juvenile justice system, based on the fundamental philosophy that children are sacred; a system with the resources to implement and support this philosophy. The Advisory Committee believes that each tribal community will use modern evidence-based and practice-based responses in concert with its cultural teachings and traditions to find the methods that are effective in preventing children's exposure to violence and treating those who have been exposed.

The Advisory Committee supports a system in which American Indian and Alaska Native children have equal protection under the law and have equal access to the services that are critical for their personal well-being. Developing local capacity through training, education, and funding is essential. Tribal cultural and family connections, coupled with culturally adapted screening and treatment interventions will ultimately save our children from the effects of exposure to violence through the development of their resiliency. Our vision includes developing and delivering a supportive juvenile justice system that is meaningful, helpful, and nurturing and that supports wellness of American Indian and Alaska Native children.

Findings and Recommendations

4.1 Congress should authorize additional and adequate funding for tribal juvenile justice programs, a grossly underfunded area, in the form of block grants and self-governance compacts that would support the restructuring and maintenance of tribal juvenile justice systems.

4.1.A Congress should create an adequate tribal set-aside that allows access to all expanded federal funding that supports juvenile justice at an amount equal to the need in tribal communities. As an initial step towards the much larger commitment needed, Congress should immediately establish a minimum 10 percent tribal set-aside, as per the Violence Against Women Act (VAWA) tribal set-aside, from funding for all Office of Justice and

Juvenile Delinquency (OJJDP) funding making clear that the tribal set-aside is the minimum tribal funding and not in any way a cap on tribal funding. President Obama's annual budget request to Congress has included a 7 percent tribal set-aside for the last few years. This is a very positive step and Congress should authorize this request immediately. However, the tribal set-aside should be increased to 10 percent in subsequent appropriations bills. Until Congress acts, the Department of Justice should establish this minimum 10 percent tribal set-aside administratively.

The funding tribes receive for juvenile justice programming must be adequate and stable. Currently, tribes need to rely on inadequate base funding from the BIA. Tribes are thus forced to compete for grant funds to support the most basic components of a juvenile justice system. It is unacceptable for federal agencies to provide grant funding for a tribal program, only to limit the funding to three years; thus requiring tribes to recompete or lose funding at the end of the grant period. It is unethical to withdraw critical services being provided to tribal children who trust that those services will help them with the trauma they have already faced. Tribes use scarce and limited resources to develop a program and establish relationships to create trust in the program. Then, when the program is most productive, it loses funding and comes to an end. Long-term stability of good programs is vital to significantly address exposure to violence and trauma that impact youth.

Flexibility in funding is important to allow local communities to utilize the funding in creative, impactful ways that focus on an individual community's needs. Funding is the key to tribal empowerment. The Overview Section, Chapter 1 of this report provides a greater explanation of the need for block grants and/or self-governance compacts.

The White House Native American Affairs Office (see Recommendation 1.2) should coordinate implementation of this recommendation along with the other recommendations in this chapter.

4.1.B Federal funding for state juvenile justice programs should require that states engage in and support meaningful and consensual consultation with tribes on the design, content, and operation of juvenile justice programs to ensure that programming is imbued with cultural integrity to meet the needs of tribal youth.

Programming offered in state juvenile justice systems is not meeting the needs of AI/AN youth and in some cases is harming these youth. Even those states with significant AI/AN populations fail to meaningfully consult with tribes about their juvenile justice systems to ensure that their programming is thoughtful and culturally based. One way to ensure that states with significant AI/AN populations involve tribes in important decisions regarding AI/AN children is to tie federal funding to meaningful consultation with tribes. Encouraging states and tribes to collaborate and cooperate on juvenile justice is imperative, even cooperation on such issues as cross-deputization of law enforcement indirectly affects youth. And states must share information about AI/AN youth involved in their juvenile systems if tribes are to be meaningfully involved in their youths' healing and development. For instance, the state of Washington maintains a database of screening of all juveniles who enter that juvenile justice system, which is readily identifiable by name and birth date. Washington State tribes should be able to access these screens of their tribal member children to better coordinate services that the tribes could provide.

In general, providing tribes with adequate funding for programs and services will also make tribal programs more attractive alternatives to state-run programs. This would ultimately encourage local courts to utilize tribal programs. Developing the tribes' ability to offer states options of culturally appropriate services through their tribal juvenile justice system could counter the impact of AI/AN youth caught in the state juvenile justice system. Some tribes have good relationships with their local county juvenile court systems and juveniles in the state system are referred to the tribal court systems. Encouragement of these collaborative ventures through funding is critically important.

4.1.C Congress should direct the Department of Justice (DOJ) and the Department of Interior (DOI) to determine which agency should provide funding for both the construction and operation of jails and juvenile detention facilities

in AI/AN communities, require consultation with tribes concerning the selection process, ensure the trust responsibilities for these facilities and services are assured, and appropriate the necessary funds.

Currently the DOJ and DOI have divided responsibilities to construct, operate, staff, and maintain jails and juvenile detention centers. This has resulted in dozens of facilities being constructed that are vacant or seriously underutilized because operating funds have not been provided. The tribes where these facilities have been constructed have significant need for both detention facilities and alternative programs to support children and youth who are in the juvenile justice system, many of whom have also been exposed to violence. These youth often need substance abuse treatment, mental health treatment, education, and other services to address their exposure to violence. These facilities must be staffed and funded for operations after construction. The split responsibility that exists now is not workable and is not in the best interest of tribes. In the future, tribes should be consulted before facilities are constructed.

4.2 Federal, state, and private funding and technical assistance should be provided to tribes to develop or revise trauma-informed, culturally specific tribal codes to improve tribal juvenile justice systems.

Developing a tribal juvenile justice system means developing tribal codes that fit the culture and community. Too often tribes have copied tribal codes from nontribal or different tribal entities, which do not fit their own tribal or community's values and beliefs. It is particularly important that tribes receive adequate funding for juvenile justice so they can develop juvenile justice systems that are not a reproduction of the failed Western systems, but a structure that respects their youth and their tribal values, as well as a system that is trauma-informed. Technical assistance should be provided to develop culturally appropriate, trauma-informed, juvenile justice codes and systems.

4.3 Federal, tribal, and state justice systems should provide publicly funded legal representation to AI/AN children in the juvenile justice systems to protect their rights and minimize the harm that the juvenile justice system may cause them. The use of technology such as videoconferencing could make such representation available even in remote areas.

"How do we continue programs for more than 5 years? When Columbus landed in 1492, he screwed us up for over 500 years. And it ain't going to take overnight."

Tracy Ching King. Testimony before the Task Force on American Indian/Alaska Native Children Exposed to Violence, Phoenix, AZ, February 11, 2014

The status of AI/AN youth is unique; they may be prosecuted in three distinct justice systems: federal, tribal, or state. Each has its own rules and procedures, which are foreign and confusing to any juvenile and their family. An AI/AN youth in juvenile court is very likely also a victim of trauma. This makes it even more important that this youth is listened to, respected, and represented by competent counsel in order to foster understanding of the process and achieve the best disposition possible. In the state and federal juvenile justice systems, the youth is entitled to some form of representation; either a *guardian ad litem* if they are under a certain age, or their own attorney to represent their interests. This right, however, does not universally exist in tribal juvenile justice systems as the Indian Civil Rights Act does not require publically funded appointed counsel for juveniles. To allow a child to be formally processed in a juvenile justice system without an advocate by their side is unconscionable. The youth's counsel is in the best position to ensure that the youth is not re-traumatized by the system, adequately advise the youth, intervene with his or her family and tribe to protect the youth's rights, help the youth recognize the need for accountability for his or her actions, promote assessment, and be an advocate for fairness and rehabilitation.

The impact of immaturity is a factor in every juvenile case. However, in those cases involving AI/AN youth, the effects of exposure to violence and trauma are more likely to also be present. Parents frequently are no more likely to understand the system, rights, and process, than the youth. It is highly likely that the parents are in the cycle of intergenerational violence and trauma exposure and are limited in their understanding about how this impacts their child. Juvenile defenders play a vital role in ensuring that all youth that enter the juvenile system are treated fairly and protected from further harm within the system. Given the over-representation of AI/AN youth in state and federal justice systems and in secure confinement, it is critical that culturally competent, well-trained defense counsel be afforded to the youth at the public expense in all federal, tribal, and state juvenile proceedings. The juvenile defender acts as the child's voice in the proceeding, representing the expressed interests of the youth. Defenders do not simply bend to any and every whim of the child. Instead, they elicit a child's perspective, counsel the child on the practical and legal consequences of any decision, and help the child arrive at informed choices and decisions, understanding the myriad of direct and collateral consequences they may face.[12]

4.4 Federal, tribal, and state justice systems should only use detention of AI/AN youth when the youth is a danger to themselves or the community. It should be close to the child's community and provide trauma-informed, culturally appropriate, and individually tailored services, including reentry services. Alternatives to detention such as "safe houses" should be significantly developed in AI/AN urban and rural communities.

The use of juvenile detention is not effective as a deterrent to delinquent behavior, risky behavior, or truancy and should only be used when there is clear evidence that the youth is a danger to themselves or the community. Federal, tribal, or state detention of AI/AN youth should be close to the juvenile's community and provide trauma-informed, culturally appropriate, and individually tailored services to each child. Detention should only be used as a last resort and culturally appropriate alternatives to incarceration such as "safe houses" should be significantly developed within AI/AN urban and rural communities.

Although most AI/AN youth in the juvenile justice system are charged with low-level offenses and normally would not be subject to detention, the lack of alternatives and diversion programs force the system to use detention as shelter. This is a poor response as younger inmates have higher rates of victimization by youth and staff. [13] Female inmates are sexually victimized at higher rates.[14] Youth with higher rates of exposure to violence who are put into detention have greater fear of future victimization and higher rates of conflict with other detainees and staff.[15]

Adequate funding would help keep children out of detention. Tribes need resources to develop appropriate juvenile codes and diversionary programs. This can include development of or revisions to Juvenile Codes as well as the creation of prevention and diversion programs to ensure children are not placed in detention, unless all other options have been exhausted by tribes.[16] Only a few tribes have the financial ability to develop services and alternatives to detention on their own. Most rely on the federal government to meet its trust obligation to tribes by providing the funding needed.

Youth returning from a detention or treatment facility must have appropriate reentry services. Too frequently there is no support available for youth returning to their homes or to their

"As a commissioner on the Indian Law and Order Commission, I asked for the better part of two years, where are our children?"

Judge Theresa Pouley, Chief Judge, Tulalip Tribal Court and Member, Indian Law and Order Commission. Testimony before the Task Force on American Indian/Alaska Native Children Exposed to Violence, Phoenix, AZ, February 11, 2014

"*I think there needs to be a safe house on every reservation, a place that is not a detention facility, a place that is not a lockdown facility, a place that is home and they can feel what it's like to have a home.*"

Jessie Deardorff, Manager, Lummi Safe House. Testimony before the Task Force on American Indian/Alaska Native Children Exposed to Violence, Phoenix, AZ, February 11, 2014

communities due in part to the limited infrastructure and the judicial limitation of tribes and funding.

Some of these alternatives were described in testimony at public hearings of the Advisory Committee. In particular, the Advisory Committee heard about "safe houses/homes" (transitional living with intensive services) in tribal communities, such as the Lummi Safe House in the Lummi Nation. This facility provides a safe place for Lummi youth in a home environment. They may take in youth who have run away from home, those returning home after treatment or transitioning from foster care, along with other children in need of safe housing.[17]

Another example is the Ain Dah Yung Center in Saint Paul, Minnesota, which provides emergency shelter to homeless AI/AN youth and could be considered a "safe house." Homeless youth are vulnerable to further trauma, and are highly likely to become involved in the juvenile justice system. These "safe houses" should provide screening and individual services needed by youth as well as culturally specific teachings, life skills, education support, employment, and transitional services. Funding restrictions limit the amount of time homeless youth may stay at the Ain Dah Yung to twenty-one days. Such short time frames should be eliminated or adjusted to allow for individualized response, recognizing that youth in need of a "safe house" are also suffering from multiple traumatic events. These youth may need long-term support to help them find a more permanent home and more stable family connections.

While most AI/AN youth are placed in detention for committing low-level offenses, there is a group of Native youth prosecuted in the federal system that may spend more time in secure confinement than youth prosecuted in state systems, sometimes by several years. Placement far from a youth's home is more likely with either the state or federal system. Federal sentences are usually longer than state sentences for identical crimes.[18] The Bureau of Prisons (BOP) contracts with state and local facilities in nine states. Many youth are placed wherever there is bed space, which means that the youth are placed in facilities far from their families and loved ones.[19] Tribes and states also place juveniles far from home, generally because there are no options available nearer to home or the options available do not provide the services needed by the youth. AI/AN youth should be detained close to home to enable family to be involved with the youth.

The BOP, a federal agency, should enter into intergovernmental agreements or contracts with Indian tribal juvenile detention centers for federally detained AI/AN juveniles to permit them to be housed in tribally eligible facilities within or near their own community. The BOP should review 18 U.S.C., Section 4006 [20]to determine if Indian tribes are eligible to enter into an agreement with the DOJ along with states and territories; and if not, the Congress should amend this section to include Indian tribes.

The DOJ should explore with the Center for Medicare and Medicaid Services (CMS), Department of Health and Human Services (HHS), what services Medicaid can provide AI/AN children in need of treatment, and determine together with the tribes, how tribes can bill for Medicaid services for AI/AN children in tribal juvenile facilities that offer direct and alternative treatment services.

All juvenile justice systems should recognize the special needs of juvenile girls and LGBTQ/2S and individually tailor services for all AI/AN juveniles. For example, AI/AN girls in detention have experienced alcohol and drug usage; educational challenges, including high dropout rates; teen pregnancy; high intentional and unintentional injury rates, including suicide attempts and completions; and high rates of sexually transmitted diseases.[21]

4.5 **Federal, tribal, and state justice systems and service providers should make culturally appropriate trauma-informed screening, assessment, and care the standard in juvenile justice systems. Indian Health Service (IHS) and tribal and urban Indian behavioral health service providers must receive periodic training in culturally adapted trauma-informed interventions and cultural competency to provide appropriate services to AI/AN children and their families.**

Children and adolescents exposed to violent or traumatic events involving serious threat of injury or death to oneself or others often results in emotional, behavioral, or psychological harm.[22] The pervasiveness of exposure to violence is the precursor to poor mental health outcomes demonstrated in the high rates of substance abuse, PTSD, and depression among AI/AN children and families.[23] One report found that the prevalence for exposure to any traumatic event ranged from 63.4 to 69.8 percent for fifteen to fifty-seven year olds for tribal participants in the study.[24] Likewise,

"Finally, there's a strong need for funding for on-reservation shelters and group homes . . . more in a family setting. Those would be places for victims and their families to live free from fear and receive the necessary treatment and life-skills types of programming and educational services that are desperately needed to help in and reuniting victims and their families. The facilities would include culturally sensitive curriculums that address everything from day treatment for substances abuse, to supervised visitation centers, to parental skills programming, to nutritional needs programming and developmental education. These are the types of programs that we take for granted in off-reservation communities and everybody in this room longs for the day when we can take those types of programs for granted on reservation communities.

Joe Vetsch, Criminal Prosecutor for the Spirit Lake Nation. Testimony before the Task Force on American Indian/ Alaska Native Children Exposed to Violence, Bismarck, ND, December 9, 2013

"What I have found is that in the tribal juvenile detention centers, the American Indian girls are at great risk for not receiving the needed services for what they come in with. A lot of them come in with prior suicide attempts.... We really need a transformation of the system. The juvenile detention centers should be a place where healing can begin. They should be able to have the youth screening for suicidality, for their strengths, for their skills, for trauma, what have they been through; for education, for health."

Ethleen Ironcloud-TwoDogs, Technical Assistance Specialist, Tribal Defending Childhood Initiative, Education Development Center, Inc. Testimony before the Task Force on American Indian/ Alaska Native Children Exposed to Violence, Phoenix, AZ, February 11, 2014

a community-based study revealed that 57 percent of AI/AN youth and young adults between the ages of fifteen and twenty-four had experienced a minimum of one traumatic event in their short lifetime.[25]

Behavioral health services for AI/AN youth may be handled by different agencies with different priorities. Youth in the juvenile justice system are typically not a priority to those community-based agencies. Reports indicate that 60 percent of Native people rely on IHS for their health care including behavioral health.[26] There are only two psychiatrists and four psychologists for every one hundred thousand tribal members who are in need of these services; and less than 5 percent of the 1.5 million of IHS-eligible tribal members receive mental health and substance abuse services.[27] IHS continues to operate at 52 percent of need and mental health and substance abuse services are funded at an appalling 7 percent of need.[28] The U.S. Commission on Civil Rights divulged that IHS spends $1,941.00 per patient for all health care services; compared to the federal prison system, which spends $3,803.00 per federal prisoner.[29]

This documented disparity in the limited availability of behavioral health services offered by IHS underscores the need for maintaining an adequate workforce for treating AI/AN children exposed to violence, and ensuring they are appropriately trained in trauma-informed interventions that are culturally relevant. IHS and other agencies providing these services must work together with a youth focus and consistently build and retrain an adequate workforce. Ensuring that culturally appropriate trauma-informed screening and care becomes the standard in all juvenile justice systems that impact AI/AN youth is critical to developing systems that treat children as sacred and promote wellness and resilience.

4.6 Congress should amend the Indian Child Welfare Act (ICWA) to provide that when a state court initiates any delinquency proceeding involving an Indian child for acts that took place on the reservation, all of the notice, intervention, and transfer provisions of ICWA will apply. For all other Indian children involved in state delinquency proceedings, ICWA should be amended to require notice to the tribe and a right to intervene. As a first step, the Department of Justice (DOJ) should establish a demonstration pilot project that would provide funding for three states to provide ICWA-type notification to tribes within

their state whenever the state court initiates a delinquency proceeding against a child from that tribe which includes a plan to evaluate the results with an eye toward scaling it up for all AI/AN communities.

States have jurisdiction over AI/AN children when a violation occurs outside of Indian country or within Indian country in PL-280 states or states that have a settlement act or other similar federal legislation. Since 64 percent[30] to 78 percent[31] of the AI/AN population resides off reservation or not on tribal land, the vast majority of AI/AN children who come to the attention of authorities are involved in the states' juvenile justice systems. An overarching concern voiced at hearings conducted by the Advisory Committee was that states are not required to notify the tribe or involve the tribe in a juvenile delinquency proceeding. That concern is exacerbated because states generally do not provide the cultural support necessary for Native youth's rehabilitation and reentry into the tribal community.[32]

Unlike the child welfare system where the state is required to notify the tribe under ICWA, there is no requirement that the child's tribe be contacted if the child is charged with a juvenile offense. The unique issues of AI/AN youth are often overlooked in the state's juvenile justice system and their outcomes are difficult to track.[33] In most states, AI/AN youth are more frequently referred to juvenile court, receive disproportionately harsher sentences, and are more likely to be removed from their homes. A 2006 Alaska study using Anchorage and Fairbanks data from 1999 to 2001, found Alaska Native youth are referred to juvenile court 3.28 times more than Caucasian youth. In Fairbanks the referral rate was 4.85 times more likely. Alaska Native youth are held in secure detention at a rate of about one and a half times the rate of Caucasian youth in Anchorage and at more than twice the rate in Fairbanks.[34] In four states (South Dakota, Alaska, North Dakota, and Montana), Native youth account for between 29 percent and 42 percent of youth in secure confinement—far above their percentage of the total population.[35]

The disparities that currently exist in the juvenile justice system are similar to the inequities that gave rise to and supported the passage of ICWA of 1978. State systems do not even record the tribal member status of youth or the Indian country location associated with the offense. Tribes find it impossible to hold the state accountable for how their youth are treated. Providing tribes with notice

"And we also have to begin to focus on the reentry and detention alternatives. What we often see is some minors are given harsher penalties than adults charged with the same offenses. And we begin to desensitize them to what it is to be in detention facilities. And it's like we're creating a better criminal. As they go through the system, the punishment of jail doesn't mean as much to them, because they've spent so much time in jail already."
Sherrie Harris, Public Defender San Carlos Apache Tribe. Testimony before the Task Force on American Indian/Alaska Native Children Exposed to Violence, Phoenix, AZ, February 11, 2014

in all state delinquency proceedings and with the right to intervene and/or transfer in all other state delinquency proceedings involving AI/AN youth when the offense occurs on the reservation would allow tribes to stay connected to their youth and to ensure the state system is accountable for treatment of tribal youth.

Not every tribe will have the ability or resources to intervene or transfer a case to tribal court, but every tribe should have the option to decide on the status of their tribal youth, particularly when the offense occurs on the reservation. Intervention can provide a unique tribal perspective to the court proceedings and additional assurance that the youth are important as tribal citizens. Tribes may offer have tribal-specific resources that the state lacks. An inadequate response will ensure that current disparities will continue and that the juvenile system will continue to be a pipeline for tribal youth to the adult criminal justice system.

Resiliency is based on connectedness to culture, family, and community. An AI/AN child's resiliency cannot be fully developed in a state's juvenile justice system without the involvement of the child's tribe. According to the literature, enculturation, spirituality, and social connections are protective factors that continue to play important roles in fostering resilience among AI/AN children and families.[36] The tribe's involvement can increase the likelihood that these factors will be central to the development of youth, enhance their sense of responsibility and understanding, and show them that they matter to their tribe and their community.

This change in the law will also undoubtedly lead to greater cooperation between states and tribes when AI/AN children are involved. Such a change will no doubt benefit AI/AN children.

States can do much to encourage cooperation and meaningful collaboration with tribes on AI/AN juvenile justice proceedings within their state boundaries. Some counties and tribes share programs and services. New Mexico has an effective practice of requiring that AI/AN children be identified when the child is involved in the juvenile justice system.[37] Once a child is identified, the tribe must be notified and consulted for purposes of disposition. Tribal customs and practices are also taken into consideration.

4.7 Congress should amend the Federal Education Rights and Privacy Act (FERPA) to allow tribes to access their members' school attendance, performance, and disciplinary records.

Almost 92 percent of tribal children attend public schools. FERPA[38] generally allows federal, state, and local education agencies to access student records and other personally identifiable information kept by state public schools without the advance consent of the parents. Tribes are excluded from this law. These records include information about a student's attendance, grades, and discipline; information critical to a tribal education department seeking to provide services to tribal member students. Early intervention is important and school absences, performance, or disciplinary problems can be a red flag indicating family or individual problems. The tribe, if notified, would have the option to intervene to help the family or youth. Through the Elementary and Secondary Education Act of 1965[39] and its 1994 reauthorization, Congress authorized U.S. Department of Education funding of Tribal Education Departments to provide educational support services to their student tribal members. It is this type of support that allows tribal education departments to direct services toward students at risk for truancy proceedings, which often can result in detention. Unfortunately, Congress has not amended FERPA[40] to include these federally supported tribal education departments along with analogous agencies of state, local, and federal governments that are able to access student information.

FERPA (20 U.S.C. 1232(g)(b); 34 C.F.R. 99.31(a).) should be amended to explicitly authorize tribal education departments to readily access information regarding their member children who are absent from school or have performance or disciplinary records. Tribes should be treated in the same manner as FERPA treats states.

Tribes that have programs for early intervention and assistance, such as the Coeur d'Alene Tribe of Idaho or the Salt River Pima Maricopa Indian Community, testified to the Advisory Committee about their problems securing the information they need because of FERPA restrictions.[41] Some schools will cooperate with information requests and others refuse to provide information due to confidentiality. It must be clarified that tribes have a right to this important information about their young tribal members.

"At the federal, state, and tribal level, we all must work to better serve the children in Indian country. It starts with embracing the spirit of cooperation and working together to find solutions. . . . But without proper support from every level of government, no amount of partnership and creative thinking can deliver the level of services that our children need and deserve."

Ned Norris Jr , Chairman, Tohono O'odham Nation. Testimony before the Task Force on American Indian/ Alaska Native Children Exposed to Violence, Phoenix, AZ, February 11, 2014

Notes

1. Carlson, B. E., "Children Exposed to Intimate Partner Violence: Research Findings and Implications for Intervention," 1(4) (2001): 321–42; Skowyra, K., and Cocozza, J. J., "A Blueprint for Change: Improving the System Response to Youth with Mental Health Needs Involved with the Juvenile System," *National Center for Mental Health and Juvenile Justice, Research and Program Brief*, June 2006; Widsom, C. S., Ireland, T., and Glynn, P. J., "Alcohol-Abuse in Abused and Neglected Children Followed-Up: Are They an Increased Risk?," *Journal of Studies on Alcohol* 56(2) (1995): 207–17.

2. Kilpatrick, D. G., et al., "Violence and Risk of PTSD, Major Depression, Substance Abuse/Dependence and Comorbidity: Results from the National Survey of Adolescents," *Journal of Consulting and Clinical Psychology* 71(4) (2003): 692–700; Cauffman, E., et al., "Posttraumatic Stress Disorder among Female Juvenile Offenders," *Journal of the American Academy of Child and Adolescent Psychiatry* 37(11) (1998): 1209–16; Abram, K. M., "Posttraumatic Stress Disorder and Trauma in Youth in Juvenile Detention," *Archives of General Psychiatry* 61(4) (2004): 403–10.

3. Sprague, C., "Informing Judges About Child Trauma," *NCTSN Service System Briefs* 2 (2008); Adams, E. J., "Healing Invisible Wounds: Why Investing in Trauma-Informed Care for Children Makes Sense," *Justice Policy Institute* (2010).

4. Petrosino, A., et al., "Formal System Processing of Juveniles: Effects on Delinquency," *Campbell Systematic Review* (2010). doi:10.4073/csr.2010.1.

5. Evans-Campbell, T., et al., "Indian Boarding School Experience, Substance Use, and Mental Health among Urban Two-Spirit American Indian/Alaska Natives," *The American Journal of Drug and Alcohol Abuse* 38(5) (2012): 421–7; Prucha, Francis Paul, *Americanizing the American Indians*. Cambridge, MA: Harvard University Press, 1973.

6. Huff, Delores J., *To Live Heroically: Institutional Racism and American Indian Education*. Albany: State University of New York Press, 1997.

7. Royster, Judith, "The Legacy of Allotment," *Arizona State Law Journal* 27 (1995): 12.

8. Act of August 15, 1953, Ch. 505, 67 Stat. 588-90 (now codified as amended in scattered sections of 18, 28 U.S.C.).

9. Alaska Tribe –The Native peoples of Alaska are commonly referred to as "Alaska Natives," and "Alaska Native Villages." For the purposes of this report, we will use the term "Alaska Tribe" to refer federally recognized tribes in the State of Alaska. 79 Fed. Reg. 4,748 (Jan. 29, 2014), *available at* http://www.gpo.gov/fdsys/pkg/FR-2014-01-29/pdf/2014-01683.pdf.

10. Testimony of Leander McDonald, Hearing of the Task Force on American Indian/Alaska Native Children Exposed to Violence, Bismarck, ND, December 9, 2013, at 108, available at: http://www.justice.gov/defendingchildhood/nd-briefingbinder.pdf; Testimony of Darla Thiele, Hearing of the Task Force on *American Indian/Alaska Native Children Exposed to Violence*, Bismarck, ND, December 9, 2013, at 61, available at: http://www.justice.gov/defendingchildhood/1st-hearing/intersection-dv-cpsa.pdf; Testimony of Lonna Hunter, Hearing of the Task Force on American Indian/Alaska Native Children Exposed to Violence, Bismarck, ND, December 9, 2013 at 17, available at: http://www.justice.gov/defendingchildhood/nd-briefingbinder.pdf.

11. See Roth, Anthony, and Fonagy, Peter, *What Works for Whom? A Critical Review of Treatments for Children and Adolescents*, New York: Guildford Press, 2005.

12. Testimony of Nadia Seeratan, Hearing of the Task Force on American Indian/Alaska Native Children Exposed to Violence, Phoenix, AZ, February 11, 2014, at 7–12, available at: http://www.justice.gov/defendingchildhood/2nd-hearing/panel4.pdf.

13. Cooley, D. "Criminal Victimization in Male Federal Prisons." *Canadian Journal of Criminology* 35 (1993): 479–95.

14. Wolff, N., and Jing Shi, "Patterns of Victimization and Feelings of Safety Inside Prison: The Experience of Male and Female Inmates." *Crime and Delinquency* 57(1) (2010): 29–55.

15. Mackenzie, D. L. "Age and Adjustment to Prison: Interactions with Attitudes and Anxiety." *Criminal Justice and Behavior* 14(4) (1987): 427–47.

16. Testimony of Governor Gregory Mendoza, Hearing of the Task Force on American Indian/Alaska Native Children Exposed to Violence, Phoenix, AZ, February 11, 2014 at 4–10, available at: http://www.justice.gov/defendingchildhood/2nd-hearing/panel2.pdf.

17. Testimony of Jessie Deerdorff, Hearing of the Task Force on American Indian/Alaska Native Children Exposed to Violence, Phoenix, AZ, February 11, 2014 at 8–14, available at: http://www.justice.gov/defendingchildhood/2nd-hearing/panel5.pdf.

18. Ibid.

19. Ibid.

20. 20

21. Testimony of Ethleen Ironclound-TwoDogs, Hearing of the Task Force on American Indian/Alaska Native Children Exposed to Violence, Phoenix, AZ, February, 11, 2014 at 192, available at: http://www.justice.gov/defendingchildhood/az-briefingbinder.pdf.

22. Cohen, J. A., Manarino, A. P., and Deblinger, E., *Treating Trauma and Traumatic Grief in Children and Adolescents*, New York: The Guilford Press, 2006.

23. Deters, P. B., et al. "Trauma and Post-Traumatic Stress Disorder Symptomatology: Patterns among American Indian Adolescents in Substance Abuse Treatment," *American Journal of Orthopsychiatry* 76(3) (2006): 335–45.

24. Manson, S. M., et al., "Social Epidemiology of Trauma among 2 American Indian Reservation Populations," *American Journal of Public Health* 95(5): 851–9.

25. Gnanadesian, M., et al., "The Relationship of Gender and Trauma Characteristics to Post-traumatic Stress Disorder in a Community Sample of Traumatized Northern Plains American Indian Adolescents and Young Adults," *Journal of Clinical Psychiatry* 66(9) (2005): 1176–83.

26. Gone, J. P., "Mental Health Services for Native Americans in the 21st Century United States," *Professional Psychology: Research and Practice* 35(1) (2004): 10–18.

27. Ibid.

28. Ibid.

29. Sarche, M., and Spicer, P., "Poverty and Health Disparities for American Indian and Alaska Native Children," *Annals of the New York Academy of Sciences* (2008).

30. Indian Law and Order Commission, *A Roadmap for Making Native America Safer: Report to the President and Congress of the United States* (November 2013): 149, available at: http://www.aisc.ucla.edu/iloc/report/index.html.

31. The percentage of AI/AN populations that live on Indian land varies substantially depending upon who self-identifies as AI/AN. The 2010 Census allows for self-identification and includes individuals of more than one race. The 2010 Census defined "American Indian or Alaska Native" as a person having origins in any of the original peoples of North and South America (including Central America) and who maintains tribal affiliation or community attachment. This is much broader than those who may be members of a tribe. See Norris, T., et al., *2010 Census Brief, The American Indian and Alaska Native Population*, available at: http://www.census.gov/prod/cen2010/briefs/c2010br-10.pdf.

32. Indian Law and Order Commission, *A Roadmap for Making Native America Safer: Report to the President and Congress of the United States* (November 2013): 156, available at: http://www.aisc.ucla.edu/iloc/report/index.html.

33. Arya, Neelum, and Rolnick, Addie C. "A Tangled Web of Justice: American Indian and Alaska Native Youth in Federal State, and Tribal Justice Systems," Washington, D.C.: *Campaign for Youth Justice Policy Brief* 1 (2008).

34. Leiber, M. J., Johnson, J., and Fox, K., *An Examination of the Factors that Influence Justice Decision Making in Anchorage and Fairbanks, Alaska, An Assessment Study*, Alaska, 2006.

35. Testimony of David Simmons, Hearing of the Tribal Law and Order Commission, Tulalip Reservation, September 7, 2011.

36. Strand, J. A., and Peacock, R., "Resource Guide for Cultural Resilience," *Tribal College Journal of American Higher Education* 14(4) (2003).

37. Wolfe, Corinne, *New Mexico Juvenile Justice Handbook*, available at: http://childlaw.unm.edu/docs/Juvenile%20Justice%20Handbook%20-%20August%202011%20Web.pdf.

38. 20 U.S.C. 1232(g).

39. PL-89-10 (1965).

40. See, Title IX, Sec. 9125 of PL-103-382 (1994).

41. Testimony of Sherri Fremont, Hearing of the Task Force on American Indian/Alaska Native Children Exposed to Violence, Fort Phoenix, AZ, April 16, 2014 at 1–6, available at: http://www.justice.gov/defendingchildhood/2nd-hearing/panel4.pdf.

CHAPTER 5

Empowering Alaska Tribes, Removing Barriers, and Providing Resources

"The state of Alaska needs a major shift in its policies and approaches to working with Alaska Native tribes and people. We are not an enemy of the state. This is our home and we love it. But we need to be respected and honored as equals."

Evon Peter, Executive Director, Indigenous Leadership Institute. Testimony before the Task Force on American Indian/ Alaska Native Children Exposed to Violence, Anchorage, AK, June 12, 2014

Problems with children exposed to violence in American Indian and Alaska Native (AI/AN) communities are severe across the United States—but they are systemically worse in Alaska. Issues related to Alaska Native children exposed to violence are different for a variety of reasons including regional vastness and geographical isolation, extreme weather, exorbitant cost of transportation, lack of economic opportunity and access to resources, a lack of respect for Alaska tribal sovereignty, and a lack of understanding and respect for Alaska Native history and culture. All of which have contributed to high levels of recurring violence. Alaska Tribes are best positioned to effectively address these problems so long as the current barriers are removed, and Alaska Tribes are empowered to protect Alaska Native children through implementation of the recommendations in this chapter.

Congress has repeatedly exempted Alaska from significant tribal legislation, including recent legislation aimed at reducing violent crime in Indian country—and thereby reducing AI/AN children's exposure to that violence. Most recently, Congress exempted Alaska from both the Tribal Law and Order Act of 2010 (TLOA)[1] and the Violence Against Women Act 2013 reauthorization (VAWA 2013)[2] which restored tribal criminal jurisdiction over all persons charged with domestic violence. The problems in Alaska are so severe and the number of Alaska Native communities affected so large, that continuing to exempt the state of Alaska from national policy change and thereby unjustifiably stigmatizing or ostracizing Alaska Tribes[3] is simply wrong. Given that violent crime—and AI/AN children exposed to that violence—is a more severe public safety problem in Alaska Native communities than in most other tribal communities in the United States, these provisions add insult to injury. In the view of the Advisory Committee, it is unconscionable and must stop.

The Advisory Committee held a series of Alaska hearings, Listening Sessions, and meetings in June 2014 to examine the scope and impact of violence facing Alaska Native children exposed to violence in their homes, schools, and communities. The Advisory Committee held a hearing in Anchorage and Listening Sessions in Bethel, Napaskiak, and Emmonak.

Remoteness and Accessibility Issues. Unless you have lived in Alaska or visited for an extended time, it is difficult to appreciate the vastness of Alaska and the extreme remoteness and accessibility issues. Cumulatively, the challenges posed by these issues contribute to difficulties in confronting the heightened levels of violence that families and Alaska Native children face.

- Alaska covers 586,412 square miles, an area greater in size than Texas, California, and Montana combined.[4]
- The 229 Alaska Tribes[5] are 40 percent of the U.S. federally recognized tribes.
- Alaska Natives represent one-fifth of the total state population.[6] Two-third of Alaska Natives live in rural and often very remote areas.[7]
- Typical Alaska villages are located off the road system with only 250 to 300 residents[8] and "more closely resemble villages in developing countries" than small towns.[9]
- Frequently, villages are accessible only by plane or, during the winter when rivers are frozen, by snow machine. Harsh weather conditions further complicate access to necessary resources, services, and supports. Food, gasoline, and other necessities are expensive and often in short supply.
- Subsistence hunting, fishing, and gathering are a part of everyday life.
- Villages are politically independent from one another, and have institutions that support that local autonomy—councils and village corporations.[10]

Alaska's True Proportion to the Continental United States
From: Indian Law and Order Commission, *A Roadmap for Making Native America Safer: Report to the President and Congress of the United States* (November 2013): 36.

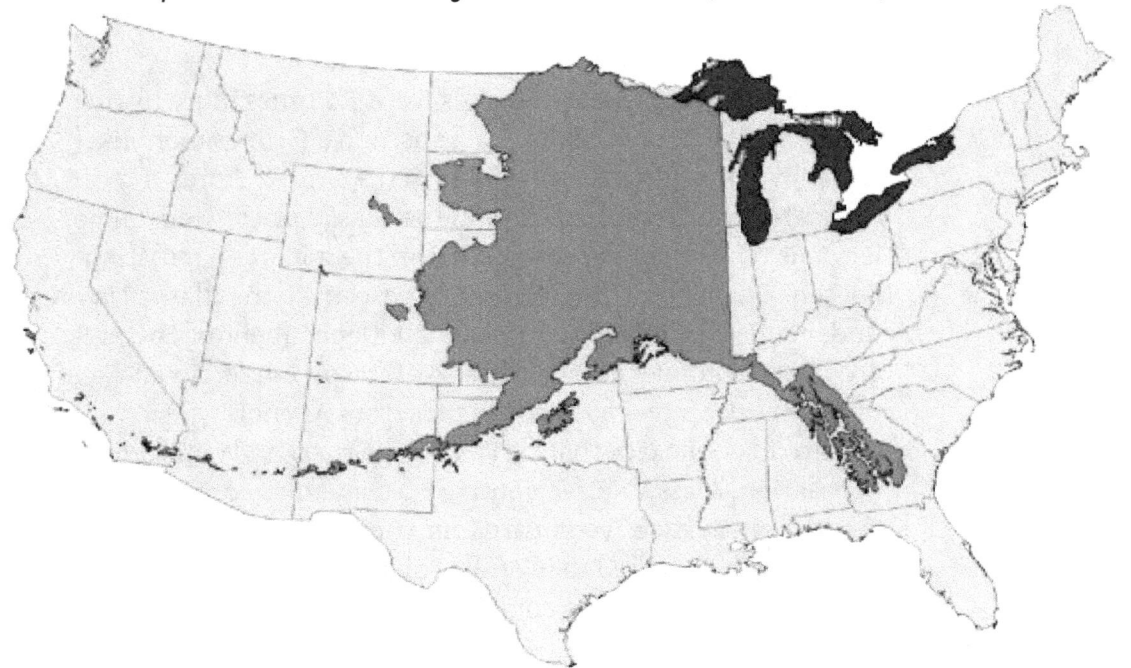

Violence in Native Alaska. Not surprisingly, these conditions pose significant challenges to the effective provision of public safety in Alaska. Alaska Natives are disproportionately affected by violent crime and Alaska Native children are, of course, disproportionately exposed to that violence. Alaska's rates of child maltreatment, domestic violence, sexual assault, and related homicides are consistently among the highest in the country with the rates for Alaska Native children significantly higher than the statewide rates.[11] Alaska Native children face multiple traumatic or Adverse Childhood Experiences (ACEs) that contribute to risky behavior such as substance abuse, suicide, and school disengagement, all of which makes them more vulnerable to domestic violence and victimization.[12]

- Compared to the overall state population, Alaska Native women are overrepresented in the domestic violence victim population by 250 percent. In tribal villages and Native communities, women have reported rates of domestic violence up to ten times higher than in the rest of the United States and physical assault victimization rates up to 12 times higher.[13]
- Alaska Native women suffer from forcible sexual assault at the highest rate of any population in the United States. They comprise 19 percent of the Alaska state females, but 47 percent of reported rape victims.[14] An Alaska Native woman is sexually assaulted every eighteen hours.[15]
- According to the Alaska Native Tribal Health Consortium, one in two Alaska Native women will experience physical or sexual violence.[16]
- Alaska's child sexual assault rate is six times the national average, and Alaska Native children experience this trauma disproportionately to the rest of the state.[17]
- From 2004 to 2007, Alaska Natives were 2.5 times more likely to die by homicide than white Alaskans, and 2.9 times more likely to die by homicide than all whites in the United States.[18]
- Alaska Natives' representation in the Alaska prison and jail population is twice their representation in the general population (36 percent vs. 19 percent).[19] Nearly 20 percent of the Alaska Natives under supervision by the Alaska State Department of Corrections are housed out of state, nearly all at Hudson Correctional Facility in New York State—4,419 road miles from Anchorage.[20]
- In Fairbanks, the city that serves a large rural and tribal village population, Alaska Native youth who come into contact with the juvenile justice system are four times more likely than non-Natives to be referred to juvenile court and three times more likely to be sentenced to confinement.[21]

Justice System Challenges. Findings in bipartisan Bill S. 1474,[22] the *Alaska Safe Families and Villages Act of 2014*—sponsored by both Alaska senators—provide a description of law enforcement and judicial challenges (which exacerbate violence exposure):

- *S. 1474 finding (9):* "less than 1/2 of remote Alaska villages are served by trained State law enforcement entities and several Indian tribes utilize peace officers or tribal police without adequate training or equipment";
- *S. 1474 finding (10):* "the centralized State judicial system relies on general jurisdiction Superior Courts in the regional hub communities, with only a handful of staffed magistrate courts outside of the hub communities"; and
- *S. 1474 finding (11):* "the lack of effective law enforcement and accessible judicial services in remote Alaska villages contributes significantly to increased crime, alcohol abuse, drug abuse, domestic violence, rates of suicide, poor educational achievement, and lack of economic development."

Levels of Exposure to Violence. A 2009 Alaska study confirmed the high level of Alaska Native children exposed to violence:

- Native mothers of three-year-olds are eight times more likely than non-Natives to report that their children had witnessed violence or abuse, and
- Alaska Native adults are almost twice as likely as non-Natives to report that as children, they witnessed parents or guardians physically fighting. Roughly one in three saw their parents hurting each other in some way, including kicking, hitting, or shoving.[23]

Impact. Children who live in a home where domestic violence is present, where they witness domestic violence, and/or where they are the direct victim of violence face many long-term effects of trauma.[24] There is ample evidence that Alaska Native children suffer from this trauma on many levels including:

- Alaska Native children constitute only 17.3 percent of the Alaska state child population; however, Alaska Native children constitute 50.1 percent of substantiated reports of child maltreatment in the state, 51.1 percent of all children in out-of-home placements, and a staggering 62.3 percent of all children in foster care. This means that Alaska Native children are represented in foster care at a rate three times greater than the general

"In Alaska where services to Natives are limited or non-existent, sexual assault rates are much higher. The National Indian Law and Order Commission visited Alaska communities where every single woman reported she'd been raped. When a 12-year old girl was raped and murdered in one village last year, it took Alaska troopers four days to respond."

Troy A. Eid, Chairman, Indian Law and Order Commission, *The Invisible Crisis Killing Native American Youth*36

"The State of Alaska frequently seeks to ignore or interpret various provisions of the Indian Child Welfare Act in a manner that seriously limits tribal jurisdiction over matters concerning tribal children. Further, tribal courts are treated differently than tribal courts in the rest of the country. As a result, hundreds of AN children are removed from their homes and placed in urban communities in non-Native care with poor prognosis for reunification or family permanency."

Sarah Hicks Kastelic, Deputy Director, National Indian Child Welfare Association. Testimony before the Task Force on American Indian/ Alaska Native Children Exposed to Violence, Anchorage, AK, June 11, 2014

"Once children are in the system they are lost, not only to their parents, but to their extended families and communities."

Andy Teuber, President/ CEO, Kodiak Area Native Association. Testimony before the Task Force on American Indian/ Alaska Native Children Exposed to Violence, Anchorage, AK, June 11, 2014

population, and this disproportionality rate has been increasing in recent years.[25]

- Children in out-of-home placement in Alaska face abuse or neglect at a rate nearly three times higher than the national rate. Because Alaska Native children are nearly two-thirds of the children in Alaska foster care, they are also more likely to be subject to child maltreatment in foster care.[26]

- Alaska Native children constituted 39 percent of the children seen in child advocacy centers throughout Alaska in 2013.[27]

- Alaska Native students—with a 50 percent high school dropout rate[28]—are twice as likely to drop out as their non-Native peers.[29]

- Rates for nine of ten leading causes of death are higher for Alaska Natives than the general U.S. population (cancer, unintentional injury, suicide, alcohol abuse, chronic obstructive pulmonary disease, cerebrovascular disease, chronic liver disease, pneumonia, influenza, and homicide).[30]

- More than 95 percent of all crimes committed in rural Alaska can be attributed to alcohol.[31] The alcohol abuse–related mortality rate was 38.7 per one hundred thousand for Alaska Natives over the period 2004 through 2008, 16.1 times higher than the rate for the U.S. white population over the same period.[32]

- The suicide rate among Alaska Natives is almost four times the U.S. general population rate, and is at least six times the national average in some parts of the state.[33] Thirteen percent of the suicides in Alaska are child suicides. Nearly 40 percent of these child suicides are Alaska Native children.[34] The alcohol-related suicide rate in remote Alaska villages is six times the average in the United States and the alcohol-related mortality rate is 3.5 times that of the general population of the United States.[35]

- The homeless population in Anchorage, both adult and youth, are disproportionately Alaska Native. Indeed, 40 percent of the youth served by Covenant House Alaska, the state's largest youth shelter, are Alaska Native. This shelter's capacity has further been challenged in recent years by an influx of young Alaska Native sex-trafficking victims.

The Advisory Committee heard repeatedly that Alaska Tribes are ready and willing to step up to address violence in their communities and serve the children exposed to that violence. It is time for Alaska and the federal government to join in partnership to remove the current barriers that inhibit their ability to do so and to empower Alaska Tribes to protect Alaska Native children.

ADVISORY COMMITTEE VISION FOR EMPOWERING ALASKA TRIBES, REMOVING BARRIERS, AND PROVIDING RESOURCES

The Advisory Committee envisions a future where Alaska Native children are raised in a supportive community rich in Alaska Native culture; where the primacy of Alaska tribal governments is recognized and respected; and where Alaska Tribes are empowered with authority and resources to prevent Alaska Native children from being exposed to violence and have sufficient tools for Alaska Tribes to respond and heal their children.

Findings and Recommendations

5.1 The federal government should promptly implement all five recommendations in Chapter 2 (*Reforming Justice for Alaska Natives: The Time is Now*) of the Indian Law and Order Commission's 2013 Final Report, *A Roadmap for Making Native America Safer*, and assess the cost of implementation. This will remove the barriers that currently inhibit the ability of Alaska Tribes to exercise criminal jurisdiction and utilize criminal remedies when confronting the highest rates of violent crime in the country.

Numerous commissions over the last several decades have received testimony and analyzed the high incidence of family violence and lack of public safety and access to justice in rural Alaska. Unquestionably, the exposure of Alaska Native children to violence is a consequence of the lack of public safety and access to justice.[37] The Alaska Sentencing Commission, the Alaska Natives Commission, the Alaska Judicial Council, the Alaska Supreme Court's Advisory Committee on Fairness and Access, the Alaska Commission on Rural Governance and Empowerment, and the Alaska Rural Justice and Law Enforcement Commission have all looked at the issues faced by small and isolated villages. As Chief Justice Dana Fabe, Alaska Supreme Court, commented, "Consistent among their recommendations is . . . the need for greater opportunities for local community leaders and organizations to engage in justice delivery at the local level . . . for courts to effectively serve the needs of rural residents, justice cannot be something delivered in a far-off court by strangers, but something in which local people . . . can be directly and meaningfully involved."[38] The conclusion reached over and over is that these issues must be addressed at the local level, with the state working in partnership with tribes, to build local capacity to address public safety and access to justice.[39]

The Indian Law and Order Commission (ILOC) reached the same conclusions in its 2013 report *A Roadmap for Making Native America Safer* and charted a path forward in Chapter 2, "Reforming Justice for Alaska Natives: The Time Is Now." The commissioners unanimously disagreed with the position of the Alaska Attorney General that state law enforcement authority is exclusive because tribes do not have a land base on which to exercise any inherent criminal jurisdiction. The ILOC report set out five specific recommendations designed to remove the current barriers in federal law that have allowed the state of Alaska to continue to marginalize—and often ignore—the potential of tribally based justice systems.

The Advisory Committee agrees with each of the five Alaska-specific ILOC recommendations and the commission's rationale for each recommendation. Until and unless these barriers are removed, the state of Alaska will continue to assert that Alaska Tribes do not have any criminal jurisdiction and thereby continue to contend that Alaska Tribes are only empowered to utilize civil courts and civil remedies when confronting the highest rates of violent crime in the country. The Advisory Committee recommends that these five ILOC recommendations be enacted as soon as possible in order to ensure that Alaska Tribes are also empowered to exercise criminal jurisdiction and criminal remedies when confronting such incredibly high rates of violent crime.

The Advisory Committee also recommends that the Congressional Budget Office or another appropriate federal entity should assess the cost to implement the five Alaska-specific recommendations of the Indian Law and Order Commission. The Advisory Committee believes that the costs must be assessed in order for these recommendations to be realized.

It is important to note that the U.S. Senate, on August 26, 2014, reported a bipartisan bill sponsored by both Alaska senators, S. 1474 to be titled *Alaska Safe Families and Villages Act of 2014*,[40] which includes a provision that would, if enacted, address ILOC Recommendation 2.4 by repealing the Alaska exclusion in Title IX of

VAWA 2013. If this bill is not enacted in the current 2014 lame duck session, it should be reintroduced and made a priority.

Unfortunately, the current version of the bill does continue to limit the potential Alaska tribal court funding to tribes exercising *civil jurisdiction* concurrent with the state of Alaska. Until the five following ILOC recommendations are implemented, the state of Alaska will likely continue asserting that Alaska Tribes are not empowered to exercise criminal jurisdiction and utilize criminal remedies when confronting violent crime and Alaska Native children exposed to it.

5.1.A **(*Indian Law and Order Commission Recommendation 2.1*): Congress should overturn the U.S. Supreme Court's decision in *Alaska v. Native Village of Venetie Tribal Government*, by amending the Alaska Native Claims Settlement Act (ANCSA) to provide that former reservation lands acquired in fee by Alaska Tribes and other lands transferred in fee to Alaska Tribes pursuant to ANCSA are Indian country.**

The U.S. Supreme Court's decision *in Alaska v. Native Village of Venetie Tribal Government* as based on an outdated and static understanding of Alaska Native Claims Settlement Act (ANCSA). Although that statute was first enacted under the influence of Termination Policy, it has been amended and reinterpreted many times since then, moving gradually but unmistakably toward a tribal self-determination model. . . . [The Federal government] confirmed recognition of Alaska Native villages [in 1993] as federally recognized Indian nations with a government-to-government relationship with the United States. Since then federal agencies have been providing services to Alaska Native villages that clearly qualify as Indian country much as they do for tribes on reservation lands. Nothing in ANCSA expressly barred the treatment of these former reservation and other tribal fee lands as Indian country. As a consequence, the *Venetie* decision has been widely criticized for failing "to honor longstanding principles of Indian law favoring the preservation of Tribal rights and powers until Congress clearly expresses its intent to terminate those rights and powers." Congress should step forward and correct the Supreme Court's misguided interpretation of ANCSA.[41]

5.1.B (*Indian Law and Order Commission Recommendation 2.2*): Congress and the President should amend the definitions of Indian country to clarify (or affirm) that Native allotments and Native-owned town sites in Alaska are Indian country.

There is an archipelago of land—individual Indian allotments and commonly held lands within Alaska Native town sites—that ANCSA did not affect. These are geographies over which the federal government retains a trust responsibility, and they should be fully recognized as Indian country. These parcels are significant—conservative estimates place their total area somewhere between four and six million acres. If a land base is what is needed to exercise criminal jurisdiction (and other kinds of land-based jurisdiction), the change would clarify that at least some Alaska Tribes do have a land base. Furthermore, these lands are a foothold from which Indian country in Alaska can be expanded.[42]

5.1.C (*Indian Law and Order Commission Recommendation 2.3*): Congress should amend the Alaska Native Claims Settlement Act to allow a transfer of lands from Regional Corporations to Tribal governments; to allow transferred lands to be put into trust and included within the definition of Indian country in the Federal criminal code; to allow Alaska Tribes to put tribally owned fee simple land similarly into trust; and to channel more resources directly to Alaska Native Tribal governments for the provision of governmental services in those communities.

To assert substantial land-based jurisdiction, Alaska Tribes need more land, with a focus on restoring and consolidating tribal authority within Native villages and town sites. Transfers of regional corporation land back to tribes and conversion of this land to trust status makes that possible. Tribes also should have the option of converting any land held in fee simple to trust status to further enlarge the reach of territorial jurisdiction.[43]

5.1.D (*Indian Law and Order Commission Recommendation 2.4*): Congress should repeal Section 910 of Title IX of the Violence Against Women Reauthorization Act of

2013 (VAWA Amendments), and thereby permit Alaska Native communities and their courts to address domestic violence and sexual assault committed by Tribal members and non-Natives, just as in the lower 48.

The special rule applying Title IX of the VAWA Amendments to only one Native community in Alaska is inimical to providing effective public safety in Alaska. A simple fix is the removal of the one section relating to Alaska, which puts Alaska Native communities on par with Native communities. Allowing tribal courts to issue protective orders, enforce them, and provide the local, immediate deterrence effect of these judicial actions may be the single-most effective tool in fighting domestic violence and sexual assault in Native communities in Alaska.[44]

5.1.E *(Indian Law and Order Commission Recommendation 2.5)*: Congress should affirm the inherent criminal jurisdiction of Alaska Native Tribal governments over their members within the external boundaries of their villages.

PL-280 does not fit well in Alaska, predicated as it was on the presence of Indian country as defined by the federal criminal code. The changes wrought by ANCSA effectively diminished any real meaning for PL-280 in Alaska, yet it is the law that the state relies on to hold that Alaska Tribes cannot exercise concurrent criminal law jurisdiction over their own members, frustrating the development of local-level criminal justice institutions. Regardless of what lands tribes own or whether they are considered Indian country, this recommendation offers an opportunity to use new tools to respond to the public safety crisis in Alaska Native communities. These changes authorize tribes to locally and immediately attend to violence and criminal activity. They make it easier to create state-tribal memorandums of understanding for law enforcement deputization and cross-deputization, cooperate in prosecution and sentencing, and apply criminal justice resources for optimal, mutual benefit. Such reforms also facilitate the ability of Alaska Tribes and Nations to work together for mutual benefit, such as creating intertribal courts and institutions. Of course, to make the most of this federal affirmation, tribes should take action to clarify and, as necessary, formalize tribal law for governing their recognized territories, especially law that relates to public safety.[45]

5.2   The Department of Justice (DOJ) and the Department of Interior (DOI) should provide recurring base funding for Alaska Tribes to develop and sustain both civil and criminal tribal court systems, assist in the provision of law enforcement and related services, and assist with intergovernmental agreements.

5.2.A   As a first step, the DOJ and the DOI should—within one year—conduct a current inventory and a needs/cost assessment of law enforcement, court, and related services for every Alaska Tribe.

5.2.B   The DOJ and the DOI should provide the funding necessary to address the unmet need identified, and ensure that each Alaska Tribe has the annual base funding level necessary to provide and sustain an adequate level of law enforcement, tribal court, and related funding and services.

5.2.C   Congress should enact legislation along the lines of the current bipartisan bill sponsored by both Alaska senators (S. 1474 to be titled Alaska Safe Families and Villages Act of 2014) that supports the development, enhancement, and sustainability of Alaska tribal courts including full faith and credit for Alaska tribal court acts and decrees and the establishment of specific Alaska tribal court base funding streams and grants to Alaska Tribes carrying out intergovernmental agreements with the state of Alaska.

5.2.D   The federal government should work together with Alaska Tribes and the state of Alaska to improve coordination and collaboration on a broad range of public safety measures that cause Alaska Native children to be exposed to high rates of violence.

The development, enhancement, and sustainment of Alaska tribal courts, and truly cooperative relationships between the state of Alaska and Alaska Tribes, are absolutely essential in reducing violent crime and protecting Alaska Native children from violence and exposure to violence. Village-based tribal courts are the culturally appropriate provider. Alaska tribal courts must be developed, enhanced, and sustained in order to effectively address issues concerning Alaska Native children exposed to violence.

In 2013, the Indian Law and Order Commission made the following findings and conclusions concerning Alaska tribal courts:

- Each of the four judicial districts in the Alaska court system serves rural Alaska, but the district courts frequently delegate responsibility to magistrates to serve low population, remote communities. Magistrates serving rural circuits visit individual communities regularly, but infrequently. Yet, often they are the sole face of the state court in Native villages.
- By federal law, Alaska Tribes may establish tribal courts. As of 2012, seventy-eight tribes in Alaska had done so; seventeen more tribes were in the process of court development. However, funding constraints and narrow jurisdiction limit Alaska tribal courts' efforts. Not all Alaska tribal courts are full-time or even operated with paid staff. These courts typically address only child welfare cases, customary adoptions, public drunkenness, disorderly conduct, and minor juvenile offenses.[47]

The *Alaska Safe Families and Villages Act of 2014* sets out the basic need for recurring base funding for Alaska Tribes to develop and sustain tribal courts. It reiterates many of the findings of the Indian Law and Order Commission, including the barriers that the centralized state judicial system imposes, as well as the lack of effective law enforcement. In addition, it found:

- *S. 1474 finding (12):* "Indian tribes that operate within remote Alaska villages should be supported in carrying out local culturally relevant solutions to effectively provide law enforcement in villages and access to swift judicial proceedings"; and
- *S. 1474 finding (13):* "increasing capacities of local law enforcement entities to enforce local tribal laws and to achieve increased tribal involvement in State law enforcement in remote villages will promote a stronger link between the State and village residents, encourage community involvement, and create greater local accountability with respect to violence and substance abuse."[48]

In addition, if enacted, S. 1474, *Alaska Safe Families and Villages Act of 2014* would establish two new Department of Justice (DOJ) grant programs: one intended to facilitate intergovernmental agreements with the state,[49] and one intended to help Alaska Tribes carry out court functions.[50]

There is a dire need for recurring base funding for all tribal courts (see recommendation 1.4), but the needs of Alaska Tribes are most acute and the current available funding is wholly inadequate:

"The single best and most effective thing Congress could do to address the serious social ills in rural Alaska is to simply confirm that our tribal governments and tribal courts have the authority to regulate and address social problems at home."

Hon. Ralph Anderson, President/CEO, Bristol Bay Native Association
Hearing on S. 1474, S. 1570, S. 1574, S. 1622, & S. 2160 before the Senate Commission on Indian Affairs
113th Congress, Second Session

- Village subsistence economies do not lend themselves to traditional means of government revenue, such as tax, limiting Alaska Natives' ability to self-fund tribal justice systems.
- BIA has historically not provided tribal justice system funding for Alaska Tribes under 638 compacts and contracts[51] (in keeping with the BIA policy of not providing tribal law enforcement and tribal court funding for PL-280 tribes or similar legislation).
- Consequently, the only current federal funding source for Alaska justice systems is the DOJ's Consolidated Tribal Assistance Solicitation (CTAS).[52] However, although they constitute 40 percent of all federally recognized tribes, Alaska Tribes have received an average of less than 9 percent of the limited CTAS funding available (see CTAS funding chart in Chapter 1). In FY 2014, the only Alaska funding under the CTAS purpose area that most directly funds tribal courts were two grant awards to Alaska organizations for a grand total of $1.4 million.[53]
- If enacted and actually funded, S. 1474 would provide only an additional $4 million per year for Alaska Tribes according to the official Congressional Budget Office estimate.[54]

The Advisory Committee recommends that the DOJ and the DOI should—within one year—conduct a current inventory and a needs/cost assessment of every Alaska Tribe to determine: (1) current level of law enforcement, tribal court, and related funding and services (such as village-based alcohol/drug abuse treatment services and village-based shelters and safe houses) available for each Alaska Tribe; (2) annual base funding level necessary for each Alaska Tribe to provide and sustain the necessary level of law enforcement, tribal court, and related funding and services; and (3) unmet need (difference between current level and base funding level needed). The White House Native American Affairs Office (see Recommendation 1.2) should coordinate this inventory along with the other activities under this recommendation.

While an additional $4 million per year under S. 1474 would be a welcome start, much more is needed. The full unmet need will not be clear until and unless the inventory and needs/cost assessment recommended in this report are completed.

Furthermore, the federal government should work together with Alaska Tribes and the state of Alaska to improve coordination and collaboration on a broad range of public safety measures that cause Alaska Native children to be exposed to high rates of violence. For example, the federal government should make grants available to Alaska Tribes to enter into and carry out intergovernmental agreements with the state of Alaska in order to provide more local tools and options to solve village public safety problems and assist with the negotiation and implementation of those intergovernmental agreements.

5.3 **The state of Alaska should prioritize law enforcement responses and related resources for Alaska Tribes, and recognize and collaborate with Alaska tribal courts.**

5.3.A **The state of Alaska should prioritize the state law enforcement response and resources for Alaska Tribes. At a minimum, there must be at least one law enforcement official onsite in each village.**

5.3.B **The state of Alaska should prioritize the provision of needed village-based services including village-based women's shelters (which allow for children to stay with their mothers), child advocacy centers, and alcohol and drug treatment services.**

5.3.C **The state of Alaska should recognize and collaborate with Alaska tribal courts including following existing federal laws designed to protect Alaska Native children and families such as VAWA protection order authority, which requires states to recognize and enforce tribal protection orders that have been issued by tribal courts–including Alaska Native tribal courts–without first requiring a state court certification of the tribal protection order.**

5.3.D **The state of Alaska should enter into self-governance intergovernmental agreements with Alaska Tribes in order to provide more local tools and options to combat village public safety issues and address issues concerning Alaska Native children exposed to violence.**

The Senate Report of S. 1474, the *Alaska Safe Families and Villages Act of 2014* found:

- Many Indian tribes and Alaska Tribes face significant public safety challenges and struggle to combat staggering rates of violent crime with inadequate resources and technology.

"Tribal courts bring not only local knowledge, cultural sensitivity, and expertise to the table, but also are a valuable resource, experience, and a have a high level of local trust. They exist in at least half the villages of our State and stand ready, willing, and able to take part in local justice delivery."
Chief Justice Dana Fabe, Alaska Supreme Court.
A Message to the First Session of the Twenty-Eighth Alaskan Legislature,
February 13, 2013

"To end the perpetrator-victim cycle we need a justice system which understands our history and has the authority to protect tribal members and deter harmful activity. That system is the tribal system."
Hon. Natasha Singh, Tribal Court Judge, Stevens Village Hearing on S. 1474, S. 1570, S. 1574, S. 1622, and S. 2160 before the Senate Commission on Indian Affairs,
113th Congress, Second Session

- Only a handful of tribes in Alaska have any law enforcement presence.
- Approximately 370 State Troopers have primary responsibility for law enforcement in rural Alaska, but have a full-time presence in less than half of the remote Alaska Native villages. Seventy-five villages lack any law enforcement at all.[55]

The 2013 ILOC report included relevant findings and conclusions concerning the very limited law enforcement available for Alaska Native Villages including:

- Alaska Department of Public Safety (ADPS) officers have primary responsibility for law enforcement in rural Alaska, but ADPS provides for only 1.0 to 1.4 field officers per million acres. Since ADPS's 370 officers cannot serve on a 24/7 basis, the actual ratio of officers to territory is much lower. According to ADPS, troopers' efforts "are often hampered by delayed notification, long response distance, and the uncertainties of weather and transportation."
- Funding is available for just more than one hundred Village Public Safety Officers (VPSOs), although only eighty-eight positions serving seventy-four communities were filled in 2011. Local Alaska Native Corporations hire VPSOs and villages have input into their selection; but, the officers actually work under Alaska State Trooper oversight. VPSO presence helps improve the coverage ratio, but technically its role is restricted to basic law enforcement and emergency first response. They do not carry firearms, although most offenders in rural villages do, a fact tragically emphasized through the death of VPSO Thomas Madole in March 2013.
- One hundred and four more officers serve fifty-two communities as village or tribal police officers, and both the Bristol Bay and North Slope Boroughs have borough-wide police departments. These officers do carry firearms, but the positions exist only in those communities with the economic resources to support them.
- The Emmonak Women's Shelter, which closed for several weeks in 2012 for lack of resources, is "one of two facilities dedicated to domestic violence protection in the State. It is also the only facility located in a Native American community." It is located "in a region in which there are few police officers, no transitional housing for women, and limited options for women seeking to escape."[56]

- Alaska funds only sixteen juvenile probation offices across all of Alaska; on average, each office's service area is the size of Tennessee.
- Of the seventy-six substance abuse treatment and/or mental health treatment centers in the state, most are in southern and southeastern Alaska, with approximately one-third in Anchorage alone; for residents of southwestern, central, and northern Alaska, help is typically provided a very long way from home.[57]

As indicated in Recommendation 5.3C (in the preceding text), the state of Alaska should recognize and collaborate with Alaska tribal courts. There have been many positive developments in recent years including Alaska Supreme Court decisions that have been increasingly supportive of Alaska tribal courts,[58] initial efforts by the state of Alaska to reach out and collaborate with Alaska tribal courts,[59] the bipartisan efforts of the Alaska senators in cosponsoring S. 1474, and increasingly supportive statements by various Alaska state officials. Much more needs to be done, however.

The state of Alaska's policy of requiring that tribal protection orders must be first "registered" or "filed" in state court before the protection order will be enforced by Alaska law enforcement authorities provides a very powerful illustration of the challenges that still remain. As Associate Attorney General Tony West explained in his July 28, 2014 response letter to Alaska Attorney General Michael Geraghty's June 26, 2014 letter:

> I wanted to follow up on one specific, but important, point that you made during our conversation. You explained that, although Alaska State Troopers do enforce domestic-violence protection orders issued by Tribal Courts, those orders must first be "registered" or "filed" in State court. You also stated that, occasionally, if confronted with an emergency or a person in imminent danger, the Troopers will enforce a Tribal-court protection order without the formality of State-court registration or filing. But if the victim has not already formally filed her Tribal-court protection order in a State court, the Troopers ordinarily will neither formally recognize the order nor enforce it by making an arrest. These statements were consistent with views that you had expressed in a letter dated December 3, 2013, which is posted on your Web site at: http://www.law.state.ak.us/press/release/2013/120613-TroyEid.html. As I mentioned during our meeting, however, that position, as you have articulated it, is inconsistent with Federal law, which requires enforcement of a Tribal-court protection orders *regardless* of whether those orders previously were registered or filed in State

"The fastest way to get law enforcement here is to shoot a moose."
Liz Medicine Crow
Quoted by Sari Horwitz
"In remote villages, little protection for Alaska Natives," *Washington Post,*
August 2, 2014

"It can mean leaving the community is an impossibility because the cost of sporadically available transportation in communities where roads don't exist can be prohibitive. Alaska can be a harsh place and weather can prevent travel for days and sometimes weeks."
Andy Teuber, President/CEO, Kodiak Area Native Association.
Testimony before the Task Force on American Indian/Alaska Native Children Exposed to Violence, Anchorage, AK, June 11, 2014

court. *See* 18 U.S.C. § 2265(d)(2). Indeed, so long as a protection order meets the other requirements of Section 2265 of the Federal Criminal Code, prior registration or filing in the state jurisdiction is not a prerequisite for state enforcement.

While Alaska statutes provide that protective orders that are filed with the clerk of the court are state enforceable, Alaska law is silent about the enforceability of Tribal-court protection orders not filed or registered in the state. Yet Federal law expressly addresses this scenario, as noted above.[60]

Unfortunately, Alaska Attorney General Michael Geraghty has not yet responded to Tony West's July 28, 2014 letter and there is no indication on the Alaska state websites that this policy has been changed to comply with federal law. Consequently, Alaska Native women and children continue to risk increased exposure to violence on a daily basis as a direct result of this misguided state of Alaska policy.

5.4 The Administration for Children and Families (ACF) in the Department of Health and Human Services (HHS) and the State of Alaska Office of Children's Services (OCS) should jointly respond to the extreme disproportionality of Alaska Native children in foster care by establishing a time-limited, outcome-focused task force to develop real-time, Native inclusive strategies to reduce disproportionality.

Alaska Native children constitute 17.3 percent of the state child population; however, Alaska Native children comprise *62.3 percent* of all children in out-of-home placements.[61] Virtually all of these children have been exposed to violence. Many of them have been direct victims of that violence. In 2012 Alaska Native children were 50.1 percent of substantiated reports of children physically abused, sexually abused, and neglected. In 2014 Alaska Native children were 50.5 percent of alleged reports of child maltreatment. Yet they were 56.5 percent of substantiated reports of child maltreatment.

Issues of foster care disproportionality are huge problems for many tribes. Inadequate numbers of Native foster families to assure compliance with ICWA impacts most state child welfare agencies as well. But this problem takes on added dimensions and particular significance in Alaska—not only due to the high rate of removals of Alaska Native children and the fact that the rate has been increasing at an alarming rate—but also due to many other factors including the remoteness of Alaska Native villages, Alaska's vast size, the exorbitant cost of transportation, the financial limitations of subsistence economy, the lack of village-based foster care options, the lack of village-based services and resources, the lack of tribal courts, and the historic refusal of the state of Alaska to collaborate with Alaska Tribes—or until recently to recognize that Alaska Tribes even exist.

In every state, to assure the safety, permanence, and well-being of children who are represented in state child welfare systems, the ACF is responsible for the oversight of state Child and Family Services Plans through periodic reviews of state child welfare systems. The Child and Family Services Reviews (CFSRs) are conducted by the Children's Bureau, within the HHS, to help states improve safety, permanency, and well-being outcomes for children and families who receive services through the child welfare system. The CFSRs monitor states' conformity with the requirements of Title IV-B and Title IV-E of the Social Security Act.

After a CFSR is completed, states develop a Program Improvement Plan (PIP) to address areas in their child welfare services that need improvement. Significant financial penalties may be assessed for failure to make the improvements needed to achieve substantial conformity.

The state of Alaska, Office of Children's Services has administrative responsibility for development and implementation of the Child and Family Services Plan, including all policies and procedures relating to child protection services in Alaska (2014 Annual Progress and Services Report, State of Alaska, Office of Children's Services).

The most recent 2014 Annual Progress and Services Report has found that the number of Alaska Native children in care has *increased* since last year, and the percent of children in out of ICWA preference placement has also *increased* from 23 percent last year to 29 percent this year.

Recent data shows that things are getting worse. The 2012 data shows that Native children were represented in foster care at 2.4 times their rate in the general population. In 2011, Alaska Native children made up 51.1 percent of all children in out-of-home placements in the state, a disproportionality rate of 2.9. In April 2014, Alaska Native children were 1,319 of the 2,106 children in out-of-home placements. This is 62.3 percent of the foster care population. The disproportionality rate for Alaska Native kids in Alaska has

"Clients with substance use treatment needs are required to leave their homes, leave their communities, leave their families to receive treatment outside, with very different cultural programming. This out of context approach to treatment without family and community support has been found to be greatly unsuccessful."
Mary David, Executive VP, Kawerak.
Testimony before the Task Force on American Indian/ Alaska Native Children Exposed to Violence, Anchorage, AK, June 11, 2014

"This culturally inappropriate intervention [removal] is extremely traumatic for children and families, and should be the last line of defense, after all other attempts have been made to strengthen the family so that a child can remain in his or her own home. However, this is not yet the practice in many state systems, and specifically the Alaska state system, for a variety of reasons, including current federal funding mechanisms. Added to this equation is the legacy of removal that Native peoples, and specifically children, have faced. The historic trauma that systematic removal has generated in Native societies makes each removal of a Native child from her home, family and community a unique form of violence."

Sarah Hicks Kastelic, Deputy Director, National Indian Child Welfare Association. Testimony before the Task Force on American Indian/ Alaska Native Children Exposed to Violence, Anchorage, AK, June 11, 2014

risen in recent years, as the percentage of Alaska Native children in foster care has increased by more than 10 percent in those years.[62]

National data indicates that at key decision points in the process of responding to reports of child maltreatment, AI/AN cases are much more likely to have the alleged abuse or neglect substantiated and to result in the child's removal from their families and placement in foster care.[63]

Efforts to address disproportionality as well as efforts to respond to child protection, family preservation and support, kinship care, foster care recruitment, and retention are outlined in all state Child and Family Services Plans, yet Alaska appears to be making little or no progress according to recent annual reports. The situation warrants an immediate, aggressive approach to address the growing number of Native children in care as well as the diminishing number of Alaska Native resource families. Federal and state governments must be held accountable for compliance with requirements of the federal Social Security Act, which are designed to support and protect children and families.

Besides Alaska, a number of states are impacted by high disproportionality rates of Native children in foster care, and most state child welfare systems do not have an adequate number of Native resource families to assure compliance with ICWA. Because *all* states are mandated to conform to the provisions of Title IV-B and Title IV-E of the Social Security Act, federal and state child welfare systems must assure that the needs of Native children in foster care are met according to federal law.

In addition, other factors that impact how Native children and families are affected by disproportionate placement include:

ICWA Compliance. When ICWA was enacted in 1978, it was intended to address identified abuses, reduce the number of out-of-home placements of AI/AN children, and provide protections to Indian families and children in both involuntary and voluntary proceedings. Although ICWA has resulted in some progress, recent analyses of national child welfare data indicate that the number of out-of-home placements of Indian children is still disproportionate to the percentage of Indian youth in the general population and that Indian children continue to be regularly placed in non-Indian homes, an indication of the continuing need for congressional intervention in this area.[64]

Increase In-Community Placements. Nationwide, the ability to place Native children within their communities is limited when no foster homes are available. But when Alaska Native children are removed from their family due to neglect or abuse, the lack of a sufficient number of licensed foster families within remote Native villages often results in the child being placed far from home in non-Native foster homes. The distance and expense of promoting family visitation often negatively impacts family reunification.

Placement within a child's own community, if safety can be assured, is generally the optimal arrangement to maintain cultural and family connections, sibling connections, and educational connections. If possible, placement with kin is the ideal placement and the first placement preference of ICWA.

Kin families can be supported in caring for relative children; however they (1) either have to be licensed (which is challenging for many Native families) and they can be paid a foster parent subsidy; or (2) they can remain unlicensed and apply for TANF-type payments[65], which are less than foster care payments. This is a fairly typical process for AI/AN families in most states.

Foster care payments are generally the better choice (generally using Title IV-E federal funds) because the foster care payments are higher than TANF child-only grants. However, licensing requirements nationwide mandate that families go through background checks, home safety checks, and other requirements. Unfortunately, some background issues prevent families from being licensed.

When no relatives are available to take in a child in an unlicensed (TANF paid) situation, the child will be sent elsewhere to be placed in a licensed (most likely, non-Native) home, generally out of the community. The system for licensing Native families in Native communities needs to be reexamined with an eye toward placing more Alaska Native children in their own communities. With the extreme disproportionality of Alaska Natives in foster care, the lack of Native resource families, and the failure of the state of Alaska Office of Children's Services to meet the federal requirements of its Child and Family Services Plan to recruit foster families who match the children in their care, ACF/HHS/CB[66] should provide tribal-specific funding resources for Alaska Native communities to develop culturally appropriate foster home recruitment and licensing services.

"Alaska Natives fear to call for help. They fear that instead of receiving genuine assistance, they might lose their children to the state welfare system that too often does not comply with the Indian Child Welfare Act. Federal and state agencies try to help but the conditions they place on assistance can be so onerous as to make it practically unworkable if not unavailable altogether. In other places people seek equal protection of the law. In many Alaska Native communities there is no protection of the law."

Andy Teuber, President/ CEO, Kodiak Area Native Association. Testimony before the Task Force on American Indian/ Alaska Native Children Exposed to Violence, Anchorage, AK, June 11, 2014

5.5 The Department of the Interior (DOI) and the State of Alaska should empower Alaska Tribes to manage their own subsistence hunting and fishing rights, remove the current barriers, and provide Alaska Tribes with the resources needed to effectively manage their own subsistence hunting and fishing.

The Advisory Committee heard many witnesses describe how regulations that limit the ability of Alaska Natives to conduct traditional subsistence hunting and fishing are directly connected to violence in Alaska Native villages and the exposure of Alaska Native children to that violence. Witnesses explained that violence is essentially nonexistent during the times in which the communities are engaging in traditional subsistence hunting and fishing activities, whereas violence spikes during times when Alaska Natives are unable to provide for their families. The Advisory Committee heard many witnesses explain that one of the most effective ways to reduce the high levels of violence in Alaska Native communities would be to empower Alaska Tribes to manage their own subsistence hunting and fishing. The need for tribes to control their own traditional hunting and fishing regulations is an important issue for all tribes, but it has particular significance for Alaska Tribes because subsistence hunting, fishing, and gathering are not only a part of everyday life for Alaska Natives, but for many Alaska Natives it is literally the subsistence on which their families survive.

Beyond providing basic food, subsistence fishing and hunting has been essential to Alaska Native families' way of life for generations. Like language and cultural traditions, it has been passed down from one generation to the next and is an important means of reinforcing tribal values and traditions and binding families together in common spirit and activity. Interfering with these traditions erodes culture, family, a sense of purpose and ability to provide for one's own, and a sense of pride. According to a significant number of Alaska Native village residents who participated in Listening Sessions with the Advisory Committee, such interference can breed alienation, frustration, anger, and family violence.

Notes

1. Tribal Law and Order Act of 2010, PL-111-211, tit. II Sec. 205.

2. Violence Against Women Reauthorization Act of 2013, PL-113-4, tit. IX Sec. 910. VAWA afforded tribes much needed added protections, including the criminal authority to prosecute non-Indian perpetrators for domestic violence, dating violence, and the violation of protection orders, and clarified the civil authority of tribes to issue protection orders against non-Indians. *See* Sec. 904 and 905. However, Sec. 910 prohibited all Alaska Tribes, except the Metlakatla Indian Community, from enjoying these added protections, despite experiencing some of the worst and most prevalent cases of domestic violence in all of Indian country.

3. The Native peoples of Alaska are commonly referred to as "Alaska Natives," and "Alaska Native Villages." For the purposes of this report, we will use the term "Alaska Tribe" to refer to federally recognized tribes in the State of Alaska. 79 Fed. Reg. 4,748 (Jan. 29, 2014), *available at* http://www.gpc.gov/fdsys/pkg/FR-2014-01-29/pdf/2014-01683.pdf.

4. The Indian Law and Order Commission, *A Roadmap for Making Native America Safer: Report to the President and Congress of the United States* (November 2013): vi, available at: http://www.aisc.ucla.edu/iloc/report/index.html.

5. Bureau of Indian Affairs, Interior, *Indian Entities Recognized and Eligible to Receive Services from the United States Bureau of Indian Affairs*, available at: http://www.indianaffairs.gov/cs/groups/public/documents/text/idc006989.pdf.

6. The Indian Law and Order Commission, *A Roadmap for Making Native America Safer: Report to the President and Congress of the United States* (November 2013): vi, available at: http://www.aisc.ucla.edu/iloc/report/index.html.

7. Written Testimony of Andy Teuber, Hearing of the Task Force on American Indian/Alaska Native Children Exposed to Violence, Anchorage, AK, June 11, 2014 at 2, available at: http://agtask-force.org/alaska/testimony/AndyTeuber.pdf.

8. The Indian Law and Order Commission, *A Roadmap for Making Native America Safer: Report to the President and Congress of the United States* (November 2013): vi, available at: http://www.aisc.ucla.edu/iloc/report/index.html (citing estimates calculated from data on the webpage "Demographic and Geographic Sketches of Alaska Natives," Alaska Natives Commission, accessed September 6, 2013, http://www.alaskool.org/resources/anc/anc07.htm).

9. The Indian Law and Order Commission, *A Roadmap for Making Native America Safer: Report to the President and Congress of the United States* (November 2013): vi, available at: http://www.aisc.ucla.edu/iloc/report/index.html (citing Alaska Federation of Natives, Alaska Day 2012, Renewable Energy Solutions for Rural Alaska: Alaska Energy Brief, May 2012, 4, accessed September 6, 2013, http://www.nativefederation.org/wp-content/uploads/2012/10/2012-afn-cap-alaska-day-brief.pdf).

10. For a description of Alaska's unique corporation model as created by the Alaska Native Claims Settlement Act of 1971, see Case, David S., and Voluck, David A., *Alaska Natives and American Laws*, Alaska: University of Alaska Press, 2012.

11. Testimony of Andy Teuber, Hearing of the Task Force on American Indian/Alaska Native Children Exposed to Violence, Anchorage, AK, June 11, 2014 at 7–8, available at: http://www.justice.gov/defendingchildhood/4th-hearing/AlaskaPanel1.pdf.

12. Testimony of Gloria O'Neill, Hearing of the Task Force on American Indian/Alaska Native Children Exposed to Violence, Anchorage, AK, June 11, 2014 at 3, available at: http://www.justice.gov/defendingchildhood/4th-hearing/AlaskaPanel1.pdf.

13. Wood, Darryl S., and Magen, Randy H., *Intimate Partner Violence Against Athabaskan Women Residing in Interior Alaska: Results of a Victimization Survey*, available at: http://justice.uaa.alaska.edu/research/2000/0026.aknativewomen/0026.02.ahtna.pdf.

14. Rivera, M., Rosay, A. B., Wood, D. S., Postle, G., and TePas, K., *Descriptive Analysis of Assaults in Domestic Violence Incidents Reported to Alaska State Troopers*, 2004 at 7, Justice Center, University of Alaska at Anchorage, JC 0601.04 (2008).

15. 3rd Finding of S. 1474, 113th Cong. 2d Sess. (2014).

16. 4th Finding of S. 1474, 113th Cong. 2d Sess. (2014).

17. Testimony of Gloria O'Neill, Hearing of the Task Force on American Indian/Alaska Native Children Exposed to Violence, Anchorage, AK, June 11, 2014 at 3, available at: http://www.justice.gov/defendingchildhood/4th-hearing/AlaskaPanel1.pdf.

18. Hagan, Kyla, and Provost, Ellen, *Alaska Native Health Status Report*, available at: http://www.anthc.org/chs/epicenter/upload/ANHSR.pdf

19. State of Alaska, *2011 Census Demographic Profile,* available at: http://labor.alaska.gov/research; State of Alaska Department of Corrections, *2011 Offender Profile,* available at: http://www.correct. state.ak.us/admin/docs/2011Profile06.pdf.

20. Indian Law and Order Commission, *A Roadmap for Making Native America Safer: Report to the President and Congress of the United States* (November 2013): 41, available at: http://www.aisc.ucla.edu/ iloc/report/index.html.

21. Leiber, Michael J., Johnson, Joseph, and Fox, Kristan, *An Examination of the Factors that Influence Justice Decision Making in Anchorage and Fairbanks, Alaska: An Assessment Study,* available at: http://dhss. alaska.gov/djj/Documents/ReportsAndPublications/DMC/06AssessmentStudy.pdf

22. S. 1474, 113th Cong. 2d Sess. (2014), Sec. 2(A)(9)-(11).

23. Kemberling, M. M., and Avellaneda-Cruz, L. D., *Healthy Native Families: Preventing Violence at All Ages,* available at: http://www.anthctoday.org/epicenter/publications/alaskanativefamilies/ dvsaBulletin_1st_ed_final.pdf.

24. Testimony of Sarah Hicks Kastelic, Hearing of the Task Force on American Indian/Alaska Native Children Exposed to Violence, Anchorage, AK, June 11, 2014 at 25, available at: http://www. justice.gov/defendingchildhood/4th-hearing/hearing4-briefing-binder.pdf.

25. Ibid., 22–25.

26. Ibid., 25.

27. Testimony of Elsie Boudreau, Hearing of the Task Force on American Indian/Alaska Native Children Exposed to Violence, Anchorage, AK, June 11, 2014 at 145, available at: http://www.justice. gov/defendingchildhood/4th-hearing/hearing4-briefing-binder.pdf.

28. *Hearing on S. 1474, S. 1570, S. 1574, S. 1622, and S. 2160 Before the S. Comm. on Indian Affairs,* 113th Cong. 2d Sess. 7 (2014) (statement of Hon. Byron L. Dorgan, U.S. Senator [Retired] from North Dakota; Founder/Chairman, Center for Native American Youth, Aspen Institute).

29. *Hearing on S. 1474, S. 1570, S. 1574, S. 1622, and S. 2160 Before the S. Comm. on Indian Affairs,* 113th Cong. 2d Sess. 66 (2014) (prepared statement of Gloria O'Neill, CEO/President, Cook Inlet Tribal Council).

30. Testimony of Cathy Baldwin-Johnson, Hearing of the Task Force on American Indian/Alaska Native Children Exposed to Violence, Anchorage, AK, June 11, 2014 at 173, available at: http://www. justice.gov/defendingchildhood/4th-hearing/hearing4-briefing-binder.pdf (citing Day, G., Holck, P., and Provost, E., *Alaska Native Mortality Update: 2004–2008,* available at: http://www.anthctoday.org/ epicenter/publications/mortality/AlaskaNativeMortalityUpdate2004_2008_17_jan_2012.pdf).

31. Alaska Rural Justice and Law Enforcement Commission, *Initial Report and Recommendations* (2006) available at: http://www.law.state.ak.us/pdf/press/040606-ARJLEC-report.pdf

32. Day, Gretchen, Holck, Peter, and Provost, Ellen M., *Alaska Native Mortality Update: 2004–2008,* Alaska Native Epidemiology Center (2011) at 15, available at: http://www.anthctoday.org/epicenter/ publications/mortality/AlaskaNativeMortalityUpdate2004_2008_17_jan_2012.pdf.

33. Centers for Disease Control and Prevention, National Center for Injury Prevention and Control, Web-based Injury Statistics Query and Reporting System (WISQARS), 2004–2008 United States Suicide Injury Deaths and Rates per 100,000, accessed March 4, 2013; and Day, Gretchen, Holck, Peter, and Provost, Ellen M., *Alaska Native Mortality Update: 2004–2008,* Alaska Native Epidemiology Center (2011) at 4, http://www.anthctoday. org/epicenter/publications/mortality/ AlaskaNativeMortalityUpdate2004_2008_17_jan_2012.pdf.

34. Testimony of Cathy Baldwin-Johnson, Hearing of the Task Force on American Indian/Alaska Native Children Exposed to Violence, Anchorage, AK, June 12, 2014 at 22, available at: http://www. justice.gov/defendingchildhood/4th-hearing/AlaskaPanel5.pdf.

35. 2nd Finding of S. 1474, 113th Cong. 2d Sess. (2014).

36. Eid, Troy A., *The Invisible Crisis Killing Native American Youth,* available at: http://www.denverpost.com/opinion/ci_25030443/invisible-crisis-killing-native-american-youth.

37. Testimony of Mary David, Hearing of the Task Force on American Indian/Alaska Native Children Exposed to Violence, Anchorage, AK, June 11, 2014 at 190, available at: http://www.justice.gov/ defendingchildhood/4th-hearing/hearing4-briefing-binder.pdf.

38. Chief Justice Dana Fabe, Alaska Supreme Court, "A Message to the First Session of the Twenty-Eighth Alaskan Legislature," February 13, 2013.

39. Testimony of Mary David, Hearing of the Task Force on American Indian/Alaska Native Children Exposed to Violence, Anchorage, AK, June 11, 2014 at 190, available at: http://www.justice.gov/ defendingchildhood/4th-hearing/hearing4-briefing-binder.pdf.

40. S. 1474, 113th Cong. 2d Sess. (2014).

41. Indian Law & Order Commission, *A Roadmap for Making Native America Safer: Report to the President & Congress of the United States* (November 2013): 51–2, available at: http://www.aisc.ucla.edu/iloc/report/index.html.

42. Ibid., 52.

43. Ibid.

44. Ibid., 55.

45. Ibid.

46. Ibid., 149.

47. Ibid., 39.

48. S. 1474, 113th Cong. 2d Sess. (2014).

49. S. Rep. No. 113-260, at 3 (2014), *to accompany* S. 1474, 113th Cong. 2d Sess. (2014).

50. S. Rep. No. 113-260, at 4 (2014), *to accompany* S. 1474, 113th Cong. 2d Sess. (2014).

51. In theory, this could change if this provision in S. 1474 is enacted "Participating Indian tribes shall be eligible for the same tribal court and law enforcement programs and level of funding from the Bureau of Indian Affairs as are available to other Indian tribes."

52. U.S. Department of Justice, "Coordinated Tribal Assistance Solicitation—FY 2014 Combined Award List," available at: http://www.justice.gov/sites/default/files/pages/attachments/2014/09/23/fy14-ctas-award-list.pdf.

53. Ibid.

54. S. Rep. No. 113-260, at 2 (2014), *to accompany* S. 1474, 113th Cong. 2d Sess. (2014), available at: http://www.gpo.gov/fdsys/pkg/CRPT-113srpt260/html/CRPT-113srpt260.htm.

55. Ibid.

56. Indian Law and Order Commission, *A Roadmap for Making Native America Safer: Report to the President and Congress of the United States* (November 2013): 41, available at: http://www.aisc.ucla.edu/iloc/report/index.html (citing Cheryl Cedar Face, Emmonak Women's Shelter Receives Emergency Funds, American Indian Report, July 6, 2012, http://www.americanindianreport.com/wordpress/2012/07/emmonak-womens-shelter-receives-emergency-funds/).

57. Indian Law and Order Commission, *A Roadmap for Making Native America Safer: Report to the President and Congress of the United States* (November 2013): 39–41, available at: http://www.aisc.ucla.edu/iloc/report/index.html.

58. See for example *Simmonds v. Parks*, 329 P.3d 995 (July 18, 2014) (Alaska Supreme Court finds that the tribal court's order to terminate parental rights is entitled to full faith and credit by the State of Alaska because the appellant failed to exhaust their tribal court remedies before collaterally attacking the trial decision in state court); also see *Alaska v. Native Village of Tanana*, 249 P.3d 734 (2011) (Alaska Supreme Court recognizes the inherent authority of tribal courts to initiate child custody proceedings under ICWA and that those tribal decisions may be entitled to full faith and credit by the state).

59. Geraghty, Michael C., *Alaska Attorney General Geraghty's June 26, 2014 Letter to U. S. Associate Attorney General Tony West*, available at: https://turtletalk.files.wordpress.com/2014/07/6-26-14-letter-from-alaska-attorney-general-to-associate-attorney-genera.pdf.

60. West, Tony, *U. S. Associate Attorney General Tony West's July 28, 2014 Response Letter to Alaska Attorney General Geraghty's June 26, 2014 Letter*, available at: https://turtletalk.files.wordpress.com/2014/07/letter-from-asg-west-to-ag-geraghty-july-28-2014.pdf.

61. Written Testimony of Sarah Hicks Kastelic, Hearing of the Task Force on American Indian/Alaska Native Children Exposed to Violence, Anchorage, AK, June 11, 2014 at 26–37, available at: http://www.justice.gov/defendingchildhood/4th-hearing/hearing4-briefing-binder.pdf.

62. Ibid.

63. Ibid., 31.

64. Written Testimony of Jacqueline Pata, Hearing of the Task Force on American Indian/Alaska Native Children Exposed to Violence, Anchorage, AK, June 11, 2014 at 100, available at: http://www.justice.gov/defendingchildhood/4th-hearing/hearing4-briefing-binder.pdf.

65. TANF, Temporary Assistance for Needy Families.

66. CB stands for Children's Bureau.

APPENDIX A

Advisory Committee Short Biographies

Dolores Subia BigFoot, PhD (*Caddo Nation of Oklahoma*)
Associate Professor, Department of Pediatrics, University of Oklahoma Health Sciences Center
Director, Native American Programs, University of Oklahoma

Dolores Subia BigFoot (enrolled member of the Caddo Nation of Oklahoma and affiliated with the Northern Cheyenne Tribe of Montana) is an Associate Professor directing the Native American Programs at the Center on Child Abuse and Neglect at the University of Oklahoma Health Sciences Center, and trained child psychologist. For twenty years she has been the Director of Project Making Medicine, a national clinical training program for mental health providers in the treatment of child physical and/or sexual abuse and related traumas. She is also the director of the Indian Country Child Trauma Center, a resource center for promoting cultural enhancement of evidence-based practices and practice-based evidence of treatment approaches for American Indian children and their families exposed to trauma. Dr. Bigfoot has over 30 years of experience and is knowledgeable about the concerns of implementation and adaptation of evidenced based practices being introduced into Indian Country. She is known for her efforts to unify traditional American Indian and Alaska Native practices and beliefs into the formal teaching and instruction of indigenous people for the professionals working with these populations.

Eric Broderick, DDS, MPH
Former Deputy Administrator of the Substance Abuse and Mental Health Services Administration
Rear Admiral

Rear Admiral Eric Broderick served for thirty-eight years in the U.S. Department of Health and Human Services (HHS) as a Commissioned Officer in the U.S. Public Health Service. He obtained his bachelor and doctoral degrees from Indiana University and then completed a general practice residency at the U.S. Public Health Service Hospital in Seattle. He accepted a position with the Indian Health Service (IHS) and worked in clinical settings in the western

United States. He was awarded a master of public health degree from the University of Oklahoma and attained diplomat status in the American Board of Dental Public Health in 1990. He has served as the Director, Division of Oral Health, and Acting Deputy Director, Office of Public Health, for the IHS. Between 2002 and 2005 he served as Senior Advisor for Tribal Health Policy in the Immediate Office of the Secretary, HHS. He joined the Substance Abuse and Mental Health Services Administration in 2006, where he served as Deputy Administrator and Acting Administrator until 2011.

Eddie F. Brown, DSW (*Pasqua Yaqui & Tohono O'odham*)
Executive Director, American Indian Policy Institute
Professor of American Indian Studies and School of Social Work
Arizona State University

Eddie F. Brown is an enrolled member of the Pasqua Yaqui Tribe and is affiliated with the Tohono O'odham Nation. His distinguished career as a leader in, and an advocate for, the American Indian community illustrates the wide range of work opportunities that can be built on advanced degrees in social work. Currently, he is a professor at Arizona State University in Tempe, where he serves as Executive Director of the American Indian Policy Institute. Brown's prior position was Associate Dean and Director of the Kathryn M. Buder Center for American Indian Studies at the George Warren Brown School of Social Work at Washington University in St. Louis. In the world of government, he has served as Director of the Arizona Department of Economic Security and Assistant Secretary - Indian Affairs for the Department of Interior.

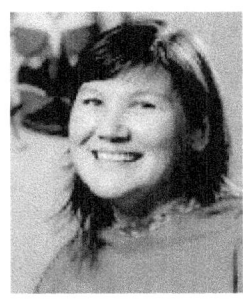

Valerie Davidson (*Yup'ik*)
Indian Health Advocate

Valerie "Nurr'araaluk" Davidson is an enrolled tribal member of the Orutsararmiut Native Council. Val has worked for over 15 years as a national policy maker on matters affecting Indian health. Most recently Val served as the Senior Director of Legal and Intergovernmental Affairs for the Alaska Native Tribal

Health Consortium, representing Alaska Native health needs at federal and state levels. Val was also the spokesperson and chief political and legal strategist for the Alaska Native Tribal Health Consortium's Dental Health Aide Therapy Program. Val served as Co-Lead Negotiator for Alaska's 229 federally recognized Tribes to negotiate the Alaska Tribal Health Compact for eleven years; was Chair of the Tribal Technical Advisory Group for the Centers for Medicare and Medicaid Services; served on the Medicare and Medicaid Policy Committee of the National Indian Health Board, the Title V Self-Governance Negotiated Rulemaking Committee, the National Steering Committee for the Reauthorization of the Indian Health Care Improvement Act, and the Medicaid Commission. Val currently serves as a Trustee of the First Alaskans Institute, working to advance Alaska Natives through community engagement, information and research, collaboration, and leadership development. Most important and bringing her the greatest joy, Val enjoys spending time at home with her children.

Senator Byron Dorgan
Chairman of the Board of Advisors Center for Native American Youth
Former U.S. Senator
Former Chairman of the Senate Indian Affairs Committee

Senator Byron Dorgan is a tireless advocate for Native American issues. While serving as the Vice Chairman in the 109th Congress and Chairman in the 110th and 111th Congresses for the Senate Committee on Indian Affairs, he brought attention to the disparities existing in Indian Country. He successfully championed efforts to reauthorize and modernize the Indian Health Care Improvement Act, authored the Tribal Law and Order Act, reauthorized the Special Diabetes Program for Indians, and fought for increased funding for Indian Country programs. Senator Dorgan is a Visiting Professor at two Universities lecturing on energy, economic policy and political affairs. He works part time as a Senior Policy Advisor with the Washington DC Law Firm Arent Fox. He is also a Senior Fellow with the Bipartisan Policy Center, a Washington DC think tank focusing primarily on energy issues. He served in the Senate leadership for sixteen years, first as Assistant Democratic Floor Leader and then as Chairman of the Democratic Policy Committee.

He was Chairman of Senate Committees and Subcommittees on the issues of energy, aviation, appropriations, water policy, and Indian affairs. He served as a U.S. Congressman and Senator for North Dakota for thirty years before retiring in 2011.

Anita Fineday, JD, MPA (*White Earth Band of Ojibwe*)
Managing Director, Indian Child Welfare Program, Casey Family Programs
Formerly Chief Judge for the White Earth Tribal Nation

Anita Fineday is the Managing Director of the Indian Child Welfare Program for the Casey Family Programs and has held this position since 2011. She previously served as the Chief Judge for the White Earth Tribal Nation for fourteen years. She holds a master's degree in public administration from Harvard University's Kennedy School of Government and a Juris Doctor from the University of Colorado School of Law. She has previously served as an associate judge for the Leech Lake Band of Ojibwe and the Grand Portage Band of Chippewa. She has also taught federal Indian law and policy at the tribal college, university, and law school levels. She is an enrolled member of the White Earth Tribal Nation.

Matthew L. M. Fletcher, JD (*Grand Traverse Band of Ottawa and Chippewa Indians*)
Director, Indigenous Law and Policy Center
Michigan State University College of Law

Matthew L. M. Fletcher is Professor of Law at Michigan State University College of Law and Director of the Indigenous Law and Policy Center; sits as the Chief Justice of the Poarch Band of Creek Indians Supreme Court; and sits as an Appellate Judge for the Pokagon Band of Potawatomi Indians, the Hoopa Valley Tribe, the Grand Traverse Band of Ottawa and Chippewa Indians, the Nottawaseppi Huron Band of Potawatomi Indians, and the Santee Sioux Tribe of Nebraska. He is a member of the Grand Traverse Band of Ottawa and Chippewa Indians. He graduated from the University of Michigan Law School in 1997 and the University of Michigan in 1994; has worked as a staff attorney for four Indian tribes—the Pascua Yaqui Tribe, the Hoopa Valley Tribe, the Suquamish Tribe, and the Grand Traverse Band; and has been a consultant to the Seneca Nation of Indians Court of Appeals. He is married to Wenona Singel, a member of the Little Traverse Bay Bands of Odawa Indians, and they have two sons, Owen and Emmett.

Jefferson Keel (*Chickasaw Nation*)
Lieutenant Governor of the Chickasaw Nation

Jefferson Keel, Lieutenant Governor of the Chickasaw Nation, is a retired U.S. Army officer with more than twenty years of active duty service. His combat experience included three years' service in Vietnam as an Infantryman, where he received the Bronze Star with "V" for valor, two purple hearts, and numerous other awards and decorations for heroism. Lt. Governor Keel has a bachelor's degree from East Central University and a master's degree from Troy University. He also completed postgraduate studies at East Central and East Texas Universities. The welfare of the Chickasaw people is his first priority. Lt. Governor Keel recently finished his second term as the President of the National Congress of American Indians. He was appointed by Senator Harry Reid to serve as a Commissioner on the Tribal Law and Order Commission; serves as Chair for the Tribal Interior Budget Committee; serves on the Department of Health and Human Services Secretary's Tribal Advisory Committee, the Indian Health Service Advisory Committee, and the Centers for Disease Control Tribal Consultation Advisory Committee. Lt. Governor Keel and his wife, Carol, have three children and eight grandchildren.

Joanne Shenandoah, PhD (*Iroquois*)
Composer and Singer

Joanne Shenandoah is one of America's most celebrated and critically acclaimed musicians. She is a Grammy Award winner, with more than forty music awards (including a record thirteen Native American Music awards) and sixteen recordings. She has captured the hearts of audiences all over the world, with praise for her work to promote universal peace. She is a board member of the Hiawatha Institute for Indigenous Knowledge. In addition to Shenandoah's musical abilities, her entire career has been dedicated to healing, and she has done thousands of events and workshops. Shenandoah recently performed for His Holiness the Dali Lama and at St. Peter's at the Vatican in Italy where she performed an original composition at the celebration for the canonization of the first Native American saint, Kateri Tekakwitha, both in October 2012. Shenandoah has performed at prestigious venues such as the White House and the National Museum of the American Indian.

Ron Whitener, JD (*Squaxin Island Tribe*)
Executive Director, Native American Law Center
Director, Tribal Court Public Defense Clinic
University of Washington School of Law

Ron Whitener is the Executive Director of the Native American Law Center, the Director of the Tribal Court Public Defense Clinic, and a Senior Law Lecturer at the University of Washington (UW) School of Law. A 1994 graduate of the UW School of Law, he worked as a tribal attorney for the Squaxin Island Tribe (of which he is a member). Professor Whitener's research interests are focused on the intersection of law and health issues for Native Americans. In 2006–7 he was a Fellow of the University of Colorado, Health Sciences Center, Native Elder Research Center. He is co-investigator on several grants with the UW Medical School and is an Associate Justice of the Northwest Intertribal Court of Appeals, a Judge of the Confederated Tribes of the Chehalis Reservation, and Counsel Attorney with Foster Pepper PLLC. In 2009 he received the American Association of Law Schools Section on Clinical Education's Shanara Gilbert Emerging Clinician Award, recognizing a clinician with ten or fewer years of teaching.

Marilyn J. Bruguier Zimmerman, MSW
(*Assiniboine-Sioux/Fort Peck Reservation*)
Director, National Native Children's Trauma Center, University of Montana

Marilyn J. Bruguier Zimmerman is an enrolled member of the Assiniboine-Sioux tribes of the Fort Peck Reservation. She is the Director of the

National Native Children's Trauma Center and serves as Associate Director of the Institute for Educational Research and Services, which allows her to work throughout the nation on culturally relevant, evidence-based interventions to treat childhood traumatic stress, reduce risk factors, and increase protective factors for substance abuse, violence, and suicide among American Indian/Alaska Native youth. In March 2013, she was invited to serve on a congressionally appointed, twelve-member commission to analyze child welfare practices across the country and to investigate and reduce the number of child fatalities in the child welfare system. She served as a member of the Indian Health Service's National Suicide Prevention Committee and the National Action Alliance for Suicide Prevention's American Indian/Alaska Native Task Force.

Individuals and Organizations that Submitted Testimony

Hearing #1: December 9, 2013 - Bismarck, ND

Dave Archambault II, Tribal Council Member, Standing Rock Sioux Tribe

Don Bartlette, Public Speaker, Social Worker

Sandra Marie Bercier, Training Director, Native American Training Institute

Barbara Bettelyoun, PhD, Psychologist, Rosebud Sioux Tribe

Sarah Deer, Assistant Professor, William Mitchell College of Law

Cecilia Firethunder, President, Oglala Lakota Nation Education Coalition; Member, Board of Directors for Little Wound School and Tasunke Wakan Okolakiciye; Former Tribal President, Oglala Sioux Nation

Donovan Foughty, State Court District Judge, North Dakota Indian Nations

Leila Kawar Goldsmith, Child Advocacy Coordinator, Tulalip Tribes of Washington

Lenny Hayes, Mental Health Therapist, Shakopee Mdewakanton Sioux Community; Psychotherapist, Tate Topa Consulting, LLC

Lisa Thompson-Heth, Executive Director, Wiconi Wawokiya, Inc.

Marilyn Hudson

Chase Iron Eyes, Attorney, Last Real Indians, Inc.

Sue Isbell, Extension Agent, Sioux County, ND

Sarah Jumping Eagle, Pediatrician, Oglala Lakota and Mdewakantowan Dakota

Cheryl Kary, PhD, Executive Director, Standing Rock Sioux Tribe

Leander "Russ" McDonald, PhD, Chairman, Spirit Lake Nation

Deborah Painte, Director, Native American Training Institute

Michelle Rivard Parks, Assistant Director, Tribal Judicial Institute; Former Tribal Prosecutor

Edward Reina, Tribal Law Enforcement Consultant, Retired Tribal Chief of Police

Jennifer Mellette TaSunke Gli Nanji Win, Freelance presenter/ negotiator, Standing Rock Sioux Tribe

Darla Thiele, Director, Sunka Wakan Ah Ku Program

Linda Thompson, Executive Director, First Nations' Women's Alliance- Tribal Domestic Violence and Sexual Assault Coalition

Joseph Vetsch, Prosecutor, Spirit Lake Tribal Court

Delores White, WS Liaison, Chairman Tex Hal, MHA Nation

Terri Yellowhammer, Technical Assistant Specialist, Native Steams Institute, Education Development Center

Hearing #2: February 11, 2014 – Phoenix, AZ

Abby Abinanti, Chief Judge, Yurok Tribal Court

Karen Allen

Daniel Cauffman, Student, Grand Valley State University, Michigan

Tracy Ching King

Jessie Deardorff, Manager, Lummi Safe House

Sheri Fremont, Director, Salt River Pima-Maricopa Indian Community Child Advocacy Center

Lea Geurts, Court Administrator; Pyramid Lake Paiute Tribal Court and Instructor, Fox Valley Technical College

Carole Goldberg, Vice Chancellor, UCLA Academic Personnel

Jonathan Hale, Chairman of Health Education and Human Services Committee, Navajo Nation Council

Sherrie Harris, Public Defender, San Carlos Apache Tribe

Candida Hunter, Manager, Hualapai Green Reentry Program, Hualapai Juvenile Detention and Rehabilitation Center

Ethleen Iron Cloud-Two Dogs, Technical Assistance Specialist; Tribal Defending Childhood Initiative, Education Development Center, Inc.

Carole Justice, Coordinator, Indian Country Methamphetamine Program, Shoshone and Arapaho Tribes

Debbie Manuel

Jose Martinez, Student, Arizona State University, Arizona

Cora Maxx Phillips, Former Executive Director, Navajo Nation Division of Social Services; CPS Worker

Gregory Mendoza, Governor, Gila River Indian Community

Ned Norris Jr., Chairman, Tohono O'odham Nation

Theresa M. Pouley, Chief Judge, Tulalip Tribal Court; Member, Indian Law and Order Commission

Addie Rolnick, Professor, William S. Boyd School of Law; Author

Herman Schultz, Counselor, Salt River Tribe

Nadia Seeratan, Senior Staff Attorney and Police Advocate, National Juvenile Defender Center

William A. Thorne Jr., Appellate Court Judge, Utah Court of Appeals, retired

Jonathan D. Varat, Distinguished Professor of Law, UCLA School of Law; Member, Indian Law and Order Commission

Erma J. Vizenor, Chairwoman, White Earth Nation

Herb Yazzie, Chief Justice, Navajo Nation Supreme Court

Hearing #3: April 16-17, 2014 – Ft. Lauderdale, FL

Brian Cladoosby, President, National Congress of American Indians (NCAI); Chairman, Swinomish Indian Tribal Community

Aisha Uwais-Savage Concha, Attorney General, Rosebud Sioux Tribe

Terry Cross, Executive Director, National Indian Child Welfare Association (NICWA)

Chris Cuestas, Consultant, National Violence Prevention Resource Center

Michael Lunderman, Prevention and Outreach Coordinator, Rosebud Sioux Tribe's Defending Childhood Initiative

Chris Meyer, Director of Education, Coeur d'Alene Tribe

Chrissi Nimmo, Assistant Attorney General, Cherokee Nation of Oklahoma

Iris PrettyPaint, Training and Technical Assistance Director and Native Aspirations Project Director, Kauffman & Associates, Inc.

Edward Reina, Tribal Law Enforcement Consultant, Retired Tribal Chief of Police

Cyril Scott, President, Rosebud Sioux Tribe

Gerald Small, Member, Chippewa Cree Tribal Business Committee

Shannon Smith, Executive Director/Attorney, Indian Child Welfare Act (ICWA) Law Center

Matthew Taylor, Associate Director, National Native Children's Trauma Center; Director, Montana Safe Schools Center; Associate Director, Institute of Education Research and Service, University of Montana

Elaine Topsky, TANF Program Director, Rocky Boy's Reservation, Montana

Jack Trope, Executive Director, Association on Indian Affairs

Erma Vizener, Chairwoman, White Earth Nation

Gerry Weisner, Tribal Prosecutor, Oklahoma and Texas; Executive Director, Native American Children's Alliance

Sandy White Hawk, Director, First Nations Repatriation Institute

Jeri Williams, Diversity and Civil Leadership Program Coordinator, Office of Neighborhood Involvement (Portland, OR)

Marlene Wong, Assistant Dean and Clinical Professor, University of Southern California School of Social Work

Sadie Young Bird, Director, Fort Berthold Coalition against Violence

Hearing #4: June 11-12, 2014 – Anchorage, AK

Ella Anagich, Attorney, Inupiat Tribe, Anchorage, Alaska

Laura Avellaneda-Cruz, Social Worker, Alaska Native Tribal Health Consortium; Epidemiologist, Alaska Native Epidemiology Center

Cathy Baldwin-Johnson, Medical Director, Alaska CARES

Diana Bline, Director of Program Services, Covenant House Alaska

Elsie Boudreau, Social Worker and Director, Alaska Native Unit within Alaska CARES, South-Central Foundation

Robin Bronen, Executive Director, Alaska Institute for Justice

Mary David, Executive Vice President, Kawerak, Inc.

Valerie Davidson

Troy Eid, Chairman, Indian Law and Order Commission

Darlene Herbert

Lenora Hootch, Founder, Native Village of Emmonak Women's Shelter; Director, Yup'ik Women's Coalition

Jerry Isaac, Vice President, Alaska NCAI; Representative, Federation of Natives Interior Villages Representative; former President, Tanana Chiefs Conference

Lisa Jaeger, Tribal Government Specialist, Tanana Chiefs Conference

Michael Jeffery, Superior Court Judge, Second Judicial District, Barrow, Alaska

Tamra Truett Jerue, Director of Social Services, Native Village of Anvik; Member, Anvik Tribal Council

Becky Judd, Rural Community Action Program

Tony Kaliss

Sarah Hicks Kastelic, Deputy Director, National Indian Child Welfare Association

Pam Karalunas, Chapter Coordinator, Alaska Children's Alliance

Julie Kitka, President, Alaska Federation of Natives

Jon Lewis

Kimberly Martus

Leotis McCormack, Member, Naspers Tribal Council, Idaho

Elizabeth Medicine Crow, President/CEO, First Alaskans Institute

Amy Modig

Walt Monegan, Former CEO, Alaska Native Justice Center; Alaska Commissioner of Public Safety; Chief of Police, Anchorage Police Department

Laurie Morton, Executive Director, Council on Domestic Violence and Sexual Assault

Myron Naneng, President, Association of Village Council Presidents

Ukallaysaaq Okleasik, Executive Director, Native Village of Kotzebue

Gloria O'Neill, President/CEO, Cook Inlet Tribal Council, Inc.

Bobbi Outten, Director, Family Wellness Warriors Initiative, South-Central Foundation

Jacqueline Pata, Executive Director, National Congress of American Indians

Diane Payne, Director, Justice for Native Children

Evon Peter, Executive Director, Indigenous Leadership Institute; CEO, Gwanzhii, LLC

Richard J. Peterson, President, Central Council Tlingit & Haida Tribes of Alaska

M. Robinson

March Runner, Tribal Administrator; ICWA Director, Galena Village, Louden Tribal Council, Alaska

Linda Sharp, Public School Teacher and Principal, retired

PJ Simon, Member, Tanana Chiefs Executive Board

David Smith, City Manager, rural Alaska, retired

Trevor J. Storrs, Executive Director, Alaska Children's Trust

Andy Teuber, President/CEO, Kodiak Area Native Association; Chairman/President, Alaska Native Tribal Health Consortium

David Voluck, Tribal Judge, Central Council of Tlingit and Haida Tribes

Listening Session, May 20-21, 2014- Minneapolis, MN

Frank Downwind, Youth Director, Little Earth of United Tribes

Carol Author, Executive Director, Domestic Abuse Project

David Campbell, Police Officer, Minneapolis, MN

Travis DeCory, Chemical Dependency Prevention Advocate

Scott DeMuth, Co-Developer, ADYC Cultural Evaluation Project

Deb Foster, Executive Director, Ain Dah Yung Center

Angela Gauthier, Family & Children's Program Director

Katie Johnson-Goodstar, Assistant Professor PhD, University of Minnesota; Co-Developer, ADYC Cultural Evaluation Project

Nancy Bordeaux, Minneapolis American Indian Center

Michael Harris, Counseling and Support Director, Indian Health Board, Minneapolis, MN

Eileen Hudon, Elder; Activist, White Earth/Ojibwe

Patina Park, Interim Executive Director, Minnesota Indian Women's Resource Center (MIWRC)

Georgette Christianson, Little Earth of United Tribes

Sheri Riemers, Residential & Administrative Operations Director

Rebecca Roepke, Oshkiniigikwe II Worker, Minnesota Indian Women's Resource Center (MIWRC)

Diane Carey, Social Worker, Minnesota Indian Women's Resource Center

Antony Stately, PhD, Psychologist, Ojibwe/Oneida

Bill Ziegler, President, Little Earth of United Tribes

Youth from Little Earth Youth Center and Ain Dah Yung Center

Listening Session, June 9, 2014- Bethel, AK

Christine Teganlakla, Outreach Coordinator, Yup'ik Women's Coalition

Janelle Vanasse, High School Principal, Bethel, AK

Ray Daw, Director of Behavioral Health

Cheryl Offt, Indian Child Welfare System

Mary Safer

Susan Taylor

Sophia Jenkins

Deborah Michael

Monica Turrentine, Teacher, Special Education, Bethel, AK

Michele DeWitt

Mardy Hanson

The Attorney General's National Task Force on Children Exposed to Violence:

Executive Summary

EXECUTIVE SUMMARY

The Attorney General's National Task Force on Children Exposed to Violence

Exposure to violence is a national crisis that affects *approximately two out of every three of our children.* Of the 76 million children currently residing in the United States, an estimated 46 million can expect to have their lives touched by violence, crime, abuse, and psychological trauma this year. In 1979, U.S. Surgeon General Julius B. Richmond declared violence a public health crisis of the highest priority, and yet 33 years later that crisis remains. Whether the violence occurs in children's homes, neighborhoods, schools, playgrounds or playing fields, locker rooms, places of worship, shelters, streets, or in juvenile detention centers, the exposure of children to violence is a uniquely traumatic experience that has the potential to profoundly derail the child's security, health, happiness, and ability to grow and learn — with effects lasting well into adulthood.

Exposure to violence in any form harms children, and different forms of violence have different negative impacts.

Sexual abuse places children at high risk for serious and chronic health problems, including posttraumatic stress disorder (PTSD), depression, suicidality, eating disorders, sleep disorders, substance abuse, and deviant sexual behavior. Sexually abused children often become hypervigilant about the possibility of future sexual violation, experience feelings of betrayal by the adults who failed to care for and protect them.

Physical abuse puts children at high risk for lifelong problems with medical illness, PTSD, suicidality, eating disorders, substance abuse, and deviant sexual behavior. Physically abused children are at heightened risk for cognitive and developmental impairments, which can lead to violent behavior as a form of self-protection and control. These children often feel powerless when faced with physical intimidation, threats, or conflict and may compensate by becoming isolated (through truancy or hiding) or aggressive (by bullying or joining gangs for protection). Physically abused children are at risk for significant impairment in memory processing and problem solving and for developing defensive behaviors that lead to consistent avoidance of intimacy.

Intimate partner violence within families puts children at high risk for severe and potentially lifelong problems with physical health, mental health, and school and peer relationships as well as for disruptive behavior. Witnessing or living with domestic or intimate partner violence often burdens children with a sense of loss or profound guilt and shame because of their mistaken assumption that they should have intervened or prevented the violence or, tragically, that they caused the violence. They frequently castigate themselves for having failed in what they assume to be their duty to protect a parent or sibling(s) from being harmed, for not having taken the place of their horribly injured or killed family member, or for having caused the offender to be violent. Children exposed to intimate partner violence often experience a sense of terror and dread that they will lose an essential caregiver through permanent injury or death. They also fear losing their relationship with the offending parent, who may be removed from the home, incarcerated, or even executed. Children will mistakenly blame themselves for having caused the batterer to be violent. If no one identifies these children and helps them heal and recover, they may bring this uncertainty, fear, grief, anger, shame, and sense of betrayal into all of their important relationships for the rest of their lives.

Community violence in neighborhoods can result in children witnessing assaults and even killings of family members, peers, trusted adults, innocent bystanders, and perpetrators of violence. Violence in the community can prevent children from feeling safe in their own schools and neighborhoods. Violence and ensuing psychological trauma can lead children to adopt an attitude of hypervigilance, to become experts at detecting threat or perceived threat — never able to let down their guard in order to be ready for the next outbreak of violence. They may come to believe that violence is "normal," that violence is "here to stay," and that relationships are too fragile to trust because one never knows when violence will take the life of a friend or loved one. They may turn to gangs or criminal activities to prevent others from viewing them as weak and to counteract feelings of despair and powerlessness, perpetuating the cycle of violence and increasing their risk of incarceration. They are also at risk for becoming victims of intimate partner violence in adolescence and in adulthood.

The picture becomes even more complex when children are "polyvictims" (exposed to multiple types of violence). As many as 1 in 10 children in this country are polyvictims, according to the Department of Justice and Centers for Disease Control and Prevention's groundbreaking National Survey of Children's Exposure to Violence (NatSCEV). The toxic combination of exposure to intimate partner violence, physical abuse, sexual abuse, and/or exposure to community violence increases the risk and severity of posttraumatic injuries and mental health disorders by at least twofold and up to as much as tenfold. Polyvictimized children are at very high risk for losing the fundamental capacities necessary for normal development, successful learning, and a productive adulthood.

The financial costs of children's exposure to violence are astronomical. The financial burden on other public systems, including child welfare, social services, law enforcement, juvenile justice, and, in particular, education, is staggering when combined with the loss of productivity over children's lifetimes.

It is time to ensure that our nation's past inadequate response to children's exposure to violence does not negatively affect children's lives any further. We must not allow violence to deny any children their right to physical and mental health services or to the pathways necessary for maturation into successful students, productive workers, responsible family members, and parents and citizens.

We can stem this epidemic if we commit to a strong national response. The long-term negative outcomes of exposure to violence can be prevented, and children exposed to violence can be helped to recover. Children exposed to violence can heal if we identify them early and give them specialized services, evidence-based treatment, and proper care and support. We have the power to end the damage to children from violence and abuse in our country; it does not need to be inevitable.

We, as a country, have the creativity, knowledge, leadership, economic resources, and talent to effectively intervene on behalf of children exposed to violence. We can provide these children with the opportunity to recover and, with hard work, to claim their birthright … life, liberty, and the pursuit of happiness. We invest in the future of our nation when we commit ourselves as citizens, service providers, and community members to helping our children recover from exposure to violence and ending all forms of violence in their lives.

To prepare this report, U.S. Attorney General Eric Holder commissioned a task force of diverse leaders dedicated to protecting children from exposure to violence and to healing those who were exposed. The report calls for action by the federal government, states, tribes, communities, and the private sector across the country to marshal the best available knowledge and all of the resources needed to defend all of our children against exposure to violence. The Attorney General's task force asks all readers of this report to imagine a safe country for our children's creative, healthy development and to join together in developing a national plan to foster that reality.

The findings and recommendations of the task force are organized into six chapters. The first chapter provides an overview of the problem and sets forth 10 foundational recommendations. The next two chapters offer a series of recommendations to ensure that we reliably identify, screen, and assess all children exposed to violence and thereafter give them support, treatment, and other services designed to address their needs. In the fourth and fifth chapters, the task force focuses on prevention and emphasizes the importance of effectively integrating prevention, intervention, and resilience across systems by nurturing children through warm, supportive, loving, and nonviolent relationships in our homes and communities. In the sixth and final chapter of this report, the task force calls for a new approach to juvenile justice, one that acknowledges that the vast majority of the children involved in that system have been exposed to violence, necessitating the prioritization of services that promote their healing.

The challenge of children's exposure to violence and ensuing psychological trauma is not one that government alone can solve. The problem requires a truly national response that draws on the strengths of all Americans. Our children's futures are at stake. Every child we are able to help recover from the impact of violence is an investment in our nation's future. Therefore, this report calls for a collective investment nationwide in defending our children from exposure to violence and psychological trauma, in healing families and communities, and in enabling all of our children to imagine and claim their safe and creative development and their productive futures. The time for action is now. Together, we must take this next step and build a nation whose communities are dedicated to ending children's exposure to violence and psychological trauma. To that end, the task force offers the following recommendations.

TASK FORCE RECOMMENDATIONS

1. Ending the Epidemic of Children Exposed to Violence

1.1 Charge leaders at the highest levels of the executive and legislative branches of the federal government with the coordination and implementation of the recommendations in this report.

The executive branch should designate leadership at the highest levels of government to implement the recommendations in this report. Working with the executive branch, Congress should take legislative action on the recommendations in this report, making these recommendations a bipartisan priority.

1.2 Appoint a federal task force or commission to examine the needs of American Indian/Alaska Native children exposed to violence.

A federal task force or commission should be developed to examine the specific needs of American Indian/Alaska Native (AIAN) children exposed to violence and recommend actions to protect AIAN children from abuse and neglect and reduce violence. The management of this task force or commission, and the selection of its members, should be carried out through an equal collaboration between the Attorney General and the Secretary of the Interior.

1.3 Engage youth as leaders and peer experts in all initiatives defending children against violence and its harmful effects.

Local, state, and regional child-serving initiatives and agencies should be directed to involve youth as leaders, planners, problem solvers, and communicators and be given the support they need to do this. Engagement with youth is essential in order to develop effective solutions to the complex problems leading to and resulting from children's exposure to violence.

1.4 Ensure universal public awareness of the crisis of children exposed to violence and change social norms to protect children from violence and its harmful effects.

Precedents exist for solving epidemic and seemingly intractable problems. Federal, state, and regional initiatives should be designed, developed, and implemented to launch a national public awareness campaign to create fundamental changes in perspective in every organization, community, and household in our country.

1.5 Incorporate evidence-based trauma-informed principles in all applicable federal agency grant requirements.

The federal government should lead the development of standards of care for identification, assessment, treatment, protection, and other crucial services for children exposed to violence and psychological trauma as well as the development of protocols for monitoring the quality of these services as measured against the national standards.

1.6 Launch a national initiative to promote professional education and training on the issue of children exposed to violence.

Standards and a curriculum must be developed to ensure that all students and professionals working with children and families are aware of the scope of the problem of children's exposure to violence as well as their responsibility to provide trauma-informed services and trauma-specific evidence-based treatment within the scope of their professional expertise.

1.7 Continue to support and sustain the national data collection infrastructure for the monitoring of trends in children exposed to violence.

Continued support for the National Survey of Children's Exposure to Violence (NatSCEV) is essential to ensure that the survey is conducted at frequent, regular intervals. The government must gather and examine additional data on a regular basis, in concert with the NatSCEV, to address related justice, education, health, and human services issues; to establish a clear picture of children's continuing exposure to violence; and to track and demonstrate the progress our country makes in ending this epidemic.

1.8 Create national centers of excellence on children's exposure to violence.

To ensure the success of this report's recommendations, national centers of excellence should be established and fully funded to support the implementation of a sustained public awareness campaign, reforms to maximize efficiencies in funding, standards for professional education and practices, and ongoing monitoring of trends and the translation of data; and to bring together the scientific, clinical, technical, and policy expertise necessary to systematically ensure the success of each of the foregoing goals.

1.9 Develop and implement public policy initiatives in state, tribal, and local governments to reduce and address the impact of childhood exposure to violence.

Every community's governing institutions and leaders should be provided with guidance from national centers of excellence to enable them to create local public policy initiatives, regulations, and services that ensure that children are protected against the harmful effects of exposure to violence and psychological trauma to the fullest extent possible.

1.10 Finance change by adjusting existing allocations and leveraging new funding.

The federal government should provide financial incentives to states and communities to redirect funds to approaches with an established record of success in defending children against exposure to violence and enabling victimized children to heal and recover.

2. Identifying Children Exposed to Violence

Every year, millions of children in this country are exposed to violence, and yet very few of these children ever receive help in recovering from the psychological damage caused by this experience. The first crucial step in protecting our children is to *identify and provide timely and effective help to those who already are being victimized by violence.* The recommendations below are offered to address identification, assessment, and screening:

2.1 Galvanize the public to identify and respond to children exposed to violence.

Sustained public information and advocacy initiatives should be implemented in every community in order to create an informed citizenry that can advocate for higher levels of services and support from policymakers for both prevention and early intervention for children exposed to violence. These initiatives are crucial to challenge the misplaced pessimism that makes violence seem like an inevitable part of life.

2.2   Ensure that all children exposed to violence are identified, screened, and assessed.

Every professional and paraprofessional who comes into contact with pregnant women and children must routinely identify children exposed to (or at risk for) violence, provide them with trauma-informed care or services, and assist them and their families in accessing evidence-based trauma-specific treatment.

2.3   Include curricula in all university undergraduate and graduate programs to ensure that every child- and family-serving professional receives training in multiple evidence-based methods for identifying and screening children for exposure to violence.

It is imperative to equip all professionals who serve children and families with the knowledge and skills they need to recognize and address the impact of violence and psychological trauma on children.

2.4   Develop and disseminate standards in professional societies and associations for conducting comprehensive specialized assessments of children exposed to violence.

Professional societies and associations of educators, law enforcement personnel, public health workers, providers of faith-based services, athletic coaches, physicians, psychologists, psychiatrists, social workers, counselors, and marriage and family therapists — and those representing specialists in child abuse and domestic violence prevention and treatment — should develop, update, and disseminate standards for training and practice in the specialized assessment of children exposed to violence.

3. Treatment and Healing of Exposure to Violence

The majority of children in our country who are identified as having been exposed to violence never receive services or treatment that effectively help them to stabilize themselves, regain their normal developmental trajectory, restore their safety, and heal their social and emotional wounds. But help isn't optional or a luxury when a child's life is at stake; it's a necessity. Even after the violence has ended, these child survivors suffer from severe problems with anxiety, depression, anger, grief, and posttraumatic stress that can mar their relationships and family life and limit their success in school or work, not only in childhood but throughout their adult lives. Without services or treatment, even children who appear resilient and seem to recover from exposure to violence still bear emotional scars that may lead them to experience these same health and psychological problems years or decades later.

3.1 Provide all children exposed to violence access to trauma-informed services and evidence-based trauma-specific treatment.

Service and treatment providers who help children and their families exposed to violence and psychological trauma *must* provide trauma-informed care, trauma-specific treatment, or trauma-focused services.

3.2 Adapt evidence-based treatments for children exposed to violence and psychological trauma to the cultural beliefs and practices of the recipients and their communities.

Federal, regional, and state funding should be dedicated to the development, testing, and distribution of evidence-based, trauma-specific treatments that have been carefully adapted to recipients' cultural beliefs and practices in order to reach the millions of children currently in need in diverse communities throughout the country.

3.3 Develop and provide trauma-informed care in all hospital-based trauma centers and emergency departments for all children exposed to violence.

Hospital-based counseling and prevention programs should be established in all hospital emergency departments — especially those that provide services to victims of violence — including victims of gang violence. Professionals and other staff in emergency medical services should be trained to identify and engage children who have been exposed to violence or to prolonged, extreme psychological trauma.

3.4 Share information and implement coordinated and adaptive approaches to improve the quality of trauma-specific treatments and trauma-focused services and their delivery by organizations and professionals across settings and disciplines to children exposed to violence.

To be effective, trauma-specific treatments and trauma-focused services must be provided in a consistent manner across the many systems, programs, and professions dedicated to helping children exposed to violence.

3.5 Provide trauma-specific treatments in all agencies and organizations serving children and families exposed to violence and psychological trauma that are suitable to their clinicians' and staff members' professional and paraprofessional roles and responsibilities.

Agencies and organizations serving children and families should have access to training on and assistance in sustained, effective implementation of widely available trauma-specific treatments that have been shown scientifically to be effective with young children, school-age children, and adolescents.

3.6 Ensure that every professional and advocate serving children exposed to violence and psychological trauma learns and provides trauma-informed care and trauma-focused services.

Treatment providers should be made available in every setting in which children spend their days — schools, youth centers, even the family's home — as well as where children receive care — clinics, hospitals, counseling centers, the offices of child protective services, homeless shelters, domestic violence programs — and where they encounter the legal system — on the street with police officers, in the courts, in probation and detention centers — to help children recover from violence and psychological trauma by providing trauma-informed care and trauma-focused services.

3.7 Grow and sustain an adequate workforce of trauma-informed service providers, with particular attention paid to the recruitment, training, and retention of culturally diverse providers.

Trauma-informed care and trauma-focused services should be taught as a required part of the curriculum for all graduate and undergraduate students enrolled in professional education programs in colleges, universities, and medical and law schools where these students are preparing for careers in the healthcare, human services, public health, child welfare, or juvenile justice fields. The same recommendation applies to technical and vocational schools in which the students are preparing to work in similar fields.

3.8 Ensure that professional societies develop, adopt, disseminate, and implement principles, practices, and standards for comprehensive evidence-based treatment of children exposed to violence or psychological trauma.

Every professional society in the United States that represents children and families should develop and formally adopt principles, practices, guidelines, and standards for evidence-based trauma-informed care, trauma-specific treatments, and trauma-focused services for violence-exposed children and their families.

3.9 Provide research funding to continue the clinical and scientific development of increasingly effective evidence-based treatments for children exposed to violence.

Research and funding infrastructures that encourage the creation and testing of innovative practices and programs that allow for the evolution of increasingly effective evidence-based treatments for children exposed to violence must be expanded or newly developed.

3.10 Provide individuals who conduct services and treatment for children exposed to violence with workforce protection to prepare them for the personal impact of this work and to assist them in maintaining a safe and healthy workplace.

All providers should receive training and resources in their workplace that enable them to maintain their own emotional and physical health and professional and personal support systems.

3.11 Incentivize healthcare providers and insurance providers to reimburse trauma-focused services and trauma-specific treatment.

Even evidence-based treatments will fail if they are poorly implemented. Treatment providers must be incentivized in their practices to routinely monitor and report on the quality, reach, and outcomes of the evidence-based or evidence-informed services they provide using established methods for doing so.

4. Creating Safe and Nurturing Homes

Each year, millions of children in this country are exposed to violence and abuse in their homes or, less often, outside the home. Violence in the home can take many forms, including, but not limited to, physical and sexual abuse of children; intimate partner violence; and violence among family members, including siblings, grandparents, or extended family. In some cases, family members may even lose their lives because of criminal violence.

Recognizing that the best place for children and adolescents to not only survive but also to thrive is in families that keep them safe and nurture their development, the task force offers 11 recommendations that are described below.

4.1 Expand access to home visiting services for families with children who are exposed to violence, focusing on safety and referral to services.

Home visitation programs should be expanded to address the dynamics of child abuse and domestic violence; to provide evidence-based safety planning for parents, including pregnant mothers who are victims of domestic violence and sexual assault; and to strengthen the connections between children and their non-offending and protective parent(s), recognizing that every violence-exposed child's well-being is inextricably linked to the safety of that child's home and the well-being of her/his parents and caregivers.

4.2   Increase collaborative responses by police, mental health providers, domestic violence advocates, child protective service workers, and court personnel for women and children who are victimized by intimate partner violence.

We need to enhance coordination between law enforcement and service providers to identify children who are traumatized by domestic violence in order to assess immediate and subsequent threats and to follow up with visits to evaluate safety and other concerns of victims.

Coordinated responses must be developed to address safety issues, basic needs, trauma-focused assessment, and identification of children needing treatment, to support children's recovery from the impact of exposure to intimate partner violence.

Models for integrated planning and intervention following initial police responses to domestic disturbances to law enforcement, mental health, child protective services, and domestic violence services agencies and courts should be disseminated nationwide.

4.3   Ensure that parents who are victims of domestic violence have access to services and counseling that help them protect and care for their children.

Parents who have experienced intimate partner violence should be provided with trauma-informed services and treatment themselves in order to assist them in providing their children with emotional security and support for healthy development.

4.4   When domestic violence and child sexual or physical abuse co-occur, ensure that the dependency and family courts, the child protection system, and domestic violence programs work together to create protocols and policies that protect children and adult victims.

When domestic violence and child abuse co-occur in a family, all victims need protection. Adult caregivers who are victimized, and their children involved in custody and dependency cases, should be provided with coordinated trauma-informed services and trauma-specific treatment appropriate to their circumstances and developmental stage. Every reasonable effort should be made to keep the violence-exposed child and non-offending parent(s) or other family caregiver(s) together.

4.5   Create multidisciplinary councils or coalitions to assure systemwide collaboration and coordinated community responses to children exposed to family violence.

Every city, county, or tribe should be directed and supported to establish and sustain a multidisciplinary network or council that includes every provider and agency that touches the lives of children exposed to violence, including key decision makers who affect policy, programs, and case management.

Coordinated multidisciplinary teams that screen, assess, and respond to victims of family violence involved in the child protection and juvenile justice systems, and standards and procedures to prevent families and children who are exposed to violence in the home from becoming unnecessarily involved in those systems, are needed in every community.

4.6   Provide families affected by sexual abuse, physical abuse, and domestic violence with education and services to prevent further abuse, to respond to the adverse effects on the family, and to enable the children to recover.

Programs should be supported and developed to engage parents to help protect and support children, ideally working to stop child sexual or physical abuse before it occurs — and also enabling parents to assist their children in recovery if sexual or physical abuse does occur. Prevention programs that equip parents and other family members with the skills needed to establish healthy, supportive, proactive relationships with children should be available to all families in every community.

4.7   Ensure that parenting programs in child- and family-serving agencies, including fatherhood programs and other programs specifically for men, integrate strategies for preventing domestic violence and sexual assault and include reparation strategies when violence has already occurred.

All agencies, programs, and providers working with fathers who have been violent toward their children, partners, or other family members must provide in-depth assessment, diagnosis, treatment planning, and educational services that are linked to the specific problems of each offender. Fathers who use violence also must be held accountable and monitored, as change does not always come easily or quickly.

4.8   Provide support and counseling to address the unique consequences for children exposed to lethal violence, both in the home as a result of domestic violence homicides and suicides, and in the community.

Evidence-based treatments that have been developed specifically to help children recover and heal from the traumatic grief of a violent death in their family should be available to all children who experience a loss due to violence, in every community in this country.

4.9 Develop interventions in all child- and family-serving agencies that build on the assets and values of each family's culture of origin and incorporate the linguistic and acculturation challenges of immigrant children and parents.

Evidence-based interventions should be created specifically for immigrant children and their families who have been exposed to violence, providing them with a network of services and supports that are grounded in the beliefs and values of their culture and language of origin rather than forcing them to renounce or relinquish those crucial ties and foundations.

4.10 Ensure compliance with the letter and spirit of the Indian Child Welfare Act (ICWA).

Thirty-five years after its passage, full implementation of the ICWA remains elusive. Because the ICWA is a federal statute, successful implementation will be best ensured through strong, coordinated support from the Department of Interior, Bureau of Indian Affairs; Department of Health and Social Services, Administration for Children and Families; and the Department of Justice, Office of Juvenile Justice and Delinquency Prevention.

4.11 Initiate a nationally sponsored program similar to the Department of Defense's community and family support programs that provides military families with specialized services focused on building strengths and resilience, new parent support, youth programs, and forging partnerships with communities.

The unique challenges of military families are widely recognized, but military families are too frequently underserved. Family support programs developed in concert with the President's "Strengthening Our Military Families" initiative should be expanded to fully provide for the safety and well-being of the children of military families and veterans living in civilian communities.

5. Communities Rising Up Out of Violence

Every year, community violence affects tens of millions of children in this country. This violence can occur in episodic incidents such as shootings in schools or other public places that cause children and families to feel terror in their own neighborhoods and schools and leave them to recover from the traumatic grief of losing friends or peers who are killed or who never fully recover. In addition, countless children are victimized when violence becomes part of the fabric of American communities as a result of gangs, or when bullying or corporal punishment is tolerated or sanctioned in schools or youth activities.

To reduce the extent of this pandemic of children's exposure to community violence, on behalf of children not yet exposed to community violence, and to help children who have been victims recover and heal from the trauma and grief caused by violence in their neighborhoods and schools, the task force proposes the following recommendations:

5.1 Organize local coalitions in every community representing professionals from multiple disciplines and the full range of service systems (including law enforcement, the courts, health care, schools, family services, child protection, domestic violence programs, rape crisis centers, and child advocacy centers) as well as families and other community members, to assess local challenges and resources, develop strategies, and carry out coordinated responses to reduce violence and the number of children exposed to violence.

Nationwide, local coalitions should be formed to increase children's safety and well-being through public awareness, wraparound support services, and immediate access to services that are tailored to meet the individual needs of children and families exposed to violence in their schools, neighborhoods, or homes.

5.2 Recognize and support the critical role of law enforcement's participation in collaborative responses to violence.

Child-serving professionals from all disciplines and law enforcement professionals should partner to provide protection and help in recovery and healing for children exposed to violence.

5.3 Involve men and boys as critical partners in preventing violence.

Initiatives must be supported and expanded to involve men and boys in using nonviolence to build healthy communities and to develop a network of men and boys across the country who are committed to creating widespread change that will help break the cycle of violence in our homes, schools, and communities.

5.4 Foster, promote, and model healthy relationships for children and youth.

Community- and school-based programs should be developed and supported to prevent violence within adolescent relationships, to promote healthy relationships, and to change social norms that tolerate and condone abuse.

5.5   Develop and implement policies to improve the reporting of suspected child sexual abuse in every institution entrusted with the care and nurturing of children.

To break the silence and secrecy that shrouds child sexual abuse, every institution entrusted with the care and safety of children must improve its policies on mandatory reporting, implement them fully, educate its employees about them, and ensure full compliance.

5.6   Train and require child care providers to meet professional and legal standards for identifying young children exposed to violence and reducing their exposure to it.

Child care providers must be trained and provided with ongoing supervision and continuing education so as to be able to recognize children in their care who have been exposed to violence and to be able to help their families to access the services and treatment that these children need in order to recover.

5.7   Provide schools with the resources they need to create and sustain safe places where children exposed to violence can get help.

Every school in our country should have trauma-informed staff and consultants providing school-based trauma-specific treatment. In addition, these professionals should help children who have severe chronic problems to access evidence-based treatment at home or in clinics.

5.8   Provide children, parents, schools, and communities with the tools they need to identify and stop bullying and to help children who have been bullied — including the bullies themselves — to recover from social, emotional, and school problems.

Trauma-informed services and support should be provided to all children who are bullies or victims of bullying in order to stop the spread of emotional and physical violence in our schools and communities.

5.9   Put programs to identify and protect children exposed to community violence who struggle with suicidality in place in every community.

Every community in the nation should have immediate access to evidence-based, trauma-informed, trauma-specific, community-adaptive suicide prevention and treatment programs for children and youth at high risk because of their severe suicidality.

5.10 Support community programs that provide youth with mentoring as an intervention and as a prevention strategy, to reduce victimization by and involvement in violence and to promote healthy development by youths.

All children's mentoring programs should provide ongoing trauma-informed training and supervision to their adult mentors to ensure the children's safety and maximize the benefits of the mentoring relationship.

5.11 Help communities learn and share what works by investing in research.

A coordinated national initiative should be created to develop public-private partnerships and funding to ensure that scientific research on the causes of children's exposure to community violence, ways to prevent such exposure, and methods of treating its adverse effects is translated into effective and efficient interventions that are available to, and used successfully in, every community in our country.

6. Rethinking Our Juvenile Justice System

The vast majority of children involved in the juvenile justice system have survived exposure to violence and are living with the trauma of those experiences. A trauma-informed approach to juvenile justice does not require wholesale abandonment of existing programs, but instead it can be used to make many existing programs more effective and cost-efficient. By correctly assessing the needs of youth in the justice system, including youth exposed to violence, and matching services directly to those needs, the system can help children recover from the effects of exposure to violence and become whole.

As a guide to addressing the needs of the vast majority of at-risk and justice-involved youth who have been exposed to violence, the task force offers the recommendations listed below.

6.1 Make trauma-informed screening, assessment, and care the standard in juvenile justice services.

All children who enter the juvenile justice system should be screened for exposure to violence. The initial screening should take place upon the child's first contact with the juvenile justice system and should include youth who meet the criteria for diversion from the system. Where feasible, juvenile justice stakeholders should develop trauma-informed care and treatment for children diverted to prevention, mental health, or dependency programs.

6.2 Abandon juvenile justice correctional practices that traumatize children and further reduce their opportunities to become productive members of society.

Juvenile justice officials should rely on detention or incarceration as a last resort and only for youth who pose a safety risk or who cannot receive effective treatment in the community. Facilities must eliminate practices that traumatize and damage the youth in their care.

6.3 Provide juvenile justice services appropriate to children's ethnocultural background that are based on an assessment of each violence-exposed child's individual needs.

Culturally sensitive role models, practices, and programs aimed at healing traumatized youth and preventing youth from being further exposed to violence in the juvenile justice system should be expanded nationwide and incorporated into statewide juvenile justice systems.

6.4 Provide care and services to address the special circumstances and needs of girls in the juvenile justice system.

Programs that provide gender-responsive services for girls healing from violence and other traumatic events, including sexual and physical abuse, should be supported and developed.

6.5 Provide care and services to address the special circumstances and needs of LGBTQ (lesbian-gay-bisexual-transgender-questioning) youth in the juvenile justice system.

Every individual who works in the juvenile justice system should be trained and provided with ongoing supervision in order to be able to deliver trauma-informed care while demonstrating respect and support for the sexual orientation of every youth.

6.6 Develop and implement policies in every school system across the country that aim to keep children in school rather than relying on policies that lead to suspension and expulsion and ultimately drive children into the juvenile justice system.

Successful school-based programs that help students develop better ways of handling emotional distress, peer pressures, and problems in family and peer relationships and that integrate recovery from trauma should be expanded and then embedded into existing school curricula and activities to increase students' abilities to have positive experiences with education, recreation, peer relationships, and the larger community.

6.7 Guarantee that all violence-exposed children accused of a crime have legal representation.

We should ensure that all children have meaningful access to legal counsel in delinquency proceedings. Screen all children who enter the juvenile and adult justice systems for exposure to violence and provide access to trauma-informed services and treatment. Train defense attorneys who represent children to identify and obtain services for clients who have been exposed to violence and to help identify and prevent abuses of children in juvenile detention and placement programs.

6.8 Help, do not punish, child victims of sex trafficking.

Child victims of commercial sex trafficking should not be treated as delinquents or criminals. New laws, approaches to law enforcement, and judicial procedures must be developed that apply existing victim protection laws to protect the rights of these child victims.

6.9 Whenever possible, prosecute young offenders in the juvenile justice system instead of transferring their cases to adult courts.

No juvenile offender should be viewed or treated as an adult. Laws and regulations prosecuting them as adults in adult courts, incarcerating them as adults, and sentencing them to harsh punishments that ignore and diminish their capacity to grow must be replaced or abandoned.

Indian Law and Order Commission:
Executive Summary

Preface

The Indian Law and Order Commission is pleased to transmit its final report and recommendations—A ROADMAP FOR MAKING NATIVE AMERICA SAFER—as required by the Tribal Law and Order Act of 2010, Public Law 111-211 (TLOA). These recommendations are intended to make Native American and Alaska Native nations safer and more just for all U.S. citizens and to reduce the unacceptably high rates of violent crime that have plagued Indian country for decades. This report reflects one of the most comprehensive assessments ever undertaken of criminal justice systems servicing Native American and Alaska Native communities.

The Indian Law and Order Commission is an independent national advisory commission created in July 2010 when the Tribal Law and Order Act was passed and extended earlier in 2013 by the Violence Against Women Act Reauthorization (VAWA Amendments). The President and the majority and minority leadership of the Congress appointed the nine Commissioners, all of whom have served as volunteers. Importantly, the findings and recommendations contained in this Roadmap represent the unanimous conclusions of all nine Commissioners—Democratic and Republican appointees alike—of what needs to be done now to make Native America safer.[1]

As provided by TLOA, the Commission received limited funding from the U.S. Departments of Justice and the Interior to carry out its statutory responsibilities. To save taxpayers' money, the Commission has operated entirely in the field—often on the road in federally recognized Indian country—and conducted its business primarily by phone and Internet email. The Commission had no offices. Its superb professional staff consists entirely of career Federal public officials who have been loaned to the Commission as provided by TLOA, and we are grateful to them and the Departments of Justice and the Interior.

TLOA has three basic purposes. First, the Act was intended to make Federal departments and agencies more accountable for serving Native people and lands. Second, TLOA was designed to provide greater freedom for Indian Tribes and nations to design and run their own justice systems. This includes Tribal court systems generally, along with those communities that are subject to full or partial State criminal jurisdiction under P.L. 83-280. Third, the Act sought to enhance cooperation among Tribal, Federal, and State officials in key areas such as law enforcement training, interoperability, and access to criminal justice information.

In addition to assessing the Act's effectiveness, this Roadmap recommends long-term improvements to the structure of the justice system in Indian country. This includes changes to the basic division of responsibility among Federal, Tribal, and State officials and institutions. The theme here is to provide for greater local control and accountability while respecting the Federal constitutional rights of all U.S. citizens.

Tribal governments, like all governments, have a moral duty to their citizens and guests to ensure the public's safety. They are also the most appropriate and capable government to ensure such safety—they employ the local police, they are the first responders, and understand the needs of their community better than all others. Unfortunately, the American legal system—through legislation and case law—has significantly hamstrung their ability to ensure safety in Indian country.

Brent Leonhard, Interim Lead Attorney, Confederated Tribes of the Umatilla Indian Reservation
Written testimony for the Indian Law and Order Commission, Hearing on the Tulalip Reservation, WA
September 7, 2011

A ROADMAP FOR MAKING NATIVE AMERICA SAFER
EXECUTIVE SUMMARY

American Indian and Alaska Native communities and lands are frequently less safe—and sometimes dramatically more dangerous—than most other places in our country. Ironically, the U.S. government, which has a trust responsibility for Indian Tribes, is fundamentally at fault for this public safety gap. Federal government policies have displaced and diminished the very institutions that are best positioned to provide trusted, accountable, accessible, and cost-effective justice in Tribal communities.

In most U.S. communities, the Federal government plays an important but limited role in criminal justice through the enforcement of laws of general application—that is, those laws that apply to all U.S. citizens—creating drug-control task forces, anti-terrorism and homeland security partnerships, and so forth. Under this system of federalism, State and local leaders have the authority and responsibility to address virtually all other public safety concerns.

Precisely the opposite is true in much of Indian country. The Federal government exercises substantial criminal jurisdiction on reservations. As a result, Native people—including juveniles—frequently are caught up in a wholly nonlocal justice system. This system was imposed on Indian nations without their consent in the late 19th century and is remarkably unchanged since that time. The system is complex, expensive, and simply cannot provide the criminal justice services that Native communities expect and deserve.

It is time for change.

Now is the time to eliminate the public safety gap that threatens so much of Native America. The United States should set a goal of closing the gap within the next decade. By 2024, coinciding with the centennial of the Indian Citizenship Act of 1924,[1] Native Americans and Alaska Natives should no longer be treated as second-class citizens when it comes to protecting their lives, liberty, and pursuit of happiness.

"A Roadmap for Making Native America Safer" (Roadmap) provides a path to make Native American and Alaska Native communities safer and more just for all U.S. citizens and to reduce unacceptably high rates of violent crime rates in Indian country.

The Roadmap is the culmination of hearings, meetings, and conversations between the Indian Law and Order Commission (Commission) and numerous Tribal, State, and Federal leaders, non-profit organization representatives, and other key stakeholders across our country.

About the Commission

In 2010, Congress passed, and the President signed, the Tribal Law and Order Act, P.L. 111-211 (TLOA), which created the Indian Law and Order Commission. The Commission is an independent national advisory commission comprised of nine members who have all served as volunteers in unanimously developing the Roadmap. The President and the majority and minority leadership of Congress appointed these commissioners.

TLOA directed the Commission to develop a comprehensive study of the criminal justice system relating to Indian country, including:

1. jurisdiction over crimes committed in Indian country and the impact of that jurisdiction on the investigation and prosecution of Indian crimes and residents of Indian land;
2. the Tribal jail and Federal prison systems with respect to reducing Indian country crime and the rehabilitation of offenders;
3. Tribal juvenile justice systems and the Federal juvenile justice system as it relates to Indian country and the effect of those systems and related programs in preventing juvenile crime, rehabilitating Indian youth in custody, and reducing recidivism among Indian youth;
4. the impact of the Indian Civil Rights Act of 1968 on the authority of Indian Tribes, the rights of defendants subject to Tribal government authority, and the fairness and effectiveness of Tribal criminal justice systems; and
5. studies of such other subjects as the Commission determines relevant to achieve the purpose of the Tribal Law and Order Act.

TLOA directed the Commission to develop recommendations on necessary modifications and improvements to the justice systems at the Tribal, State, and Federal levels. TLOA prescribed consideration of:

1. simplifying jurisdiction in Indian country;
2. improving services and programs to prevent juvenile crime on Indian land, to rehabilitate Indian youth in custody, and to reduce recidivism among Indian youth;
3. adjusting the penal authority of Tribal courts and exploring the alternatives to incarceration;
4. enhancing use of the Federal Magistrates Act in Indian country;
5. identifying effective means of protecting the rights of victims and defendants in Tribal criminal justice systems;
6. recommending changes to the Tribal jails and Federal prison systems; and
7. examining other issues that the Commission determines would reduce violent crime in Indian country.

TLOA provided the Commission with 2 years in which to complete this task, making the report due in 2012. However, due to Federal budget limitations, the Commission could not begin its work until late summer 2011. Congress provided the Commission a 1-year statutory extension when it passed the Violence Against Women Reauthorization Act of 2013, P.L. 113-4.

As provided by TLOA, the Commission received limited funding from the U.S. Departments of Justice and the Interior to carry out its statutory responsibilities. To save taxpayers' money, the Commission operated entirely in the field—often in federally recognized Indian country—and completed its business primarily by phone and email. The Commission had no offices. Its professional staff consists entirely of career Federal public officials who have been loaned to the Commission as provided by TLOA. The Commission recruited each of its three staff members; when asked to serve, all three graciously did so.

Upon completing these field hearings and meetings, the Commission developed this report. The report is called a "Roadmap" because the Commission has a particular destination in mind—to eliminate the public safety gap that threatens so much of Native America.

ABOUT THE ROADMAP

TLOA has three basic purposes. First, it was intended to make Federal departments and agencies more accountable for serving Tribal lands. Second, the Act was designed to provide greater freedom for Indian Tribes and nations to design and run their own justice systems. This includes Tribal court systems generally, along with those communities that are subject to full or partial State criminal jurisdiction under P.L. 83-280. Third, the Act sought to enhance cooperation among Tribal, Federal, and State officials in key areas such as law enforcement training, interoperability, and access to criminal justice information. This Roadmap assesses the effectiveness of these provisions.

Additionally, the Roadmap recommends long-term improvements to the structure of the justice system in Indian country. This includes the basic division of responsibility among Federal, State, and Tribal officials and institutions. Some of these recommendations require legislative action. Others are matters of executive branch policy. Still others will require action by the Federal judiciary. Finally, much of what the Commission has proposed will require enlightened and energetic leadership from the governments of the several States and, ultimately, Indian Tribes and nations themselves.

A major theme of this Roadmap is that public safety in Indian country can improve dramatically once Native nations and Tribes have greater freedom to build and maintain their own criminal justice systems. The Commission sees breathtaking possibilities for safer, strong Native communities achieved through homegrown, tribally based systems that respect the civil rights of all U.S. citizens. The Commission rejects outmoded command-and-control policies, favoring increased local control, accountability, and transparency.

The Roadmap contains six chapters, addressing: (1) Jurisdiction; (2) Reforming Justice for Alaska Natives; (3) Strengthening Tribal Justice; (4) Intergovernmental Cooperation; (5) Detention and Alternatives; and (6) Juvenile Justice.

Each chapter contains a full discussion of the aforementioned topics, providing background information, data, and on-the-ground examples about the current challenges facing Indian country. Below is a summary of each chapter. **All recommendations in this Roadmap represent the unanimous views of all nine members of the Commission, Republicans and Democrats alike.**

CHAPTER 1 - JURISDICTION: BRINGING CLARITY OUT OF CHAOS

Under the United States' Federal system, States and localities have primary responsibility for criminal justice. They define crimes, conduct law enforcement activity, and impose sanctions on wrongdoers. Police officers, criminal investigators, prosecutors, public defenders and criminal defense counsel, juries, and magistrates and judges are accountable to the communities from which victims and defendants hail. Jails and detention centers are often located within those same communities.

This framework contrasts with Indian country, where U.S. law requires Federal or State governments' control of the vast majority of criminal justice services and programs over those of local Tribal governments. Federal courts, jails, and detention centers are often located far from Tribal communities.

Disproportionately high rates of crime have called into question the effectiveness of current Federal and State predominance in criminal justice jurisdiction in Indian country. Because the systems that dispense justice in their communities originate in Federal and State law, rather than in Native nation choice and consent, Tribal citizens tend to view them as illegitimate: they do not align with Tribal citizens' perceptions of the appropriate way to organize and exercise coercive authority.

The current framework is institutionally complex. Deciding which jurisdiction delivers criminal justice to Indian country depends on a variety of factors, including but not limited to: where the crime was committed, whether or not the perpetrator is an Indian or non-Indian, whether or not the victim is Indian or non-Indian, and the type of crime committed.

The extraordinary waste of governmental resources resulting from the so-called Indian country "jurisdictional maze" can be shocking, as is the cost in human lives.

While problems associated with institutional illegitimacy and jurisdictional complexities occur across the board in Indian country, the Commission found them to be especially prevalent among Tribes subject to P.L. 83-280 or similar types of State jurisdiction. Distrust between Tribal communities and criminal justice authorities leads to communication failures, conflict, and diminished respect.

Many Tribal governments have been active in seeking ways to make do with the current jurisdictional structure. However, working around the current jurisdictional maze will continue to deliver suboptimal justice because of holes in the patchwork system and these "work-arounds" still do not provide Tribal governments with full authority over all crime and all persons on their lands.

The Commission has concluded that criminal jurisdiction in Indian country is an indefensible morass of complex, conflicting, and illogical commands, layered in over decades via congressional policies and court decisions and without the consent of Tribal nations.

Ultimately, the imposition of non-Indian criminal justice institution in Indian country extracts a terrible price: limited law enforcement; delayed prosecutions, too few prosecutions, and other prosecution inefficiencies; trials in distant courthouses; justice system and players unfamiliar with or hostile to Indians and Tribes; and the exploitation of system failures by criminals, more criminal activity, and further endangerment of everyone living in and near Tribal communities. When Congress and the Administration ask why the crime rate is so high in Indian country, they need look no further than the archaic system in place, in which Federal and State authority displaces Tribal authority and often makes Tribal law enforcement meaningless.

The Commission strongly believes, as the result of listening to Tribal communities, that for public safety to be achieved effectively in Indian country, Tribal justice systems must be allowed to flourish, Tribal authority should be restored to Tribal governments when they request it, and the Federal government, in particular, needs to take a back seat in Indian country, enforcing only those crimes that it would otherwise enforce on or off reservation.

Accordingly, the Commission recommends:

1.1: *Congress should clarify that any Tribe that so chooses can opt out immediately, fully or partially, of Federal Indian country criminal jurisdiction and/or congressionally authorized State jurisdiction, except for Federal laws of general application. Upon a Tribe's exercise of opting out, Congress would immediately recognize the Tribe's inherent criminal jurisdiction over all persons within the exterior boundaries of the Tribe's lands as defined in the Federal Indian Country Act.² This recognition, however, would be based on the*

"When Congress and the Administration ask why the crime rate is so high in Indian country, they need look no further than the archaic system in place, in which Federal and State authority displaces Tribal authority and often makes Tribal law enforcement meaningless."

understanding that the Tribal government must also immediately afford all individuals charged with a crime with civil rights protections equivalent to those guaranteed by the U.S. Constitution, subject to full Federal judicial appellate review as described below, following exhaustion of Tribal remedies, in addition to the continued availability of Federal habeas corpus remedies.

1.2: To implement Tribes' opt-out authority, Congress should establish a new Federal circuit court, the United States Court of Indian Appeals. This would be a full Federal appellate court as authorized by Article III of the U.S. Constitution, on par with any of the existing circuits, to hear all appeals relating to alleged violations of the 4th, 5th, 6th, and 8th Amendments of the U.S. Constitution by Tribal courts; to interpret Federal law related to criminal cases arising in Indian country throughout the United States; to hear and resolve Federal questions involving the jurisdiction of Tribal courts; and to address Federal habeas corpus petitions. Specialized circuit courts, such as the U.S. Court of Appeals for the Federal Circuit, which hears matters involving intellectual property rights protection, have proven to be cost effective and provide a successful precedent for the approach that the Commission recommends. A U.S. Court of Indian Appeals is needed because it would establish a more consistent, uniform, and predictable body of case law dealing with civil rights issues and matters of Federal law interpretation arising in Indian country. Before appealing to this new circuit court, all defendants would first be required to exhaust remedies in Tribal courts pursuant to the current Federal Speedy Trial Act, 18 U.S.C. § 3161, which would be amended to apply to Tribal court proceedings so as to ensure that defendants' Federal constitutional rights are fully protected. Appeals from the U.S. Court of Indian Appeals would lie with the United States Supreme Court according to the current discretionary review process.

1.3: The Commission stresses that an Indian nation's sovereign choice to opt out of current jurisdictional arrangements should and must not preclude a later choice to return to partial or full Federal or State criminal jurisdiction. The legislation implementing the opt-out provisions must, therefore, contain a reciprocal right to opt back in if a Tribe so chooses.

1.4: Finally, as an element of Federal Indian country jurisdiction, the opt-out would necessarily include opting out from the sentencing restrictions of the Indian Civil Rights Act (IRCA). Critically, the rights protections in the recommendation more appropriately circumscribe Tribal sentencing authority. Like Federal and State governments do, Tribal governments can devise sentences appropriate to the crimes they define. In this process of Tribal code development, Tribes may find guidance in the well-developed sentencing schemes at the State and Federal levels.

CHAPTER 2—REFORMING JUSTICE FOR ALASKA NATIVES: THE TIME IS NOW

Congress exempted Alaska from legislation aimed at reducing crime in Indian country, such as the Tribal Law and Order Act of 2010 and the Violence Against Women Act 2013 reauthorization (VAWA Amendments). Yet, the problems in Alaska are so severe and the number of Alaska Native communities affected so large, that continuing to exempt the State from national policy change is wrong. It sets Alaska apart from the progress that has become possible in the rest of Indian country. The public safety issues in Alaska—and the law and policy at the root of those problems—beg to be addressed. These are no longer just Alaska's issues; they are national issues.

The strongly centralized law enforcement and justice systems of the State of Alaska are of critical concern. Devolving authority to Alaska Native communities is essential for addressing local crime. Their governments are best positioned to effectively arrest, prosecute, and punish, and they should have the authority to do so—or to work out voluntary agreements with the State and local governments on mutually beneficial terms.

Forty percent of the federally recognized tribes in the United States are in Alaska, and Alaska Natives represent one-fifth of the total State population. Yet these simple statements cannot capture the vastness or the Nativeness of Alaska. The State covers 586,412 square miles, an area greater than Texas, California, and Montana combined. Many of the 229 recognized tribes in Alaska are villages located off the road system, often resembling villages in developing countries. Frequently, Native villages are accessible only by plane, or during the winter when rivers are frozen, by snow-machine. Food, gasoline, and other necessities are expensive and often in short supply. Subsistence hunting, fishing, and gathering are a part of everyday life. Villages are politically independent from one another, and have institutions that support that local autonomy—village councils and village Corporations.[3] Unsurprisingly, these conditions pose significant challenges to the effective provision of public safety for Alaska Natives.

Problems with safety in Tribal communities are severe across the United States—but they are systemically worst in Alaska. Most Alaska Native communities lack regular access to police, courts, and related services. Alaska Natives are disproportionately affected by crime, and these effects are felt most strongly in Native communities. High rates of suicide, alcohol abuse, crimes attributed to alcohol, and alcohol abuse-related mortality plague these communities.

In Alaska's criminal justice system, State government authority is privileged over all other possibilities: the State has asserted exclusive criminal jurisdiction over all lands once controlled by Tribes, and it exercises this jurisdiction through the provision of law enforcement and judicial services from a set of regional centers, under the direction and control of the relevant State commissioners. This approach has led to a dramatic under-provision of criminal justice services in rural and Native regions of the State. It also has limited collaboration with local governments (Alaska Native or not), which could be the State's most valuable partners in crime prevention and the restoration of public safety.

This is emphatically not to criticize the many dedicated and accomplished State officials who serve Alaska Native communities day in and day out. They deserve the nation's respect, and they have the Commission's.

Nonetheless, it bears repeating that the Commission's findings and conclusions represent the unanimous view of nine independent citizens, Republicans and Democrats alike, that Alaska's approach to criminal justice issues is fundamentally on the wrong track. The status quo in Alaska tends to marginalize—and frequently ignores—the potential of tribally based justice systems, as well as intertribal institutions and organizations to provide more cost-effective and responsive alternatives to prevent crime and keep all Alaskans safer. If given an opportunity to work, Tribal approaches can be reasonably expected to work better—and at less cost.

Because of the Alaska Native Claims Settlement Act of 1971 (ANCSA) and *Alaska v. Native Village of Venetie Tribal Government*[4], the Alaska Attorney General takes the view that there is very little Indian country in Alaska and thus, its law enforcement authority is exclusive throughout the State because Tribes do not have a land base on which to exercise any inherent criminal jurisdiction.

The Commission respectfully and unanimously disagrees.

Accordingly, the Commission recommends:

> **2.1:** *Congress should overturn the U.S. Supreme Court's decision in* Alaska v. Native Village of Venetie Tribal Government, *by amending ANCSA to provide that former reservation lands acquired in fee by Alaska Native villages and other lands transferred in fee to Native villages pursuant to ANCSA are Indian country.*

> **2.2:** *Congress and the President should amend the definitions of Indian country to clarify (or affirm) that Native allotments and Native-owned town sites in Alaska are Indian country.*

> **2.3:** *Congress should amend the Alaska Native Claims Settlement Act to allow a transfer of lands from Regional Corporations to Tribal governments; to allow transferred lands to be put into trust and included within the definition of Indian country in the Federal criminal code; to allow Alaska Native Tribes to put tribally owned*

fee simple land similarly into trust; and to channel more resources directly to Alaska Native Tribal governments for the provision of governmental services in those communities.

2.4: *Congress should repeal Section 910 of Title IX of the Violence Against Women Reauthorization Act of 2013 (VAWA Amendments), and thereby permit Alaska Native communities and their courts to address domestic violence and sexual assault, committed by Tribal members and non-Natives, the same as now will be done in the lower 48.*

2.5: *Congress should affirm the inherent criminal jurisdiction of Alaska Native Tribal governments over their members within the external boundaries of their villages.*

CHAPTER 3—STRENGTHENING TRIBAL JUSTICE: LAW ENFORCEMENT, PROSECUTION, AND COURTS

Parity in Law Enforcement. A foundational premise of this report is that Indian Tribes and nations throughout our country would benefit enormously if locally based and accountable law enforcement officers were staffed at force levels comparable to similarly situated communities off-reservation. From 2009-2011, the Office of Justice Services (OJS) in the Bureau of Indian Affairs (BIA) increased staffing levels on four Indian reservations to achieve such parity. This approach—through a "High Performance Priority Goal" (HPPG) Initiative—on average, reduced crime significantly on the selected reservations.

While the HPPG Initiative demonstrates what can work in Indian country, the Commission hastens to note that HPPG's results can neither be replicated nor sustained on very many other Tribal reservations due to the extremely limited Federal and State funding options currently available to Indian country. Despite the current budget reality, the results of the HPPG Initiative should not be forgotten: parity in law enforcement services prevents crime and reduces violent crime rates.

In P.L. 83-280 States, the Federal government has transferred Federal criminal jurisdiction on Indian lands to State governments and approved the enforcement of a State's criminal code by State and local law enforcement officers in Indian country. As a consequence of P.L. 83-280 and similar settlement acts, Federal investment in Tribal justice systems has been even more limited than elsewhere in Indian country. Nor is much help forthcoming from State governments; they have found it difficult to satisfy the demands of what is essentially an unfunded Federal mandate.

Accordingly, the Commission recommends:

> **3.1:** *Congress and the executive branch should direct sufficient funds to Indian country law enforcement to bring Indian country's coverage numbers into parity with the rest of the United States. Funding should be made equally available to a) Tribes whose lands are under Federal criminal jurisdiction and those whose lands are under State jurisdiction through P.L. 83-280 or other congressional authorization; b) Tribes that contract or compact under P.L. 93-638 and its amendments or not; and c) Tribes that do or do not opt out (in full or in part) from Federal or State criminal jurisdiction as provided in Recommendation 1.1 of this report.*

Data Deficits. When Tribes have accurate data, they can plan and assess their law enforcement and other justice activities. Without data and access to such data, community assessment, targeted action, and norming against standards are impossible. The Commission found that systems for generating crime and law enforcement data about Indian country either are nascent or undeveloped.

Accordingly, the Commission recommends:

> **3.2:** *To generate accurate crime reports for Indian country, especially in Tribal areas subject to P.L. 83-280, Congress should amend the Federal Bureau of Investigation (FBI) Criminal Justice Information Services reporting requirements for State and local law enforcement agencies' crime data to include information about the location at which a crime occurred and on victims' and offenders' Indian status. Similarly, it should require the U.S. Department of Justice (DOJ) to provide reservation-level victimization data in its annual reports to Congress on Indian country crime. Congress also should ensure the production of data and data reports required by the Tribal Law and Order Act of 2010, which are vital to Tribes as they seek to increase the effectiveness of their law enforcement and justice systems, by allowing Tribal governments to sue the U.S. Departments of Justice and the Interior should they fail to produce and submit the required reports.*

Special Assistant U.S. Attorneys ("SAUSAs"). The Indian country SAUSA program makes it possible for U.S. Attorneys to appoint appropriately qualified prosecutors to work in the capacity of an Assistant U.S. Attorney for the prosecution of certain Indian country cases. The SAUSA model is a positive and worthwhile development in making Indian country safer. SAUSAs boost Tribal prosecutors' ability to protect and serve. SAUSAs sometimes work with their respective U.S. Attorney's Offices to refer cases arising on Indian lands so that the investigations do not fall through the cracks. Further, all Tribal SAUSAs are required to undergo a rigorous FBI background check prior to their appointment. This vetting allows SAUSAs to legally obtain access to Law Enforcement Sensitive information. Such information helps determine how Tribal prosecutors allocate resources and implement their public safety priorities.

Despite better utilization of the SAUSA program in recent years, a more fundamental issue remains: Federal agencies' stingy support of Tribal court proceedings. Many Federal officials still see information sharing with Tribal prosecutors' offices as more or less optional. Routine refusal by many Federal law enforcement officials to testify as witnesses in Tribal court proceedings stymies the successful prosecution of Indian country crime.

Accordingly, the Commission recommends:

> **3.3:** *The Attorney General of the United States should affirm that federally deputized Tribal prosecutors (that is, those appointed as Special Assistant U.S. Attorneys or "SAUSAs" by the U.S. Department of Justice pursuant to existing law) should be presumptively and immediately entitled to all Law Enforcement Sensitive information needed to perform their jobs for the Tribes they serve.*

> **3.4:** *The U.S. Attorney General should clarify the ability and importance of Federal officials serving as witnesses in Tribal court proceedings and streamline the process for expediting their ability to testify when subpoenaed or otherwise directed by Tribal judges.*

> **3.5:** *To further strengthen Tribal justice systems, the Commission suggests that Federal public defenders, who are employees of the judicial branch of the Federal government within the respective judicial districts where they serve, consider developing their own program modeled on Special Assistant U.S. Attorneys.*

Federal Magistrate Judges. TLOA directs the Commission to consider enhanced use of Federal magistrate judges to improve justice systems. The Commission has considered the concept of cross-deputizing Tribal court judges to serve as "Special Federal Magistrate Judges" to help expedite Federal criminal investigations, arrests, and indictments of crimes occurring in Indian country. However, despite repeated attempts to garner opinions on this topic, there was no public testimony on this topic.

While Federal magistrate judges play an important role in Indian country, there are obviously many instances where only an Article III judge can perform certain functions in Indian country that are required by law. Yet, not one U.S. District Court Judge is permanently based in Indian country, nor are there any Federal courthouses there.

Accordingly, the Commission recommends:

> **3.6:** *Congress and the executive branch should encourage U.S. District Courts that hear Indian country cases to provide more judicial services in and near Indian country. In particular, they should be expected to hold more judicial proceedings in and near Indian country. Toward this end, the U.S. Supreme Court and the Judicial*

*Conference of the United States should develop a policy aimed at
increasing the Federal judicial presence and access to Federal judges
in and near Indian country.*

3.7: *Congress and the executive branch should consider
commissioning a study of the usefulness and feasibility of creating
Special Federal Magistrate Judges.*

Federal Funding and Federal Administrative Reform. The Roadmap sets
forth a vision of Tribal governments having the lead role in strengthening
Tribal justice. To achieve this goal, they must be able to communicate
clearly and effectively with their Federal and State government partners
about their justice capabilities and needs.

Most Tribal governments need financial support and a more rational
Federal administrative structure for the management of criminal justice
programs in Indian country. The need for resources is obvious if Tribes are
to pursue successful strategies such as the HPPG Initiative. Administrative
changes at the Federal level should make it possible to redirect spending
that at present is duplicative, over managed, and misallocated. Thus,
reform may not only improve information sharing, but also generate
savings so that less "new money" is needed for investment in ideas that
work.

Since the late 1980s, the U.S. Department of Justice (DOJ) has
become a major funder of Indian country criminal justice system activities.
DOJ's involvement has been of great benefit to Tribes in areas such as
program development and opening certain funding streams.

Despite these benefits, DOJ's grant-based funding approach creates
uncertainties in system planning; Tribal governments legitimately ask
why—unlike their State and local counterparts—should they rely on such
inconsistent sources to pay for governmental functions. Grant funding also
requires Tribal governments to compete for and "win" grant funds, which
means other Tribes did not. Further, small Tribes and Tribes with thinly
stretched human capital lack the capacity to write a "winning" application,
yet these Tribes often have disproportionate criminal justice needs. Finally,
many grants awarded to Tribes contain so much bureaucratic red tape that
the balance of the Federal funds awarded goes unused.

Additionally, Tribes must navigate the separate DOJ and U.S.
Department of Interior (DOI) systems, which have substantial roles in the
administration of Indian country justice programming. This arrangement
creates costly duplication, confusion concerning lines of accountability,
and wasteful outcomes. For example, the Commission learned of detention
facilities built with DOJ funds that, once completed, could not be staffed
because they were not included in the DOI budget for facilities operations
and maintenance.

Some of these problems could be resolved if Tribal governments were able to access DOJ Indian country resources that allow Tribal governments to manage Federal funds. An alternative and preferred route would be to merge or combine these Federal responsibilities for Indian country criminal justice in a single Federal department.

Accordingly, the Commission recommends:

> **3.8:** *Congress should eliminate the Office of Justice Services (OJS) within the Department of the Interior Bureau of Indian Affairs, consolidate all OJS criminal justice programs and all Department of Justice Indian country programs and services into a single "Indian country component" in the U.S. Department of Justice (including an appropriate number FBI agents and their support resources), and direct the U.S. Attorney General to designate an Assistant Attorney General to oversee this unit. The enacting legislation should affirm that the new agency retains a trust responsibility for Indian country and requires Indian preference in all hiring decisions; amend P.L. 93-638 so that Tribal governments have the opportunity to contract or compact with the new agency; and authorize the provision of direct services to Tribes as necessary. Congress also should direct cost savings from the consolidation to the Indian country agency and continue to appropriate this total level of spending over time.*

> **3.9:** *Congress should end all grant-based and competitive Indian country criminal justice funding in DOJ and instead pool these monies to establish a permanent, recurring base funding system for Tribal law enforcement and justice services, administered by the new Tribal agency in DOJ. Federal base funding for Tribal justice systems should be made available on equal terms to all federally recognized Tribes, whether their lands are under Federal jurisdiction or congressionally authorized State jurisdiction and whether they opt out of Federal and/or State jurisdiction (as provided in Recommendation 1.1). In order to transition to base funding, the enacting legislation should:*

> a. *Direct the U.S. Department of Justice to consult with Tribes to develop a formula for the distribution of base funds (which, working from a minimum base that all federally recognized Tribes would receive, might additionally take account of Tribes' reservation populations, acreages, and crime rates) and develop a method for awarding capacity-building dollars.*

> b. *Designate base fund monies as "no year" so that Tribes that are unable to immediately qualify for access do not lose their allocations.*

> c. *Authorize the U.S. Department of Justice to annually set aside five (5) percent of the consolidated former grant monies as a designated Tribal criminal justice system capacity-building fund,*

which will assist Tribes in taking maximum advantage of base funds and strengthen the foundation for Tribal local control.

3.10: *Congress should enact the funding requests for Indian country public safety in the National Congress of American Indians (NCAI) "Indian Country Budget Request FY 2014," and consolidate these funds into appropriate programs within the new DOJ Tribal agency. Among other requests, NCAI directs Congress to fully fund each provision of the Tribal Law and Order Act of 2010 that authorizes additional funding for Tribal nation law and order programs, both for FY 2014 and future years; to finally fund the Indian Tribal Justice Act of 1993, which authorized an additional $50 million per year for each of seven (7) years for Tribal court base funding; and to create a seven (7) percent Tribal set-aside from funding for all discretionary Office of Justice Programs (OJP) programs, which at a minimum should equal the amount of funding that Tribal justice programs received from OJP in FY 2010. In the spirit of NCAI's recommendations, Congress also should fund the Legal Services Corporation (LSC) at a level that will allow LSC to fulfill Congress' directives in the Tribal Law and Order Act of 2010 and Violence Against Women Act 2013 reauthorization.*

CHAPTER 4—INTERGOVERNMENTAL COOPERATION: WORKING RELATIONSHIPS THAT TRANSCEND JURISDICTIONAL LINES

Stronger coordination among Federal, State, and Tribal law enforcement can make Native nations safer and close the public safety gap with similarly situated communities. It also is a proven way to combat off-reservation crime. The Federal government cannot and should not force Tribal and State leaders to work together. Local priorities and concerns ought to drive cooperation, and it needs to be voluntary. But the President and Congress can take steps to promote and support the conditions in which more positive forms of collaboration can take root.

A principal goal in intergovernmental cooperation is to find the right mechanisms to facilitate the entry into Tribal-State and Tribal-Federal law enforcement agreements and Memoranda of Understanding, including Special Law Enforcement Commission and local deputization and cross-deputization agreements.

Special Law Enforcement Commission (SLEC). With a SLEC, a Tribal police officer, employed by a Tribal justice agency, can exercise essentially the same arrest powers of a Bureau of Indian Affairs (BIA) officer assigned to Indian country without compensation by the Federal government. The SLEC enables a Tribal police office to make an arrest for a violation of the General Crimes Act or the Major Crimes Act in the non-P.L. 83-280 States or Tribal jurisdictions. While the SLEC appears to be precisely the kind of intergovernmental cooperation that would greatly enhance public safety in

Indian country, the Commission heard testimony that the BIA certification of the SLEC commissions is often delayed far too long.

State and Local Agreements. The Commission believes the recognition of Tribal government and jurisdictional powers through agreements with State and local jurisdictions will develop partnerships, allow the sharing of knowledge and resources, and result in better chances to coordinate police enforcement. Greater intergovernmental cooperation often results in better services for Indian country, is more cost effective, culturally compatible, and provides better arrest and prosecution rates.

The use of Memoranda of Understanding (MOUs) or other similar agreements between local law enforcement agencies and Tribal public safety permit, or "deputize," the Tribal officers to enforce State criminal law. In most cases, this mechanism has served to ease the burden on non-Indian police forces. It also allows a full arrest of a suspect, which is necessary to secure a crime scene, protect evidence and witnesses, and ensure an appropriate arraignment and prosecution. However, liability concerns can hinder adoption of such agreements.

Accordingly, the Commission recommends:

> **4.1:** *Federal policy should provide incentives for States and Tribes to increase participation in deputization agreements and other recognition agreements between State and Tribal law enforcement agencies.*
>
> *Without limitation, Congress should:*
>
> *a) Support the development of a model Tribal-State law enforcement agreement program that addresses the concerns of States and Tribes equally, to help State legislatures and Governors to formulate uniform laws to enable such MOUs and agreements, in both P.L. 83-280 and non-P.L. 83-280 States;*
>
> *b) Support the training costs and requirements for Tribes seeking to certify under State agencies to qualify for peace office status in a State in a deputization agreement;*
>
> *c) Create a federally subsidized insurance pool or similar affordable arrangement for tort liability for Tribes seeking to enter into a deputization agreement for the enforcement of State law by Tribal police;*
>
> *d) For Tribal officers using a SLEC, amend the Federal Tort Claims Act[5] to include unequivocal coverage (subject to all other legally established guidelines concerning allowable claims under the Act), not subject to the discretion of a U.S. Attorney or other Federal official; and*

e) Improve the SLEC process by shifting its management to the U.S. Department of Justice and directing DOJ to streamline the commissioning process (while retaining the requirements necessary to ensure that only qualified officers are provided with SLECs). (Also see Recommendation 4.8.)

Tribal Notification of Arrest, Court Proceedings, and Reentry. On the Federal side, United States Attorney's Offices sometimes do not communicate effectively, or at all, with Tribal jurisdictions when declining cases for Federal prosecution. Without notification, local Tribal courts often do not take up the case in Tribal court by exercising their concurrent jurisdiction.

Tribal government notification at the time of a Tribal citizen's arrest—and appropriate Tribal government involvement from that point forward (during trial, detention, and reentry)—can reasonably be expected to improve outcomes for the offender and for the offender's family and Tribe, as well as improve law enforcement outcomes overall.

> **4.2:** *Federal or State authorities should notify the relevant Tribal government when they arrest Tribal citizens who reside in Indian country.*

> **4.3:** *When any Tribal citizen resident in Indian country is involved as a criminal defendant in a State or Federal proceeding, the Tribal government should be notified at all steps of the process and be invited to have representatives present at any hearing. Tribes should similarly keep the Federal or State authorities informed of the appropriate point of contact within the Tribe. These mutual reporting requirements will help ensure the effective exercise of concurrent jurisdiction, when applicable, and the provision of wrap-around and other governmental services to assist the offender, his or her family, as well as the victims of crime.*

> **4.4:** *All three sovereigns—Federal, State, and Tribal—should enter into voluntary agreements to provide written notice regarding any Tribal citizens who are reentering Tribal lands from jail or prison. This requirement should apply regardless if that citizen formerly resided on the reservation. This policy will allow the Tribe to determine if it has services of use to the offender, and to alert victims about the offender's current status and location.*

Intergovernmental Data Collection and Sharing. Good criminal justice information—and, as necessary, sharing of information—are key to the effective operation of a criminal justice program. Indian country is seen as a data gap. Some Tribes are working with State and Federal law officials on innovative ways to collect and distribute data. However, more can and should be done to encourage data sharing, particularly at the State and local level.

Accordingly, the Commission recommends:

> **4.5:** *Congress should provide specific Edward J. Byrne Memorial Justice Assistance Grants (Byrne grants) or COPS grants for data-sharing ventures to local and State governments, conditioned on the State or local government entering into agreements to provide criminal offenders' history records with federally recognized Indian Tribes with operating law enforcement agencies that request to share data about offenders' criminal records; any local, State, or Tribal entity that fails to comply will be ineligible for COPS and Byrne grants.*

CHAPTER 5—DETENTION AND ALTERNATIVES: COMING FULL CIRCLE, FROM *Crow Dog* TO TLOA AND VAWA

In August 1881, *Crow Dog*, a Brule Lakota man, shot and killed Spotted Tail, a fellow member of his Tribe. The matter was settled according to long-standing Lakota custom and tradition, which required Crow Dog to make restitution by giving Spotted Tail's family $600, eight horses, and a blanket. After a public outcry that the sentence was not harsher, Federal officials charged *Crow Dog* with murder in a Dakota Territory court. He was found guilty and sentenced to death. The U.S. Supreme Court ultimately affirmed Tribal jurisdiction in this case, noting that the territorial court had inappropriately measured Lakota standards for punishment "by the maxims of the white man's morality."[6] Members of Congress, outraged by the Supreme Court's ruling, overturned the decision by enacting the Major Crimes Act of 1885, which for the first time extended Federal criminal jurisdiction to a list of felonies committed on reservations by Indians against both Indians and non-Indians.

In the 130 years since, detention and imprisonment have risen in prominence as responses to crime in Indian country, and Tribal governments have struggled to reassert their views about the value of reparation, restoration, and rehabilitation.

In recent years, the TLOA and VAWA Amendments have allowed Tribal governments to regain significant authority over criminal sentencing. But more could be done. By investing in alternatives to incarceration, the Commission also is hopeful that significant cost savings in Federal and State resources can be realized.

Deficiencies in Detention. Indians who offend in Indian country and are sentenced to serve time may be held in Tribal, Federal, or State facilities. While there are hardships associated with any incarceration, American Indians and Alaska Natives serving time in State and Federal detention systems experience a particular set of problems. One is systemic disproportionality in sentencing. The other is distance from their homes.

Further, such detention systems fail to provide culturally relevant support to offenders and community reentry becomes more difficult and may be ill coordinated.

Indians offenders also could be placed in an Indian country detention facility. There is an increasing number of exemplary facilities that serve as anchors along a continuum of care from corrections to community reentry and that are able to connect detainees with core rehabilitation services. For many Tribes, financial assistance from the Federal government for facility planning, renovation, expansion, staffing, and operations has been important in these efforts.

On the other hand, eight Tribal detention facilities permanently closed between 2004 and 2012. In most cases, deficiencies in funding, staff, and appropriate space proved their undoing. Indeed, the Commission visited detention facilities with deplorable living conditions. Funding for new jails and funding for operations remains a challenge. And while the number of violent offenders in Indian country detention facilities has fallen slightly in recent years, new sentencing authorities provided by TLOA and the VAWA Amendments may result in an increased the number of violent offenders in Indian country detention facilities.

Opportunities in Alternatives. "Alternatives to incarceration" or "alternatives to detention" are programs in which a judge may send criminal offenders elsewhere instead of sentencing them to jail. By addressing the core problems that lead offenders to crime (which may include substance abuse, mental health problems, and limited job market skills) and by helping them develop new behaviors that support the choice to not commit crimes, alternative sentencing aims to create pathways away from recidivism. Jail may still be part of an offender's experience with an alternative sentence, but it would be used more sparingly and as a shorter-term measure, functioning as a component in a more comprehensive program involving intensive supervision, coordinated service provision, and high expectations for offender accountability.

A considerable amount of data demonstrates the effectiveness of some alternatives to detention across a wide range of court settings and offense categories. Effectiveness can translate to cost savings. Governments save money by diverting offenders away from jail and into alternative programs.

Accordingly, the Commission recommends:

> **5.1:** *Congress should set aside a commensurate portion of the resources (funding, technical assistance, training, etc.) it is investing in reentry, second-chance, and alternatives to incarceration monies for Indian country, and in the same way it does for State governments, to help ensure that Tribal government funding for these purposes is ongoing. In line with the Commission's overarching*

recommendation on funding for Tribal justice, these resources should be managed by the recommended Indian country unit in the U.S. Department of Justice and administered using a base funding model. Tribes are specifically encouraged to develop and enhance drug courts, wellness courts, residential treatment programs, combined substance abuse treatment-mental health care programs, electronic monitoring programs, veterans' courts, clean and sober housing facilities, halfway houses, and other diversion and reentry options, and to develop data that further inform the prioritization of alternatives to detention.

To increase intergovernmental collaboration, as suggested elsewhere in this report, Tribal, State, and Federal governments should collaborate to ensure that Tribal governments are knowledgeable about which of its citizens are in the custody of non-Tribal governments. This would afford each offender's Tribal government the option to be engaged in decision making regarding corrections placement and supervision and allow the nation to be informed about, and prepared for, the offender's eventual reentry to the Tribal community.

Accordingly, the Commission recommends:

5.2: *Congress should amend the Major Crimes Act, General Crimes Act, and P.L. 83-280 to require both Federal and State courts exercising transferred Federal jurisdiction 1) to inform the relevant Tribal government when a Tribal citizen is convicted for a crime in Indian country, 2) to collaborate, if the Tribal government so chooses, in choices involving corrections placement or community supervision, and 3) to inform the Tribal government when that offender is slated for return to the community.*

Tribes must receive a fair share of funds available at the Federal level for corrections systems creation and operation. While some corrections funds are specifically designated for Tribes, most are allocated in a manner that privileges State and local governments above Tribal governments. Savings realized through the creation and increased use of alternatives to detention should not be lost to Tribal governments, which is the case today. Instead, funding should "follow the offender," so that if an offender's time served is reduced, money that would have been spent on detention is then available for service provision.

Accordingly, the Commission recommends:

5.3: *Recognizing that several Federal programs support the construction, operation, and maintenance of jails, prisons, and other corrections programs that serve offenders convicted under Tribal law, appropriate portions of these funds should be set aside for Tribal governments and administered by a single component of the U.S. Department of Justice. This includes any funds specifically intended* *for Tribal jails and other Tribal corrections programs (e.g., those available through the Bureau of Indian Affairs) and a commensurate Tribal share of all other corrections funding provided by the Federal government (e.g., Bureau of Prisons funding and Edward J. Byrne Memorial Justice Assistance Grants/JAG program funding). To the extent that alternatives to detention eventually reduce necessary prison and jail time for Tribal-citizen offenders, savings should be reinvested in Indian country corrections programs and not be used as a justification for decreased funding.*

5.4: *Given that even with a renewed focus on alternatives to incarceration, Tribes will continue to have a need for detention space:*

a) Congress and the U.S. Department of Justice should provide incentives for the development of high-quality regional Indian country detention facilities, capable of housing offenders in need of higher security and providing programming beyond "warehousing," by prioritizing these facilities in their funding authorization and investment decisions; and,

b) Congress should convert the Bureau of Prisons pilot program created by the Tribal Law and Order Act into a permanent programmatic option that Tribes can use to house prisoners.

CHAPTER 6—JUVENILE JUSTICE: FAILING THE NEXT GENERATION

Indian country juvenile justice exposes the worst consequences of our broken Indian country justice system. Native youth are among the most vulnerable group of children in the United States. In comparison to the general population, poverty, substance abuse, suicide, and exposure to violence and loss disproportionately plague Native youth. Not surprisingly, and detailed in the Roadmap, these conditions negatively influence how Native children enter adulthood.

The same complexities and inadequacies of the Indian country adult criminal justice impair juvenile justice as well. The Federal court system has no juvenile division—no specialized juvenile court judges, no juvenile probation system. The U.S. Bureau of Prisons has no juvenile detention, diversion, or rehabilitation facilities. For Indian country youth who become part of State juvenile justice systems, there is generally no requirement that a child's Tribe be contacted if an Indian child is involved. Thus, the unique circumstances of Native youth are often overlooked and their outcomes are difficult to track. Juveniles effectively "go missing" from the Tribe.

Although data about Indian country juveniles in Federal and State systems are limited, the available data reveal alarming trends regarding processing, sentencing, and incarceration of Native youth. Native youth are overrepresented in both Federal and State juvenile justice systems and receive harsher sentences.

Jurisdiction Reforms for Native Youth. Just as Tribal self-determination and local control are the right goals for adult criminal matters, they are the right goals for juvenile matters.

Accordingly, the Commission recommends:

> **6.1:** *Congress should empower Tribes to opt out of Federal Indian country juvenile jurisdiction entirely and/or congressionally authorized State juvenile jurisdiction, except for Federal laws of general application.*

Analogous to the mechanism set forth in Chapter 1 (Jurisdiction: Bringing Clarity Out of Chaos), for any Tribe that exercises this option, Congress would recognize the Tribe's inherent jurisdiction over those juvenile matters, subject to the understanding that the Tribe would afford all constitutionally guaranteed rights to the juveniles brought before the Tribal system, and the juveniles would be entitled to Federal civil rights review of any judgments entered against them in a newly created United States Court of Indian Appeals. As in adult criminal court, the Tribe opting for this exclusive jurisdiction could offer alternative forms of justice, such as a juvenile wellness court, a teen court, or a more traditional peacemaking process, as long as the juvenile properly waived his or her rights.

If Tribes choose not to opt out entirely from the Federal criminal justice system for offenses allegedly committed by their juvenile citizens, Tribal governments should still be provided with a second option:

> **6.2:** *Congress should provide Tribes with the right to consent to any U.S. Attorney's decision before Federal criminal charges against any juvenile can be filed.*

The U.S. Criminal Code already provides for such Tribal governmental consent in adult cases where Federal prosecutors are considering seeking the death penalty. The same reasoning ought to apply to U.S. Attorneys' decisions to file Federal charges against Native juveniles for Indian country offenses.

Strengthening Tribal Justice for Native Youth. Similarly, in the interests of achieving parity between Tribal and non-Indian justice systems, resources for Indian country juvenile justice must be more effectively deployed.

Accordingly, the Commission recommends:

6.3: *Because resources should follow jurisdiction, and the rationale for Tribal control is especially compelling with respect to Tribal youth, resources currently absorbed by the Federal and State systems should flow to Tribes willing to assume exclusive jurisdiction over juvenile justice.*

6.4: *Because Tribal youth have often been victimized themselves, and investments in community-oriented policing, prevention, and treatment produce savings in costs of detention and reduced juvenile and adult criminal behavior, Federal resources for Tribal juvenile justice should be reorganized in the same way this Commission has recommended for the adult criminal justice system. That is, they should be consolidated in a single Federal agency within the U.S. Department of Justice, allocated to Tribes in block funding rather than unpredictable and burdensome grant programs, and provided at a level of parity with non-Indian systems. Tribes should be able to redirect funds currently devoted to detaining juveniles to more demonstrably beneficial programs, such as trauma-informed treatment and greater coordination between Tribal child welfare and juvenile justice agencies.*

6.5: *Because Tribal communities deserve to know where their children are and what is happening to them in State and Federal justice systems, and because it is impossible to hold justice systems accountable without data, both Federal and State juvenile justice systems must be required to maintain proper records of Tribal youth whose actions within Indian country brought them into contact with those systems. All system records at every stage of proceedings in State and Federal systems should include a consistently designated field indicating Tribal membership and location of the underlying conduct within Indian country and should allow for tracking of individual children. If State and Federal systems are uncertain whether a juvenile arrested in Indian country is in fact a Tribal member, they should be required to make inquiries, just as they are for dependency cases covered by the Indian Child Welfare Act.*

6.6: *Because American Indian/Alaska Native children have an exceptional degree of unmet need and the Federal government has a unique responsibility to these children, a single Federal agency should be created to coordinate the data collection, examine the specific needs, and make recommendations for American Indian/ Alaska Native youth. This should be the same agency within the U.S. Department of Justice referenced in Recommendation 6.4. A very similar recommendation can be found in the 2013 Final Report of the Attorney General's National Task Force on Children Exposed to Violence.*

"*... data show that Federal and State juvenile justice systems take Indian children, who are the least well, and make them the most incarcerated. Furthermore, conditions of detention often contribute to the very trauma that Native children experience. Detention is often the wrong alternative for Indian country youth and should be the last resort.*"

Detention and Alternatives for Native Youth. Alternatives to detention are even more imperative for Tribal youth than for adult offenders. Experts in juvenile justice believe detention should be a rare and last resort for *all* troubled youth, limited to those who pose a safety risk or cannot receive effective treatment in the community. More specifically, data show that Federal and State juvenile justice systems take Indian children, who are the least well, and make them the most incarcerated. Furthermore, conditions of detention often contribute to the very trauma that Native children experience. Detention is often the wrong alternative for Indian country youth and should be the last resort.

Accordingly, the Commission recommends:

> **6.7:** *Whether they are in Federal, State, or Tribal juvenile justice systems, children brought before juvenile authorities for behavior that took place in Tribal communities should be provided with trauma-informed screening and care, which may entail close collaboration among juvenile justice agencies, Tribal child welfare, and behavioral health agencies. A legal preference should be established in State and Federal juvenile justice systems for community-based treatment of Indian country juveniles rather than detention in distant locations, beginning with the youth's first encounters with juvenile justice. Tribes should be able to redirect Federal funding for construction and operation of juvenile detention facilities to the types of assessment, treatment, and other services that attend to juvenile trauma.*

> **6.8:** *Where violent juveniles require treatment in some form of secure detention, whether it be through BOP-contracted State facilities, State facilities in P.L. 83-280 or similar jurisdictions, or BIA facilities, that treatment should be provided within a reasonable distance from the juvenile's home and informed by the latest and best trauma research as applied to Indian country.*

Intergovernmental Cooperation for Native Youth. Where juveniles are involved, intergovernmental cooperation can enable Tribes to ensure that their often-traumatized youth receive proper assessment and treatment that is attentive to the resources and healing potential of Tribal cultures. Yet, Federal law, as prescribed by the Federal Delinquency Act, limits the ability to consider Tribal law and the unique needs and circumstances of a juvenile offender, particularly if that offender may be tried as an adult.

Accordingly, the Commission recommends:

> **6.9:** *The Federal Delinquency Act, 18 U.S.C. § 5032, which currently fosters Federal consultation and coordination only with States and U.S. territories, should be amended to add "or tribe" after the word "state" in subsections (1) and (2).*

6.10: *The Federal Delinquency Act, 18 U.S.C. § 5032, should be amended so that the Tribal election to allow or disallow transfer of juveniles for prosecution as adults applies to all juveniles subject to discretionary transfer, regardless of age or offense.*

6.11: *Federal courts hearing Indian country juvenile matters should be statutorily directed to establish pretrial diversion programs for such cases that allow sentencing in Tribal courts.*

Finally, there are two key mechanisms of enhanced Tribal-State cooperation: notice to Tribes when their children enter State juvenile justice systems and opportunities for Tribes to participate more fully in determining the disposition of juvenile cases.

Accordingly, the Commission recommends:

6.12: *The Indian Child Welfare Act[7] should be amended to provide that when a State court initiates any delinquency proceeding involving an Indian child for acts that took place on the reservation, all of the notice, intervention, and transfer provisions of ICWA will apply. For all other Indian children involved in State delinquency proceedings, ICWA should be amended to require notice to the Tribe and a right to intervene.*

CONCLUSION

These recommendations are the result of Commission field hearings and site visits to all 12 of the Bureau of Indian Affairs' regions across the United States, along with hundreds of letters, emails, and other input from every corner of our country. They are intended to make Native America safer and more just for all U.S. citizens and to save taxpayers' money by replacing outdated top-down policies and bureaucracies with locally based approaches that are more directly accountable to the people who depend on them most and can make them work.

Many of these recommendations will require Federal legislation. Others are matters of internal executive branch policy. Still others will require action by the Federal judiciary. And much of what the Commission has proposed will demand enlightened and energetic leadership from the affected State governments. This includes the development of model and uniform State codes and best practices. Ultimately, Indian Tribes, nations, pueblos, villages, and rancherias must choose if and when to implement these reforms.

This is a defining moment for our nation and for this generation. How we choose to deal with the current public safety crisis in Native America—a crisis largely of the Federal government's own making over more than a century of failed laws and policies—can set our generation apart from the legacy that remains one of great unfinished challenges of the Civil Rights Movement.

Public safety in Indian country can and will improve dramatically once Native American nations and Alaska Native Tribes have greater freedom to build and maintain their own criminal justice systems. We see breathtaking possibilities for safer, strong Native communities achieved through home-grown, tribally based systems, respective of the civil rights of all U.S. citizens, systems that reject outmoded command-and-control policies in favor of increased local control, accountability, and transparency. Lives are at stake, and there is no time to waste.

ENDNOTES

[1] Also known as the Snyder Act, the Indian Citizenship Act, 43 Stat. 253, conferred U.S. citizenship on "all non citizen Indians born within the territorial limits of the United States," thereby enabling Native Americans to vote in Federal elections.

[2] 18 U.S.C § 1151.

[3] Alaska Native Corporations are discussed in Chapter 2, notably at endnote 9.

[4] 522 U.S. 520 (1998).

[5] 28 U.S.C. § 1346(b)

[6] *Ex parte Crow Dog,* 109 U.S. 556, 571 (1883).

[7] 25 U.S.C. § 1901 *et seq.*

Glossary Terms and Acronyms

638 (aka 638 Contract): Refers to the Indian Self-Determination and Education Assistance Act, Public Law 93-638 (January 1975). Tribal programs operating under a 638 Contract receive the funds from the Bureau of Indian Affairs (BIA) and/or the Indian Health Service (IHS) to operate those programs, which BIA and/or IHS would have used to operate a direct service program for the tribe. For example many tribes receive funding that the BIA would have used to operate a law enforcement program, and use those funds to finance their own tribal police department under a 638 contract.

Adverse Childhood Experience Study (ACE): The largest investigations ever conducted to assess associations between childhood maltreatment and later-life health and well-being. The study is a collaboration between the Centers for Disease Control and Prevention and Kaiser Permanente's Health Appraisal Clinic in San Diego. The ACE Study findings suggest that certain experiences are major risk factors for illness, death, and poor quality of life in the United States.

Allotment: The policy subdividing Indian reservations into individual privately owned parcels of land, eliminating communal ownership of tribal land and resources. The federal policy was ended in 1934, but left a "checkerboard" landownership on Indian reservations where the tribe, non-Natives, and allottees own scattered properties.

American Indian/Alaska Native: As a general principle, an Indian is a person who is of some degree Indian blood and is recognized as an Indian by a tribe and/or the United States. No single federal or tribal criterion establishes a person's identity as an Indian. Government agencies use differing criteria to determine eligibility for programs and services. Tribes also have varying eligibility criteria for membership. It is important to distinguish between the ethnological term *Indian* and the political/legal term *Indian*. The protections and services provided by the United States for tribal members flow not from an individual's status as an American Indian in an ethnological sense, but because the person is a member of a tribe recognized by the United States and with which the United States has a special trust relationship. (Please see http://www.justice.gov/otj/nafaqs.htm.)

Batterer: A person that commits acts of domestic violence.

Braided Funding: Braided funding involves multiple funding streams within—or across—state, tribal, and federal agencies to support a program or special initiative. The term *braided* is used because multiple funding streams are brought together to pay for more than any one stream can support alone.

Child Abuse Prevention and Treatment Act (CAPTA): The law (PL 93-247) that provides a foundation for a national definition of child abuse and neglect. CAPTA defines child abuse and neglect as "at a minimum, any recent act or failure to act on the part of a parent or caretaker, which results in death, serious physical or emotional harm, sexual abuse or exploitation, or an act or failure to act which presents an imminent risk of serious harm."

Child Exposed to Violence: Any individual who is not yet an adult (typically from birth to either eighteen or twenty-one years old) who is exposed to violence that poses a threat to the individual's or an affiliated person's life or bodily integrity. Children exposed to violence are at much greater risk of developing lethal medical illnesses in their early adult years; utilizing disproportionately costly medical, psychological, and public health services; and dying prematurely.

Child Maltreatment: Any act or series of acts of commission or omission by a parent or other caregiver (e.g., clergy, coach, teacher) that results in harm, potential for harm, or threat of harm to a child.

Child Protective Services: The agency of the federal government, of a state, or of an Indian tribe that has the primary responsibility for child protection on any Indian reservation or within any community in Indian country.

Cultural-Based Practice: Reviewing and changing the structure of a program or practice to more appropriately fit the needs and preferences of a particular cultural group or community.

Domestic Violence: Domestic violence is a pattern of abusive behavior in any relationship that is used by one partner to gain or maintain power and control over another intimate partner. Domestic violence can be physical, sexual, emotional, economic, or psychological actions or threats of actions that influence another person. This includes any behaviors that intimidate, manipulate, humiliate, isolate, frighten, terrorize, coerce, threaten, blame, hurt, injure, or wound someone. Other terms used to describe this pattern of behavior are *battering*, *intimate partner violence*, and *interpersonal violence*.

Evidence-Based Practice: An intervention that has been consistently shown in several research studies to assist consumers in achieving their desired goals of health and wellness.

Evidence-Based Treatment: Interventions and services provided by a credentialed professional or paraprofessional to serve as a therapy or community-based service to promote recovery from psychosocial, psychological, or medical problems or to prevent these problems altogether. These interventions and services:

(a) Have been scientifically tested and demonstrated to be effective;
(b) Have clearly defined procedures that can be taught and implemented consistently with fidelity;
(c) Are feasible and useful for clinical practitioners and programs; and
(d) Are credible and acceptable to the recipients.

Expert Testimony: Opinions stated during trial or deposition by a specialist qualified as an expert on a subject relevant to the lawsuit or a criminal case.

Failure to Protect: Some states have attempted to protect children by including exposure to domestic violence as "failure to protect" under child abuse and neglect laws. Charges have been brought against domestic violence victims for failure to act or fulfill a duty recognized by the law to protect children from exposure to domestic violence.

Foster Care: Supervised care for orphaned, neglected, or delinquent children in a substitute home or an institution.

Historical Trauma: Historical trauma refers to cumulative emotional and psychological wounding, exceeding over an individual life span and across generations, caused by significant group traumatic experiences.

Holistic: Refers to a method of healing and focuses on the whole person (physical, mental, emotional, and spiritual aspects), not just one aspect.

Indian Country: A legal term of art set forth in 18 U.S. Code Section 1151 defined as: *(a) all land within the limits of any Indian reservation under the jurisdiction of the United States Government, notwithstanding the issuance of any patent, and, including rights-of-way running through the reservation, (b) all dependent Indian communities within the borders of the United States whether within the original or subsequently acquired territory thereof, and whether within or without the limits of a state, and (c) all Indian allotments, the Indian titles to which have not been extinguished, including rights-of-way running through the same.*

Intimate Partner Violence: Used interchangeably in this report with *domestic violence.* Term includes physical violence, sexual violence, threats of physical or sexual violence, and psychological/emotional violence between intimate partners.

Jurisdiction: The authority given by law to a court to try cases and rule on legal matters within a particular geographic area and/or over certain types of legal cases.

Juvenile Court: A special court or department of a trial court that deals with civil and criminal issues involving minors. The typical age of these defendants is less than eighteen, but juvenile court does not have jurisdiction in cases in which minors are charged as adults. While attorneys may be present, the procedure in juvenile court is not always adversarial. Juvenile court can involve parents, social workers, and probation officers in the process to achieve positive results and save the minor from involvement in future crimes. However, serious crimes and repeated offenses can result in sentencing juvenile offenders to prison. Where parental neglect or loss of control is a problem, the juvenile court may seek out foster homes for the juvenile, treating the child as a ward of the court.

Juvenile Delinquent: A person who is under age (usually less than eighteen), who is found to have committed a crime in states that have declared by law that a minor lacks responsibility and thus may not be sentenced as an adult.

Mediation: The attempt to settle a legal dispute through active participation of a third party (mediator) who works to find points of agreement and make those in conflict agree on a fair result. Mediation differs from arbitration, in which the third party (arbitrator) acts much like a judge in an out-of-court, less formal setting but does not actively participate in the discussion. Mediation has become very common in trying to resolve domestic relations disputes (divorce, child custody, visitation) and is often ordered by the judge in such cases.

Multidisciplinary Team (MDT): Multiagency, multijurisdictional team that is responsible for the coordination of investigations involving child abuse and/or neglect cases. A key responsibility of the MDT is to reduce trauma to the child victim. The MDT shall have members who have experience and training in prevention, identification, investigation, and treatment of incidents of child abuse and neglect.

Offender: An accused defendant in a criminal case or one convicted of a crime.

Parent: A person's father or mother to include by adoption.

Parent-Child Interaction Therapy (PCIT): An empirically supported treatment for young children with emotional and behavioral disorders that places emphasis on improving the quality of the parent-child relationship and changing parent-child interaction patterns.

Practice-Based Evidence: A range of interventions and services that are derived from, and supportive of, the positive cultural attributes of the local society and traditions. Practice based evidence services are accepted as effective by the local community, through community consensus, and address the therapeutic and healing needs of individuals and families from a culturally-specific framework. Practitioners of practice based evidence models draw upon cultural knowledge and traditions for treatment and services. Practice –based evidence is distinct from evidenced based practices. Many promising practices for Native populations do not have the level of evidence necessary to be deemed an evidence based practice, but nonetheless, they have shown to be effective for tribal populations.

Posttraumatic Stress Disorder (PTSD): A debilitating psychological condition triggered by a major traumatic event, such as rape, war, a terrorist act, death of a loved one, a natural disaster, or a catastrophic accident. It is marked by upsetting memories or thoughts of the ordeal, "blunting" of emotions, increased arousal, and sometimes severe personality changes.

Protocol: A set of policies, procedures, and agreements. Typically, a protocol is a written document outlining each agency's role and responsibility. The agencies and individuals signing the document signify their mutual commitment to the team and the team's mission statement.

Public Law 280 Tribes: Public Law 280 (1953) transferred criminal and civil jurisdiction in Indian country from the federal government to the states of Alaska, California, Minnesota, Nebraska, Oregon, and Wisconsin. Other states were given the option to assume jurisdiction by legislation. The act was amended in 1968, requiring tribal consent to the transfer of jurisdiction.

Regional Corporation: Created by the Alaska Native Claims Settlement Act, which divided Alaska into twelve regions with one Regional Corporation for each region. These corporations were authorized to select lands and hold subsurface rights to "Village Corporations" lands. Later, a thirteenth Regional Corporation was formed for non-resident Alaska Natives.

Resilience: Capacity to adapt successfully and to function competently despite adversity.

Safe House: A place for sanctuary from hostile actors or actions, or from retribution, threats, or perceived danger.

Screening: Asking brief questions or gathering existing information to determine if an individual should be identified as having a specific need or problem.

Silo: A mind-set present wherein certain agencies or individuals do not wish to share information with others in the same service.

Stovepipe: An organization that has a structure that largely or entirely restricts the flow of information within the organization to up-down through lines of control, inhibiting or preventing cross-organizational communication. Many traditional, large (especially governmental or transnational) organizations have, or risk falling into having, a stovepipe pattern.

Subsistence: A form of food hunting and gathering, including fishing, that many American Indian/ Alaska Native tribes still depend on to supplement their diet and to conduct traditional tribal ceremonies.

Title IV-E Agency: The state or tribal Title IV-E agency designated to administer or supervise the administration of the programs under this plan. It is also the agency that administers or supervises the administration of the State/Tribal Child Welfare Services Plan under subpart 1 of Title IV-B of the act.

Title IV-E Funding: Annual appropriated funding authorized by Title IV-E of the Social Security Act, as amended, and implemented under the Code of Federal Regulations (CFR) at 45 CFR parts 1355, 1356, and 1357 with specific eligibility requirements and fixed allowable uses of funds. Funding is awarded by formula as an open-ended entitlement grant and is contingent upon an approved Title IV-E plan to administer or supervise the administration of the program.

Trauma: A deeply distressing or disturbing experience.

Trauma-Focused Cognitive Behavioral Therapy: A model of psychotherapy that effectively combines trauma-sensitive interventions with cognitive behavioral therapy. It is designed to address the needs of children with posttraumatic stress disorder or other significant behavioral problems related to traumatic life experiences.

Trauma-Focused Services: Services are considered trauma-focused when caregivers (such as biological, foster, or adoptive parents; mentors, spiritual advisors, or coaches; or line staff in child-serving programs) or professionals providing services:

(a) *Realize* (understand) the impact that exposure to violence and trauma have on victims' physical, psychological, and psychosocial development and well-being;

(b) *Recognize* when a specific person who has been exposed to violence and trauma is in need of help to recover from trauma's adverse impacts; and

(c) *Respond* by helping in ways that reflect awareness of trauma's adverse impacts and consistently support the person's recovery from them and actively seeks to resist re-traumatization.

Trauma-Informed Care: This is a new form of evidence-based interventions and service delivery, implemented by multiple service providers, that identifies, assesses, and heals people injured by, or exposed to, violence and other traumatic events.

Trauma-Specific Treatment: Medical, physiological, psychological, and psychosocial therapies that are:

(a) Free from the use of coercion, restraints, seclusion, and isolation;

(b) Provided by a trained professional to an individual, a family, or a group adversely affected by violence exposure and trauma; and

(c) Designed specifically to promote recovery from the adverse impacts of violence exposure and trauma on physical, psychological, and psychosocial development, health, and well-being.

Toxic Stress: Experiences, particularly in childhood, that can affect brain architecture and brain chemistry. These typically are experiences that are bad for an individual during development, such as severe abuse.

Violence: The World Report on Violence and Health (WRVH) (http://www.who.int/violence_injury_prevention/violence/world_report/en/) defines violence as "the intentional use of physical force or power, threatened or actual, against oneself, another person, or against a group or community that either results in or has a high likelihood of resulting in injury, death, psychological harm, maldevelopment, or deprivation."

Violence Exposure: Violence exposure can be *direct*, where the victim or community of victims is the direct target of the intentional use of force or power, but it can also be *indirect*, where the victim or community of victims is witness to the intentional use of force or power or has lost a loved one to violence. In both cases, more than twenty years of scientific literature on the impact of violence demonstrates that violence exposure results in significant short- and long-term debilitating and costly impacts on the victim's physical, emotional, cognitive, and social health and well-being.

Frequently Used Acronyms

ACE	Adverse Childhood Experience Study
ACF	Administration of Children and Families
AFCARS	Adoption and Foster Care Analysis and Reporting System
AI/AN	American Indian/Alaska Native
ANCSA	Alaska Native Claims Settlement Act
ASFVA	Alaska Safe Families and Villages Act of 2014
BIA	Bureau of Indian Affairs
BIE	Bureau of Indian Education
CAPTA	Child Abuse Prevention Treatment Act
CBO	Congressional Budget Office
CFSR	Child and Family Services Review
CTAS	Coordinated Tribal Assistance Solicitation
DHHS	Department of Health and Human Services
DOI	Department of Interior
DOJ	Department of Justice
FERPA	Federal Education Right and Privacy Act
HHS	Health and Human Services
HUD	Housing Urban Development
ICRA	Indian Civil Rights Act
ICWA	Indian Child Welfare Act
IHS	Indian Health Service
ILOC	Indian Law and Order Commission
LGBTQ/2S	Lesbian, Gay, Bisexual, Transgender, Queer/Questioning, and Two-Spirit
MOU	Memorandum of Understanding
NCAI	National Congress of American Indians
NCANDS	National Child Abuse and Neglect Data System
OJP	Office of Justice Programs
OJJDP	Office of Juvenile Justice and Delinquency Prevention
TLOA	Tribal Law and Order Act
VOCA	Victims of Crime Act

Suggested Further Reading Print and Internet Sources

Tribal Sovereignty and Federal Indian Policy

Cadawalader, S., Deloria Jr., V., *Aggressions of Civilization: Federal Indian Policy since the 1880s,* Philadelphia: Temple University Press (1984).

Canby Jr., William C., *American Indian Law, In a Nutshell,* 5th ed., St. Paul, MN: West (2009).

Carpenter, K., Fletcher, M., Riley, A., eds., *The Indian Civil Rights Act at Forty,* Los Angeles: UCLA American Indian Studies Center (2012).

Clark, B., *Lone Wolf v. Hitchcock: Treaty Rights and Indian Law at the End of the 19th Century,* Lincoln: University of Nebraska Press (1994).

Clinton, Robert N., et al., American *Indian Law: Cases and Materials,* 5th ed., San Francisco: Lexis Nexis, (2007).

Cooter, Robert, *Indian Common Law: The Role of Custom in American Indian Tribal Courts,* available at: http://www.americanbar.org/content/newsletter/publications/gp_solo_magazine_home/gp_solo_magazine_index/indianchildwelfareact.html.

Deer, S., Garrow, C. E., *Tribal Criminal Law and Procedure,* Walnut Creek, CA: Alta Mira Press (2004).

Deer, S., Richland, J., *Introduction to Tribal Legal Studies,* 2nd ed., Lanham, MD: Rowman and Littlefield (2010).

Fixico, Donald, *Termination and Relocation: Federal Indian Policy (1945–1960),* Albuquerque: University of New Mexico Press (1990).

Fletcher, Matthew, *Rethinking Customary Law in Tribal Court Jurisprudence,* available at: http://www.law.msu.edu/indigenous/papers/2006-04.pdf.

Fletcher, Matthew L. M., *American Indian Tribal Law,* New York: Aspen Publishers (2011).

Fortin, Seth J., *The Two-Tiered Program of the Tribal Law and Order Act,* available at: http://www.uclalawreview.org/?p=4439.

Gardner, J., Melton, A., *Public Law 280: Issues and Concerns for Victims of Crime in Indian Country,* available at: http://www.tribal-institute.org/articles/gardner1.htm.

Getches, David, et al., *Cases and Materials on Federal Indian Law,* 6th ed., St. Paul, MN: West (2011).

Goldberg, Carole, *Questions and Answers about Public Law 280,* available at: http://www.tribal-institute.org/articles/goldberg.htm.

Goldberg-Ambrose, Carole, *Planting Tail Feathers: Tribal Survival and Public Law 280,* Los Angeles: American Indian Studies Center Publications (1997).

Indian Law—Tribal Courts—Congress Recognizes and Affirms Tribal Courts' Special Domestic Violence Jurisdiction over Non-Indian Defendants—The Violence Against Women Reauthorization Act of 2013, available at: http://cdn.harvardlawreview.org/wp-content/uploads/2014/03/violence_against_women_reauthorization_act1.pdf.

Jones, B. J., et al., *The Indian Child Welfare Act Handbook: A Legal Guide to the Custody and Adoption of Native American Children,* American Bar Association (2009).

Krakoff, Sarah, *Inextricably Political: Race Membership, and Tribal Sovereignty,* available at: http://digital.law.washington.edu/dspace-law/bitstream/handle/1773.1/1184/87WLR1041.pdf?sequence=1.

National American Indian Court Judges Association, *Indian Courts and the Future,* Ann Arbor: University of Michigan Library (repr., 1978).

Native American Rights Fund, *A Practical Guide to the Indian Child Welfare Act,* Boulder, CO: Native American Rights Fund (2007).

Newton, Nell Jessup, ed. *Cohen's Handbook of Federal Indian Law,* San Francisco: Lexis Nexis (2012).

Pevar, Stephen L., *The Rights of Indians and Tribes,* Carbondale: Southern Illinois University Press (1992).

Philp, Kenneth, "Stride towards Freedom: The Relocation of Indians to Cities, 1952–1960," *Western Historical Quarterly* 16(2) (1985): 175-190.

Pommersheim, Frank, *Tribal Courts: Providers of Justice and Protectors of Sovereignty,* available at: http://www.tribal-institute.org/articles/pommer~1.htm.

Prucha, F., *American Indian Policy in Crisis: Christian Reformers and the Indian, 1865–1900,* Norman: University of Oklahoma Press (1976).

Prucha, F., ed., *Americanizing the American Indians,* Cambridge, MA: Harvard University Press (1973).

Resnik, Judith, *Multiple Sovereignties: Indian Tribes, States, and the Federal Government,* available at: http://www.tribal-institute.org/articles/resnik1.htm.

Ross, Jeffrey I., ed., *American Indians at Risk,* Vols. 1 and 2, Santa Barbara, CA: ABC-CILO (2013).

Shoemaker, Nancy, "Urban Indians and Ethnic Choices: American Indian Organizations in Minneapolis, 1920–1950," *Western Historical Quarterly* 19(4) (1988): 431-447.

Tatum, M., et al., *Structuring Sovereignty: Constitutions of Native Nations,* Los Angeles: American Indian Studies Center Publications (2014).

Tatum, Melissa, *Law Enforcement Authority in Indian Country,* available at: http://tlj.unm.edu/tribal-law-journal/articles/volume_4/tatum/.

Tribal Law and Policy Institute, *Promising Strategies: Public Law 280,* available at: http://www.walkingoncommonground.org/files/TLPI%20Promising%20Strategies%20280_FINAL_Updated%20%208-16-13.pdf.

Tribal Law and Policy Institute, *Promising Strategies: Tribal-State Court Relations,* available at: *http://www.walkingoncommonground.org/files/TLPI%20Promising%20Strategies%20Tribal-State%20Court%20Relations_FINAL_Updated%208-15-13.pdf.*

U.S. Commission on Civil Rights, *A Quiet Crisis: Federal Funding and Unmet Needs in Indian Country,* Washington, D.C.: U.S. Commission on Civil Rights (2003).

Domestic Violence, Sexual Abuse, and Child Maltreatment

Agtuca, Jacqueline, *Safety for Native Women: VAWA and American Indian Tribes*, Lame Deer, MT: National Indigenous Women's Resource Center (2014).

Amnesty International USA, *Maze of Injustice: The Failure to Protect Indigenous Women from Sexual Violence in the United States*, New York: Amnesty International Publications (2007).

Bancroft, L., Silverman, J., *The Batterer as Parent: Addressing the Impact of Domestic Violence on Family Dynamics,* Thousand Oaks, CA: Sage Publications (2002).

BigFoot, Dolores S., *Dealing with Disclosure of Child Sexual Abuse, Native American Topic*, available at: http://www.icctc.org/Disclosuremonograph.pdf.

BigFoot, Dolores S., *History of Victimization Issues in Native Communities*, available at: http://www.unifiedsolutions.org/Pubs/history_of_victimization_in_native_communities.pdf.

Deer, Sarah, *Expanding the Network of Safety: Tribal Protection Orders for Survivors of Sexual Assault*, available at: http://tlj.unm.edu/tribal-law-journal/articles/volume_4/violence,%20women/index.php.

Deer, Sarah, *Relocation Revisited: Sex Trafficking of Native Women in the United States*, available at: http://open.wmitchell.edu/cgi/viewcontent.cgi?article=1157&context=facsch.

Deer, Sarah, *Sovereignty of the Soul: Exploring the Intersection of Rape Law Reform and Federal Indian Law*, available at: http://papers.ssrn.com/sol3/papers.cfm?abstract_id=987702.

Deer, Sarah, et al., *Final Report: Focus Group on Public Law 280 and the Sexual Assault of Native Women*, available at: http://www.tribalinstitute.org/download/Final%20280%20FG%20Report.pdf.

Deer, Sarah, et al., ed., *Sharing Our Stories of Survival: Native Women Surviving Violence*, Lanham, MD: Rowman and Littlefield (2008).

Deluzio, Christopher, *Tribes and Race: The Court's Missed Opportunity in Adoptive Couple v. Baby Girl*, available at: http://digitalcommons.pace.edu/plr/vol34/iss2/1.

Dobie, Kathy, *Tiny Little Laws, A Plague of Sexual Violence in Indian Country*, available at: http://harpers.org/archive/2011/02/tiny-little-laws/2/.

EchoHawk, Larry, *Child Sexual Abuse in Indian Country: Is the Guardian Keeping in Mind the Seventh Generation?*, available at: http://www.unified-solutions.org/pubs/child_sexual_abuse_in_ic_larry_echohawk.pdf.

EchoHawk, L., Meyer Santiago, T., *What Indian Tribes Can Do to Combat Child Sexual Abuse,* available at: http://lawschool.unm.edu/tlj/tribal-law-journal/articles/volume_4/abuse/index.php.

Edleson, Jeffrey, et al., *Report of the Attorney General's National Advisory Committee on Violence Against Women*, Washington, D.C.: U.S. Department of Justice, Office on Violence Against Women (2012).

Farley, Melissa, et al., *Garden of Truth: The Prostitution and Trafficking of Native Women in Minnesota,* available at: http://miwsac.org/images/pdf/Garden%20of%20Truth%20Final%20Project%20WEB.pdf.

Garrow, C., Hollebeke, M., *Adoptive Couple v. Baby Girl: A Summary,* available at: http://www.srmt-nsn.gov/_uploads/site_files/Garrow-Hollebeke-Mar-Apr2014.pdf.

Hart, William, et al., *Report of the Attorney General's National Task Force on Family Violence*, Washington, D.C.: U.S. Department of Justice (1984).

Herrington, Lois, et al., *Report of the President's National Task Force on Victims of Crime*, Washington, D.C.: U.S. Department of Justice (1982).

Jones, B. J., *Indian Child Welfare Act: The Need for a Separate Law,* available at: http://www.americanbar.org/content/newsletter/publications/gp_solo_magazine_home/gp_solo_magazine_index/indianchildwelfareact.html.

McCold, P., Wachtel, B., *Community Is Not a Place: A New Look at Community Justice Initiatives,* available at: http://www.iirp.edu/article_detail.php?article_id=NDc1.

National Council of Juvenile and Family Court Judges, *Checklist to Promote Perpetrator Accountability in Dependency Cases Involving Domestic Violence,* available at: http://www.icadvinc.org/wp-content/uploads/2011/11/2011-checklist-for-CHINS-ct..pdf.

Simoni, Jane M., et al., "Triangle of Risk: Urban American Indian Women's Sexual Trauma, Injection Drug Use, and HIV Sexual Risk Behaviors," *AIDS and Behavior* 8(1) (2004): 33–45.

Stoof, Melvin R., *Domestic Violence, Child Welfare and Supervised Visitation in Native American Communities,* available at: http://mshoop.org/brochurespdf/DV%20Child%20Welfare%20and%20SVC%20in%20Native%20communities.pdf.

Trope, J., Smith, A., *The Continued Protection of Indian Children and Families after Adoptive Couple v. Baby Girl: What the Case Means and How to Respond,* available at: http://www.law.seattleu.edu/Documents/ailj/Spring%202014/Trope-and-Smith.pdf.

Weber, G., Zuni, C., *Domestic Violence and Tribal Protection of Indigenous Women in the United States,* available at: http://www.law-lib.utoronto.ca/Diana/fulltext/zuni.htm.

White, H., Larrington, J., *Intersection of Domestic Violence and Child Victimization in Indian Country*, available at: http://www.swclap.org/pdfs/INTERSECTIONDVANDKIDS.pdf.

White Eagle, Maureen, *Keeping Native Children Safe When Sexual Abuse Allegations Are Raised in Custody Disputes*, available at no cost by calling Minnesota Indian Women's Sexual Assault Coalition at 651-646-4800.

White Eagle, Maureen, et al., *Responses to the Co-Occurrence of Domestic Violence and Child Maltreatment in Indian Country: Repairing the Harm and Protection Children and Mothers*, available at: http://www.tribalinstitute.org/download/OVWGreenbookReportHVS_TD_7-18.pdf.

Issues on Community Violence

BigFoot, Dolores S., ed., *Multidisciplinary Teams and Child Protection Teams*, available at: https://www.oumedicine.com/docs/ad-pediatrics-workfiles/mdtcpt.pdf?sfvrsn=2.

Bureau of Justice Statistics, *American Indians and Crime, 1992–2002*, available at: http://www.bjs.gov/content/pub/pdf/aic02.pdf.

Craig, J., Hull-Jilly, D., "Characteristics of Suicide among Alaska Native and Alaska Non-Native People, 2003–2008," *State of Alaska Epidemiology Bulletin* 15(1) (2012).

Elton, P., Stewart, M., *How Multidisciplinary Teams Achieve Success in Indian Country*, available at: http://www.policechiefmagazine.org/magazine/index.cfm?fuseaction=display_arch&article_id=2889&issue_id=32013.

Gardner, Jerry, *Improving the Relationship between Indian Nations, the Federal Government, and State Governments*, available at: http://www.tribal-institute.org/articles/mou.htm.

Lucero, Nancy, *Working with Urban Indian Families with Child Protection and Substance Abuse Challenges*, available at: http://www.nrc4tribes.org/files/Urban%20Indian%20guide.pdf.

Major, Aline K., Egley Jr., Arlen, Howell, James C., et al., "Youth Gangs in Indian Country," *OJJDP Juvenile Justice Bulletin*, U.S. Department of Justice, Office of Juvenile Justice and Delinquency Prevention (2004).

Reyhner, Jon, *Family, Community and School Impacts on AI/AN Students' Success*, available at: http://jan.ucc.nau.edu/jar/AIE/Family.html.

Sarche, M. C., Whitesell, N. R., "Child Development Research in North American Native Communities—Looking Back and Moving Forward: Introduction." *Child Development Perspectives* 6 (2012): 42–8.

Stiffman, A. R., et al. "American Indian Youth: Southwestern Urban and Reservation Youth's Need for Services and Whom They Turn to for Help," *Journal of Child and Family Studies* 12 (2005): 319–33.

Trujillo, O., Alston, D., *A Report on the Status of American Indians and Alaska Natives in Education: Historical Legacy to Cultural Empowerment,* Washington, D.C.: National Education Association (2005).

U.S. Department of Education, National Center for Education, *Statistics Status and Trends in the Education of American Indians and Alaska Natives,* available at: http://nces.ed.gov/pubs2005/nativetrends/ind_3_2.asp.

Volkow, Nora, "Substance Abuse in American Indian Youth Is Worse Than We Thought," *Nora's Blog,* National Institute on Drug Abuse (2014), available at: http://www.drugabuse.gov/about-nida/noras-blog/2014/09/substance-use-in-american-indian-youth-worse-than-we-thought.

Trauma and Healing

Barnes, Patricia M., et al., "Health Characteristics of the American Indian or Alaska Native Adult Population: United States, 2004–2008," *National Health Statistics Reports* 20, Hyattsville, MD: National Center for Health Statistics (2010).

Bartgis, J., BigFoot, D.S., *The State of Best Practice in Indian Country,* available at: http://www.icctc.org/Bartgis-Bigfoot%20The%20State%20of%20Best%20Practices%20in%20Indian%20Country%20(2).pdf.

BigFoot, Dolores S., Schmidt, Susan, *Honoring Children, Mending the Circle: Cultural Adaptation of Trauma-Focused Cognitive-Behavior Therapy for American Indian and Alaska Native Children,* available at: http://www.itcmi.org/wp-content/uploads/2013/04/TBCAC-cultural-adaptation-article2010.pdf.

Buller, Ed, *Aboriginal Community Healing Process in Canada,* available at: http://www.iirp.edu/pdf/man05/man05_buller.pdf.

Colmant, Stephen, et al., "Constructing Meaning to the Indian Boarding School Experience," *Journal of American Indian Education* 43(3) (2004): 22–40.

Dickerson, Daniel L., et al., "Mental Health and Substance Abuse Characteristics among a Clinical Sample of Urban American Indian/Alaska Native Youths in a Large California Metropolitan Area: A Descriptive Study," *Community Mental Health Journal,* Springerlink.com (2010).

Federal Partners Committee on Women and Trauma, *Trauma Informed Approaches: Federal Activities and Initiatives,* available at: http://www.nasmhpd.org/docs/Women%20and%20Trauma/2013FederalPartnersReportFinal.pdf.

Finkelhor, David, et al., "Trends in Childhood Violence and Abuse Exposure," *Arch Pediatr Adolesc Med* 164(3) (2010): 238–42.

Indian Law and Order Commission, *A Roadmap for Making Native America Safer: Report to the President and Congress of the United States* (2013), available at: http://www.aisc.ucla.edu/iloc/report/index.html.

James, Cara, et al., "A Profile of American Indians and Alaska Natives and Their Health Coverage," *Race, Ethnicity and Health Care*: Issue Brief, available at: http://kaiserfamilyfoundation.files.wordpress.com/2013/01/7977.pdf.

Koltko-Rivera, Mark E., "The Psychology of Worldviews," *Review of General Psychology* 8 (2004): 3–58.

Koss M. P., et al., "Adverse Childhood Exposures and Alcohol Dependence among Seven Native American Tribes," *American Journal of Preventative Medicine* (2003): 238-244.

LaFromboise, Teresa D., et al., "Family, Community, and School Influences on Resilience among American Indian Adolescents in the Upper Midwest," *Journal of Community Psychology* 34(2) (2006): 193–209.

Listenbee Jr., Robert L., et al., *Report of the Attorney General's National Task Force on Children Exposed to Violence*, Washington, D.C.: U.S. Department of Justice, Office of Juvenile Justice and Delinquency Prevention (2012).

Mihesuah, Devon A., "Commonalty of Difference: American Indian Women and History," Special Issue: Writing about American Indians, *American Indian Quarterly* 20 (1996): 15–27.

Sarche, Michelle C., et al., *American Indian and Alaska Native Children and Mental Health: Development, Context, Prevention, and Treatment*, Santa Barbara, CA: ABC-CILO (2011).

Sawatsky, J., Ross, R., *The Ethic of Traditional Communities and the Spirit of Healing Justice, Studies from Hollow Water, the Iona Community and Plum Village*, Philadelphia: Jessica Kingsley Publisher (2007).

Shonle, Ruth, "The Christianizing Process among Preliterate Peoples," *The Journal of Religion* 4 (1924): 261–80.

Smith, Andrea, "Soul Wound: The Legacy of Native American Schools," *Amnesty International Magazine*, available at: http://www.amnestyusa.org/node/87342.

Stamm, B. Hudnall, et al., "Considering a Theory of Cultural Trauma and Loss," *Journal of Loss and Trauma* 9 (2001): 1–22.

Strand, J. A., Peacock, R., "Resource Guide for Cultural Resilience," *Tribal College Journal of American Indian Higher Education* 14(4) (2003): 28-31.

Thurman, Pamela J., et al., "The Circles of Care Evaluation: Doing Participatory Evaluation with American Indian and Alaska Native

Communities," *American Indian and Alaska Native Mental Health Research, Journal of the National Center* 11(2) (2004): 139–54.

United Nations Department of Economic and Social Affairs, *State of the World's Indigenous Peoples*, New York: United Nations (2009).

Wilkins, Natalie, et al., *Connecting the Dots: An Overview of the Links among Multiple Forms of Violence*, Atlanta: National Center for Injury Prevention and Control, Centers for Disease Control and Prevention and Prevention Institute (2014).

Yellow Horse Braveheart, Maria, *Historical Trauma*, available at: http://www.historicaltrauma.com/.

Zvolensku, Michael J., et al., "Assessment of Anxiety Sensitivity in Young American Indians and Alaska Natives," *Behavior of Research and Therapy* 39 (2001): 477–93.

Juvenile Justice

Adams, E. J., "Healing Invisible Wounds: Why Investing in Trauma-Informed Care for Children Makes Sense," *Justice Policy Institute*, available at: http://www.justicepolicy.org/images/upload/10-07_REP_HealingInvisibleWounds_JJ-PS.pdf.

Alexie, Sherman, *Flight: A Novel*, New York: Black Cat (2007).

The Annie E. Casey Foundation, *Juvenile Detention Alternatives Initiative Annual Results Report* (2009), available at: http://jdaiannualreports.com/pastreports.php .

The Annie E. Casey Foundation, *Planning for Juvenile Detention: A Structured Approach*, available at: http://www.aecf.org/resources/planning-for-juvenile-detention-reforms/.

Arya, Neelum, Rolnick, Addie, "A Tangled Web of Justice: American Indian and Alaska Native Youth in Federal, State, and Tribal Justice Systems," Washington, D.C.: *Campaign for Youth Justice Policy Brief* 1 (2008): n6.

Bonnie, Richard J., ed., et al., *Reforming Juvenile Justice: A Developmental Approach*, National Research Council, Committee on Assessing Juvenile Justice Reform, Committee on Law and Justice, Division of Behavioral and Social Sciences and Education, Washington, D.C.: The National Academies Press (2013).

Cauffman, Elizabeth, "Understanding the Female Offender," *Future of Children* (18) (2008): 119-142.

Center for Children's Law and Policy, *Understanding the BJS Study of Sexual Victimization in Juvenile Facilities,* available at: http://www.cclp.org/documents/PREA/Fact%20Sheet%20--%202012%20BJS%20Sexual%20Victimization%20Study.pdf.

Declaration on the Rights of a Child, United Nations General Assembly Resolution 1386(XVI) (1959), available at: http://www.unicef.org/malaysia/1959-Declaration-of-the-Rights-of-the-Child.pdf.

Henning, Kris, "Loyalty, Paternalism, and Rights: Client Counseling Theory and the Role of Child's Counsel in Delinquency Cases," *Notre Dame L. Rev.* 81 (2005): 245-324.

Holman, B., Ziedenberg, J., *The Dangers of Detention: The Impact of Incarcerating Youth in Detention and Other Secure Congregate Facilities*, available at: http://www.justicepolicy.org/images/upload/06-11_REP_DangersOfDetention_JJ.pdf.

Indian Law and Order Commission, *A Roadmap for Making Native America Safer: Report to the President and Congress of the United States* (2013): 149–80, available at: http://www.aisc.ucla.edu/iloc/report/files/Chapter_6_Juvenile_Justice.pdf.

Levick, Marsha, et al., "The Eighth Amendment Evolves: Defining Cruel and Unusual Punishment through the Lens of Childhood and Adolescence," *U. Pa. J.L. and Soc. Change* 15 (2012): 285-337.

Majd, Katayoon, et al., *Hidden Injustice: Lesbian, Gay, Bisexual, and Transgender Youth in Juvenile Courts*, available at: http://www.equityproject.org/pdfs/hidden_injustice.pdf.

Melton, Ada P., *Building Culturally Relevant Youth Court in Tribal Communities*, available at: http://aidainc.net/Publications/monograph.pdf.

Melton, Ada P., *Collaboration and Resource Sharing to Improve Services to Indian Youth*, available at: http://aidainc.net/Publications/collaboration.htm.

Mendel, Richard, *No Place for Kids: The Case for Reducing Juvenile Incarceration*, available at: http://www.aecf.org/resources/no-place-for-kids-full-report/.

No Turning Back: Promising Approaches to Reducing Racial and Ethnic Disparities Affecting Youth of Color in the Justice System, available at: http://www.cclp.org/documents/BBY/ntb_fullreport.pdf.

Sherman, Francine, *Testimony before Congress on Meeting the Needs of Girls in the Juvenile Justice System*, available at: http://www.youtube.com/watch?v=-vP6GRSC8Yc.

Smink, J., Zorn, J., *Legal and Economic Implications of Truancy*, Clemson, SC: National Dropout Prevention Center/Network, College of Health, Education, and Human Development, Clemson University (2005).

Soler, Mark, et al., "Juvenile Justice: Lessons for a New Era," *Georgetown J. Poverty Law and Pol'y* 16 (2009): 483-541.

Sprague, C., "Informing Judges About Child Trauma," *NCTSN Service System Briefs* 2 (2008): 396-404.

Taylor, R. W., Fritsch, E. J., *Juvenile Justice: Policies, Programs, and Practices*, 3rd ed., New York: McGraw-Hill (2011).

Teske, Steve, et al., *Collaborative Role of Courts in Promoting Outcomes for Students: The Relationship between Arrests, Graduation Rates, and School Safety,* available at: http://school-justicesummit.org/pdfs/journal-web_paper_9.pdf.

Walton, Stephanie, *New Ways to Address Truancy,* Denver, CO: National Conference of State Legislatures (2006).

Alaska Special Issues

Carlson, B. E., "Children Exposed to Intimate Partner Violence: Research Findings and Implications for Intervention," *Trauma, Violence, and Abuse* 1(4) (2000): 321-342.

Case, D. S., Voluck, D. A., *Alaska Natives and American Laws*, 3rd ed., Fairbanks: University of Alaska Press (2012).

Denetsosie, Warren, *Alaska v. Native Village of Venetie Tribal Government: Redefining "Indian Country,"* available at: http://www.tribal-institute.org/articles/denetsosie.htm.

Goodkind, J. R., et al., "Promoting Healing and Restoring Trust: Policy Recommendations for Improving Behavioral Health Care for American Indian/Alaska Native Adolescents," *American Journal of Community Psychology* 46 (2010): 386-394.

Indian Law and Order Commission, *A Roadmap for Making Native America Safer: Report to the President and Congress of the United States* (2013): 55–61, available at: http://www.aisc.ucla.edu/iloc/report/files/Chapter_2_Alaska.pdf.

Leiber, M. J., et al., *An Examination of the Factors That Influence Justice Decision Making in Anchorage and Fairbanks, Alaska,* available at: http://dhss.alaska.gov/djj/Documents/ReportsAndPublications/DMC/06AssessmentStudy.pdf.

Strommer, G., Osborne, S., *"Indian Country" and the Nature and Scope of Tribal Self-Government in Alaska,* available at: http://scholarship.law.duke.edu/cgi/viewcontent.cgi?article=1093&context=alr.

Internet Sources

ACE Study Summary: http://www.cdc.gov/violenceprevention/
acestudy/index.html

Alaska Native Issues: http://www.tribal-institute.org/lists/alaska.htm

Alaska Rural Justice Commission: http://www.akjusticecommission.org/

The Annie E. Casey Foundation: http://www.aecf.org/resources/
urban-indian-america/

Center for Native American Youth at the Aspen Institute, *Fast Facts:
Native American Youth and Indian Country*, available at: http://www.
aspeninstitute.org/sites/default/files/content/upload/Native%20
Youth%20Fast%20Facts%20Update_04-2014.pdf

Child Abuse and Neglect Resources: http://www.tribal-institute.org/
lists/child.htm

Domestic Violence Resources: http://www.tribal-institute.org/lists/
domestic.htm

Indian Child Protection and Family Violence Prevention: http://www.
law.cornell.edu/uscode/text/25/chapter-34

Indian Child Welfare Act: http://www.tribal-institute.org/lists/icwa.htm

Indian Country Child Trauma Center: http://www.icctc.org/

Indian Self-Determination Act: http://www.tribal-institute.org/lists/
pl93-638.htm

Juvenile Justice: http://www.tribal-institute.org/lists/juvenile.htm

National Indian Education Association: http://www.niea.org/

National Native Children's Trauma Center: http://iers.umt.edu/
National_Native_Childrens_Trauma_Center/

Tribal Court Clearinghouse: http://www.tlpi.org

Tribal Jurisdiction: http://www.tribal-institute.org/lists/jurisdiction.htm

Tribal Law and Order Act: http://www.narf.org/nill/resources/tloa.html

Violence Against Women Act: http://www.tribal-institute.org/lists/
vawa_2013.htm

Walking On Common Ground: http://www.WalkingOnCommonGround.org